Dante Alighieri, Emelia Russell Gurney

Dante's Pilgrim's Progress

Or, The passage of the blessed soul from the slavery of the present corruption to the liberty

of eternal glory

Dante Alighieri, Emelia Russell Gurney

Dante's Pilgrim's Progress
Or, The passage of the blessed soul from the slavery of the present corruption to the liberty of eternal glory

ISBN/EAN: 9783743407831

Manufactured in Europe, USA, Canada, Australia, Japa

Cover: Foto ©ninafisch / pixelio.de

Manufactured and distributed by brebook publishing software (www.brebook.com)

Dante Alighieri, Emelia Russell Gurney

Dante's Pilgrim's Progress

DANTE'S PILGRIM'S PROGRESS;

OR,

'THE PASSAGE OF THE BLESSED SOUL
FROM
THE SLAVERY OF THE PRESENT CORRUPTION
TO
THE LIBERTY OF ETERNAL GLORY.'

WITH
NOTES ON THE WAY

BY
EMELIA RUSSELL GURNEY.

LONDON:
ELLIOT STOCK, 62, PATERNOSTER ROW, E.C.
1893.

Dedicated,

BY HIS PERMISSION,

TO THE

LORD BISHOP OF RIPON,

IN MOST GRATEFUL MEMORY OF THREE LECTURES GIVEN BY HIM

IN 1884 ON THE

DIVINE COMEDY,

WHICH AWAKENED THE LONG SLUMBERING DESIRE IN THE MIND

OF THE COMPILER OF THIS VOLUME TO ENDEAVOUR TO

APPROPRIATE SOME PART, AT LEAST, OF OUR

GREAT MEDIÆVAL INHERITANCE.

['*La Divine Comédie ressemble à ces vastes héritages tombés entre les mains d'une postérité débile et appauvrie, qui les morcelle pour les cultiver.*'—A. F. OZANAM.]

I am permitted to quote from a letter written by the Bishop of Ripon, to whom I submitted my incomplete MS., some words expressing his valuable approbation of the general intention and aim of this volume:

'*The Palace, Ripon,*
'*November* 6, 1892.

'*Dear Mrs. Russell Gurney,*

. . . .

'*I must thank you for your manuscript; it is helpful and exhilarating; its spirit and purpose are what we need to see more of in this literal and over-dogmatizing age.*

'*Most of all, I am pleased that you have gone to the heart of the poem.*

'*In Dante, as in more sacred literature, "The letter killeth, and the spirit giveth life."*

'*Very truly yours,*
'*W. B. RIPON.*'

THE ILLUSTRATIONS.

THE Frontispiece is a Photograph of Dante, taken from an oil picture, painted by Domenico il Michelino, 1465, now in the Duomo at Florence. It has been necessary to omit a part of the background, of Florence, and of the Entrance to the Inferno, to fit the proportions of this volume.

The Chromo-lithograph depicts three conditions of the heart of Man. These are described in the Preface. Mr. Frederic Shields has generously endowed the volume with this expressive sketch. The designs on the Cover are also given by the same Master's hand.

On one side the scallop-shell represents the Pilgrim's Way, in its descent and climb; the added wings denote his Ascension through the Heavens to his Goal. On the other side the three Circles enclose illustrations from the Vegetable Kingdom, used by Dante in his three Books. These signify the degrees of life in that Kingdom, corresponding with the same degrees in the Moral Order.

The rigid and poisonous Thorns of the Suicides' Wood manifest a bitter outgrowth, due to conditions starved of the sap and light of Nature. The humble Reed, swayed by waves or wind, has its place and its voice in the Kingdom, where nothing less obedient to Nature's shocks could grow.

Finally, we are shown the White Rose, the Sunshine's Blossom:

> 'The bright, transcendent flower,
> Spirits odorous breathes.'

The colours of the Book, white, green, and flame-colour, are the hues in which Dante clothes Faith, Hope, and Charity, and the Celestial Wisdom Herself.

TO THE READER.

WE are told that our Creeds 'may be said or sung.' To sing them, as a great Poet sings, loosens their bonds from the utterance of historical statements and logical inferences, and sends them forth as expressions of the divinely taught and living human heart, tinctured with its rich experience of sorrow and wrong, and joy and love.

Dante thus gave forth the sublimated creed of the Mediæval Church, and through six centuries his song has maintained its hold upon the hearts of men. In this age, when it is increasingly felt that spiritual truth is too vast to be forced through any portal that opens on the realm of the understanding alone, his music is very welcome to the listener whose faith seeks an entrance into other and larger haunts of the Spirit.

Amongst such as these there may be a few whom Dante would call 'Anime pellegrine' . . . 'who know themselves to be out of their own country' (Vita Nuova, XLII.). It is for these, who may lack time and opportunity for the study of the whole Poem, that the Compiler has ventured to separate the ensuing fragments from their context.

They are fragments from the Poet's song that relate especially to the 'Pilgrim's Progress'; or, to use Dante's own words, to the 'Passage of the blessed Soul from the

To the Reader.

Slavery of the present corruption to the liberty of Eternal Glory.'

The rich accompaniments of dramatic incident, of Biographies, of History and of Politics, that belong to his music, have been disregarded, in order to concentrate the Pilgrim's attention on this 'progress of the soul,' which might be called the 'Motif' of his Symphony—its oft recurring, never forgotten 'motif'—like that of the Holy Grail in Parsifal.

It is hoped that the vibrating notes of this strain, in his own untranslatable words, may prove a spell to arrest the scattered thoughts of some who desire to concentrate a short half hour in their busy day to unseen realities.

Dante's own words, in some measure, authorize us to make a study by itself of his mystical meaning, which he indicates as the pith of the Divina Commedia. He says, in his letter to Can Grande, that his Poem is to be taken in many senses, and marks out for us four among the many, as the literal, the allegorical, the moral, and the anagogical (or mystical). He cites Ps. cxiv. as an example of the mode of applying these four interpretations, and, I think, implies that this Psalm is an epitome of his Poem, when he declares its mystical significance to be 'the passage of the blessed soul from the slavery of the present corruption to the liberty of Eternal Glory.'

Once, in the Inferno, he bids us[*] 'look behind the veil for the teaching of his "strange verses."' Again, in the Purgatorio, he begs his reader to fix his eyes carefully on the Truth 'that he may penetrate through his subtle veil,'[†] and using another metaphor, he says, in the Paradiso,[‡] 'as he voyages singing across the sea, never yet traversed,' that only 'those few who hunger in Time for the Bread of Angels

---

[*] Inferno, IX. 60.   [†] Purgatorio, VIII. 19.
[‡] Paradiso, XI. 1-15.

To the Reader.

should use his wake on the trackless Element, while others would do well to return to their own shores. His primary subject, he says, is 'Man in the exercise of his free will, with the consequences of his action'; or, Man in his passage from corruption to glory, learning, through the exercise of choice, his true destiny.

The human heart, then, is the Arena of the Divine Comedy, whether in the conditions of the flesh, or freed from the restraints and sheltering concealments the flesh provides. The three Realms of the Inferno, the Purgatorio, and the Paradiso should, it is believed, be studied as three pictures of the human heart; or of three attitudes of the Will of Man in relation to the Central source of his being and of the Universe.

These three conditions of the human heart have been delineated at the end of this Preface by a Master's hand, and speak with an appealing force of their own. They are drawn on a background of gold, reminding us that in God each lives and moves and has his being. In the first (Superbia) we see the heart, either through ignorance, or through pride and self-will, in antagonism to the laws of its essential being, with labyrinths within and battlements around, shutting out the circulation of light and of life. In the second (Umiltà), we see it enlightened through the acceptance of the Cross, the Light flowing in upon that Wood and bringing in its stream the vernal Hope of adjustment, or of At-one-ment with the laws of its essential being. In the third (Amore) the heart is seen through accepted Love and Wisdom, the Shechinah at its Centre, and the true life-blood circulating within it.

'In the foreground of the Divina Commedia, indeed, Dante describes 'allegorically,' or perhaps even, he may have believed, in some degree 'literally,' the three places of habitation appointed to spirits who leave the mortal condition in the three attitudes of Will described above. He sees such spirits stript of all that hinders and hides in this world, manifesting in corresponding environment the outcome of essential character.

No doubt these habitations are pictured in most respects in accordance with his contemporaries' belief, and probably with his own; yet his deeper vision evidently led him within the arena of the human heart, rather than into its arbitrary and more external surroundings.

We desire to follow him into this deeper and more universal vision, and to learn with him our right relationship with the indwelling Spirit of Truth.

'From within,' says our Lord, 'out of the heart of men proceed evil thoughts, adulteries, murders,' etc., 'all these evil things come from within,' Mark viii. 21. Again, He tells us that 'the Kingdom of Heaven is within.' And we know that the Pilgrimage from one Realm to another is made in 'heart and mind' through the God-given graces of Repentance and Aspiration.

In attempting to follow the words of the 'Sacred Poem, to which Heaven and Earth have contributed,' we are not likely to find more meanings than were in the mind of the Singer. Should we, however, read into Dante's words an interpretation caught from the 'fresher stamp of the time-bettering days,' it would be only what we might hope to receive from the vitality of a work of genius.

'A work of genius,' it has been well said, 'is a living organism of a high and complex character, mobile and sensitive to its surroundings. It has latent correspondence with human nature, which time alone discovers; it has the spontaneous activity, the unconscious self-adapting power of genius.

To the Reader.

'The greater the genius of the writer, the more responsive will the book be to its environment; the greater will be the area over which its relations extend, the more far-reaching, both in time and space, the range of its correspondences. For genius is, in fact, life, and the faculty of engendering life in others.'—From Professor Butcher on 'Some Aspects of Greek Genius.'

It has been thought desirable to keep the thread of the 'Pilgrim's Progress' as unbroken as possible in the Selection of these Fragments. The universally known passages (such as the story of Francesca and Paolo da Rimini, the Fate of Ugolino, etc.) have been, therefore, for the most part omitted.

Hints towards the spiritual meaning to be sought, or, as they have been entitled, 'Notes on the Way,' are on the pages opposite to the Italian text. These may be looked upon as prosaic Sign-posts for the unaccustomed traveller through the mystic Wood. Originality is not claimed for them, nor has it been attempted to fathom or define all the significance of the passage selected for study; on the contrary, full space is left for the insight and experience of each reader. The interpretations of the Poet's symbolism are often patent and generally accepted; or little more than a paraphrase has been suggested, with an added emphasis or illustration from the words of the Sacred Writers, or those of later Seers.

Readers, though unacquainted with the Italian language (especially if they know something of either Latin or French), are earnestly counselled to read the words aloud in the original, and to catch the rhythm of the lines; they will, it is believed, in so doing enter much more into the spirit of the Poem than by confining themselves even to the best translations. 'Let each one know,' Dante has said, 'that nothing that is harmonized by the bonds of music can be transmuted

To the Reader.

into another tongue without breaking all its sweetness and harmony.'—'Convito,' I. 7.

Longfellow's excellent and almost literal line-by-line translation (price one shilling, Routledge) should be procured, and the passages selected marked for reference.

To say nothing of earlier Commentators, the notes to Dean Plumptre's poetic Translation of the 'Divine Comedy,' Mr. Wicksteed's Lectures, and Six Sermons on Dante, and Mr. W. T. Harris's 'Spiritual Sense of Dante' (New York), have been, it is thankfully acknowledged, especially helpful to the compiler of these fragments.

It need scarcely be added that this little book is not offered to any student of Dante, nor even to any who may hope to become students of the Poet; for such, ampler and far better modes of approach are open. Not as a contribution towards acquaintance with his great work of Art have these pages been put together, but rather as subjects for meditation *with* Dante on the Eternal verities he unfolds, and on our abiding portion in God.

SVPERBIA — VMILTÀ

INFERNO.

THE DESCENDING WAY OF THE INFERNO.

> 'I sent my Soul through the Invisible
> Some letter of that After-life to spell:
> And by-and-by my Soul returned to me,
> And answer'd, "I myself am Heav'n and Hell."'

NOT as a future Torture Chamber for souls after death do we propose to study the following extracts from the Inferno. Rather, as Dante's own words instruct us, we seek here his portrayal of 'Man endowed with free-will' placing himself, either through Ignorance or through wilful Pride, in antagonism to the laws of his own being.

We see him represented in the moral world as we should see him in the world of Nature, were he to place himself, as some maniac might do, in opposition to all the laws of Nature; burying his face in the mud, feeding on stones, or casting himself into the destructive elements of Fire or Water.

Only in obedience to the laws of Nature, we know, can man escape destruction and become the dominant Lord of Nature, making her forces his own ministers.

In the moral world, as in the physical world, a man in his right reason will adjust himself to these laws of his being. This is Dante's theme.

The Descending Way of the Inferno.

'From within,' says our Lord, 'out of the heart of men, proceed evil thoughts, adulteries, fornications, murders, thefts, covetousness, wickedness, deceit, an evil eye, blasphemy, pride, foolishness: all these evil things come from within, and defile the man.'—Mark vii. 21-23.

These evil things, scattered and mitigated by the presence of good, by public opinion, and by the concealments of the world of sense, are gathered together in the Inferno in one fearful knot, laid bare and focussed under the piercing ray of Truth's righteous judgment.

Not, then, as everlastingly enduring and cunningly-devised punishments should we regard the tortures unveiled before us, but as the pictures of evil things with which we are acquainted in their germs, set full-grown before our eyes in root and branch and blossom and fruit.

Beatrice, when she meets Dante in Eden, tells him that it was only by the light of truth concerning the nature and consequences of evil that he could escape from the abode of corruption, towards which she had watched his down-tending steps.—Purg. xxx.

When his senses are 'exercised to discern both good and evil,' he must needs of his own free will choose the good and refuse the evil.

When we find our true element, we must needs throw ourselves therein.

We may look at Dante as he is guided through the Inferno by his divinely-appointed Mentor (Reason or Conscience personified by Virgil), as the *Representative of the awakening consciousness of Humanity* in relation to corruption within and without.

We see him instructed first in the borderland of Hell concerning the feebleness of moral fibre that is parent to cowardly

The Descending Way of the Inferno.

selfishness. We see selfishness more fully developed, leading downwards through the three Circles of Avarice, Anger, and Malice into the more and more complete subjugation of Reason to Appetite; then, passing into a further deliberate choice of evil for self-ends, through the yet lower circles of Fraud, Treachery, and Betrayal. At last the stagnation of Death is reached, in the frozen pool of self-worshipping and inhuman Isolation and Pride.

Throughout the descent, Self is discovered at the Centre of all action. First, rather as self-preservation; later, as self-appropriation in every stage and degree; and lastly, as self-aggrandisement, it crowds out every other consideration, and is seen to be the monster that is the Betrayer, Murderer, and Death of all else.

Force without Love is the false conception regarding the Supreme Being throughout this deepening darkness and chaos. His Name is never uttered, for his character is unknown. Virgil himself can only speak of GOD to the disciple as 'He who can, what He wills.' Once alone he alludes to Christ without naming Him, as 'the Powerful One crowned with Victory.'

The defiant who will not bend even in their extremity of suffering before such arbitrary and torturing Force (as He is conceived to be), unlike the cowardly-selfish, excite some sort of admiration, as evidencing in their indomitable, though depraved, Will the nobility of their origin, even in this wrecked condition.*

Dante in such an atmosphere, true to his own creative imagination, becomes at times even cruel and vindictive himself.

The walls, battlements, dykes, and bridges of the Inferno

* *Vid.* Capaneus, Inf. xiv. 43-66; Farinata, Inf. x. 22.

mark its stony, rigid nature as the outward expression of the hardened, heartless, and exclusive consciousness of self-centred man.

The terrible words graven on the Gates that enclose this Land of Darkness express the absolute hopelessness of Evil as an element for Man to inbreathe. They assert the Eternal Decree of Divine Righteousness, Power, Wisdom, and Love, that Man, made by and for this fourfold Unity, cannot exist as Man in antagonism to this Unity. Man made for Justice or Righteousness cannot live in unrighteousness; Man made for Power cannot live in subjugation to his own wayward impulses; Man made for Wisdom cannot live in Foolishness; Man made for Love cannot live in Hatred. We shall find that he may appear to live—'he may eat and drink, and sleep and put on clothes' (Inf. xxxiii. 141); but he is only the semblance of a man; he himself is dead.

The City of Dis, the metropolis of the Inferno, named after its king, has no sign of social life within its turreted, luridly-gleaming walls. Its battlements rise from the putrescent fen of Styx; they are garrisoned by the Furies, who alone give signs of combined action, and this is used to keep out the living Intelligences of Dante and Virgil; while, at the same time, these Furies imprison the Sepulchred Souls of Infidels and Heretics. It is the City of the Dead —of the Murderers of Truth; in awful contrast to the City of interwoven Love and Wisdom, at unity with itself, whose only confines are Light and Love.

The Inferno is full of such introversions or travesties of Man's Home and Element in the Heart of God, shown to us in the Heavenly Commonwealth of the Paradiso.

Outside this Element the deluded and tormented are lost.

The Descending Way of the Inferno.

In Dante we view the Pioneer, or Forerunner of men 'remembering themselves' and returning from darkness into light; or, in his own words, we see 'the blessed soul in his passage from the slavery of the present corruption into the Liberty of Eternal Glory.' God's lost Son is found; He that was dead is alive.

'Know ye not that the unrighteous shall not inherit the Kingdom of God? . . . And such were some of you: but ye are washed, but ye are sanctified, but ye are justified in the name of the Lord Jesus, and by the Spirit of our God.' —1 Cor. vi. 9-11.

Dante awakens in a dark forest, his way lost. He looks upward, and sees the Sun's rays illuminating a Mountain.

INFERNO, CANTO I. 1-21.

NEL mezzo del cammin di nostra vita
   Mi ritrovai per una selva oscura,
   Che la diritta via era smarrita.
Ahi quanto, a dir qual era, è cosa dura,
   Questa selva selvaggia ed aspra e forte,   5
   Che nel pensier rinnova la paura !
Tanto è amara, che poco è più morte :
   Ma per trattar del ben ch' i' vi trovai,
   Dirò dell' altre cose ch' io v' ho scorte.
I' non so ben ridir com' io v' entrai ;   10
   Tant' era pien di sonno in su quel punto
   Che la verace via abbandonai.
Ma poi ch' io fui appiè d' un colle giunto,
   Là ove terminava quella valle
   Che m' avea di paura il cuor compunto,   15
Guardai in alto, e vidi le sue spalle
   Vestite già de' raggi del pianeta,
   Che mena dritto altrui per ogni calle.
Allor fu la paura un poco queta,
   Che nel lago del cuor m' era durata   20
   La notte, ch' io passai con tanta pièta.

Those unacquainted with the Italian language are advised to procure Longfellow's almost literal translation ; a vol. of Morley's Universal Library, published by Routledge. 1s.

'And the Lord God called unto the Man, and said unto him, Where art thou?'—GEN. iii. 9, 10 (N.V.).

(I)

AT some crisis in life, probably after the illusions of early youth have vanished, the Pilgrim perceives he has lost his way. He knows he must have slept and wandered, but cannot tell whence he came, nor whither he goes. The savage, pathless forest in which he finds himself fills him with bitterness and dismay, and the vision of an unattainable Ideal is presented in the Mountain before him. The difficulties and burdens and perplexities which entangle him are insurmountable. The dark and savage Forest seems to picture the chaotic life within, and the disorganized condition of the political life around him. The divine Ruler within and without is sighed for, and 'That Sun which leads others right by every path' (throughout the Poem ever the symbol of Divine illumination) a little quiets the terror which throughout the night of anguish had brooded over the deep lake of his heart like Death.

The awakening, or the preparation for the new Birth, is accompanied with travail pangs. 'O wretched man that I am, who shall deliver me from the body of this death?' has often been the cry of the soul.

To awaken and to be in pain is the same thing at some stages of the spiritual growth. This fact exists by some deep necessity in the disorder of this world. Pain awakens from unreal and self-centred dreams. Blessed, then, may be pain, for through it we may be born out of Self into the progressive life of Truth and Love.

'Till Life is coming back, our death we do not feel:
Light must be entering in, our darkness to reveal.'—TRENCH.

*At the foot of the Mountain Dante is impeded and terrified
by a Panther, a Lion, and a She-Wolf.*

INFERNO, CANTO I. 31-54.

ED ecco, quasi al cominciar dell' erta,
   Una lonza leggiera e presta molto,
   Che di pel maculato era coperta.
E non mi si partia dinanzi al volto ;
   Anzi impediva tanto 'l mio cammino,   35
   Ch' io fui per ritornar più volte vôlto.
Temp' era dal principio del mattino,
   E il Sol montava in su con quelle stelle
   Ch' eran con lui, quando l' Amor divino
Mosse da prima quelle cose belle ;   40
   Sì ch' a bene sperar m' era cagione
   Di quella fera alla gaietta pelle,
L' ora del tempo, e la dolce stagione :
   Ma non sì, che paura non mi desse
   La vista, che m' apparve, d' un leone.   45
Questi parea che contra me venesse
   Con la test' alta, e con rabbiosa fame,
   Sì che parea che l' aer ne tremesse :
Ed una lupa, che di tutte brame
   Sembiava carca nella sua magrezza,   50
   E molte genti fe già viver grame.
Questa mi porse tanto di gravezza
   Con la paura ch' uscia di sua vista,
   Ch' io perdei la speranza dell' altezza.

'*Who shall ascend unto the Hill of the Lord?*'

(II)

THE impulses of the Pilgrim's animal nature within, and such appeals from without, oppose any movement, upwards. He would fain return and sleep as before.

Carnality, Violence, and avaricious Self-love drive him back from his new Enterprise of climbing the Mountain. The hungering She-wolf especially causes him to relinquish the heights he has been impelled to ascend.

Yet a glimmer of hope is kept alive by Nature's beautiful things. The Morning air, the rising Sun, the Stars, the sweet Spring season, and even the beauty of the spotted Panther whom he knew to be the foe in his upward path, all witnessed to the divine hope awakened faintly within.

Man requires the animal element in him to exercise his strength to rise above it. We are to overcome, not to destroy, the animal within by the power of divine Wisdom, *i.e.*, 'Christ in us, the hope of glory.' 'He who has nothing to overcome can gain no victory.'

We know not yet what the animal nature and world is to become to us within and without, till they and we are in right and orderly relationship.

Even the rapacious hungering She-wolf, who leaves us no peace, the Self that would grasp all and never be satisfied, is to be tamed into obedience and gathered into Service rather than to be annihilated.

When the true man is restored in all his powers, we shall say, 'Nor soul helps flesh more, now, than flesh helps soul.'

The political significance of the 'many-sensed Allegory' in this passage is not contradicted, while we dwell on its spiritual interpretation; for this interpretation reveals the underlying root and cause of the political disorder, as moral disorder.

Dante is driven back by the Wolf from the ascent, and Terror takes the place of Hope; when Virgil appears.

──────── (III) ────────

INFERNO, CANTO I. 55-66, 76-78.

E QUALE è quei, che volentieri acquista,
    E giugne 'l tempo che perder lo face,
    Che in tutti i suoi pensier piange e s'attrista;
Tal mi fece la bestia senza pace,
    Che, venendomi incontro, a poco a poco,
    Mi ripingeva là dove 'l Sol tace.   60
Mentre ch' io ruinava in basso loco,
    Dinanzi agli occhi mi si fu offerto
    Chi per lungo silenzio parea fioco.
Quand' i' vidi costui nel gran diserto,
    'Miserere di me,' gridai a lui,   65
    'Qual che tu sii, od ombra, od uomo certo.'
   *   *   *   *   *   *
Ma tu perchè ritorni a tanta noia?   76
    Perchè non sali il dilettoso monte,
    Ch' è principio e cagion di tutta gioia?

'*My heart throbbeth, my strength faileth me :*
As for the light of my eyes, it also is gone from me.'
PSA. xxxviii. 10 (N.V.).

(III)

BEAUTIFUL Nature-visions are not enough to enable the Pilgrim to overcome the opposing forces he finds within and without as he endeavours to make his way upwards. Discouraged, even despairing, he rushes downwards to a level lower than the one he had reached before. The She-wolf described on last page and here again (lines 58 to 60), we know too well 'coming on against us by degrees'; ever greedy of attention, flattery, and indulgence, and ever more lean and hungry through our feeding her; thrusting us back into the gloom, where the 'Sun is silent' to our souls, and causing us to be indifferent to any higher life than that of Self's encroaching dominion. But the first progress of the newly-awakened Soul cannot be upwards. That delectable Mount, though seen in vision, is unattainable by one who has wandered so far as the Pilgrim. In this extremity Help is at hand. The voice of Conscience, or right Reason, represented by Virgil (weak through silence), though long disregarded, is heard again, declaring the Mount of Benediction as the Source of all joy—but another path than the one apparent to the Pilgrim will be pointed out.

Virgil foretells Dante's Way to the Holy City, and speaks of a worthier Soul who must introduce him there.

(IV)

INFERNO, CANTO I. 112-129.

<blockquote>
OND' io per lo tuo me' penso e discerno,
  Che tu mi segui; ed io sarò tua guida,
  E trarrotti di qui per luogo eterno,
Ov' udirai le disperate strida   115
  Di quegli antichi spiriti dolenti,
  Che la seconda morte ciascun grida.
E vederai color che son contenti
  Nel fuoco, perchè speran di venire,
  Quando che sia, alle beate genti: 120
Alle qua' poi se tu vorrai salire,
  Anima fia a ciò di me più degna:
  Con lei ti lascerò nel mio partire;
Chè quell' Imperador, che lassù regna,
  Perch' io fui ribellante alla sua legge,   125
  Non vuol che 'n sua città per me si vegna.
In tutte parti impera, e quivi regge:
  Quivi è la sua cittade, e l' alto seggio:
  O felice colui, cui ivi elegge!
</blockquote>

The Pilgrim is instructed that he must go through Death and Resurrection unto Life.

— (IV) —

THE Pilgrim must learn what man is in wilful captivity to corruption, its results unhindered by any counteracting environment; he must see that this corruption disintegrates every bond of the human family, and separates from all life, before his debased will can be content to pass through purifying Fire towards Union with the Highest. He is here taught, also, to expect a more perfect and heavenly Guide than his present but partially enlightened Mentor to lead him into the Holy City.

Observe line 127 as pointing out the advance to be made in truer relationship with God. It is said, 'He governs everywhere, and there (in the Holy City) He reigns—or rules.' The word 'imperare' implies an exercise of force or external authority; while the word 'reggere' may be used for an internal rule or law of life.

He who rules on Earth should 'discern at least the Towers of the Holy City,' Dante has said—should at least have some ideal of a righteous polity.

'Solid food is for full-grown men, even those who by reason of use have their senses exercised to discern good and evil.'—Heb. v. 14 (N.V.).

Dante, through much questioning, doubts whether the Enterprise set before him be not beyond his powers.

(V)

INFERNO, CANTO II. 1-6, 10-12, 31-42.

LO giorno se n' andava, e l' aer bruno
    Toglieva gli animai, che sono in terra,
    Dalle fatiche loro; ed io sol uno
M' apparecchiava a sostener la guerra
    Sì del cammino e sì della pietate,   5
    Che ritrarrà la mente, che non erra.

*   *   *   *   *

Io cominciai: Poeta, che mi guidi,   10
    Guarda la mia virtù, s' ell' è possente,
    Prima ch' all' alto passo tu mi fidi.

*   *   *   *   *

Ma io perchè venirvi? o chi 'l concede?   31
    Io non Enea, io non Paolo sono:
    Me degno a ciò nè io nè altri crede.
Perchè, se del venire i' m' abbandono,
    Temo che la venuta non sia folle: 35
    Se' savio, e intendi me' ch' io non ragiono.
E quale è quei che disvuol ciò ch' e' volle,
    E per nuovi pensier cangia proposta,
    Sì che dal cominciar tutto si tolle;
Tal mi fec' io in quella oscura costa: 40
    Per che, pensando, consumai l' impresa,
    Che fu nel cominciar cotanto tosta.

'*My Son, glorify thy Soul in meekness, and give it honour according to the dignity thereof.*'—ECCLUS. x. 28.

(V)

THE time of repose invites the Pilgrim, and he longs to accept it like the animal world around him.

Energy, that should have been expended on the first step, has been consumed by many thoughts concerning the Enterprise viewed as an appalling whole.

Doubts of personal sufficiency for the high calling he has received, and the counsels of flesh and blood, sap away the divinely-implanted heroism that would choose the Best.

> '*Our doubts are traitors
> And make us lose the good we oft might win
> By fearing to attempt.*'—'*Measure for Measure.*'

'The man who is great of soul is one who counts himself worthy, being worthy of great things.'—'Il Convito.'

'You . . . judge yourselves unworthy of Eternal Life.'—Acts xiv. 46.

'Blessed is he who heals us of our self-despisings!'—MARK RUTHERFORD.

Virgil warns Dante against Cowardice. He describes Beatrice, moved by Love, electing himself as Dante's Guide upwards.

(VI)

INFERNO, CANTO II. 43-72.

SE io ho ben la tua parola intesa,
    Rispose del Magnanimo quell' ombra,
    L' anima tua è da viltate offesa: 45
La qual molte fïate l' uomo ingombra
    Sì, che da onrata impresa lo rivolve,
    Come falso veder bestia, quand' ombra.
Da questa tema acciocchè tu ti solve,
    Dirotti perch' io venni, e quel ch' io intesi   50
    Nel primo punto che di te mi dolve.
Io era intra color che son sospesi,
    E donna mi chiamò beata e bella,
    Tal che di comandare i' la richiesi.
Lucevan gli occhi suoi più che la Stella: 55
    E cominciommi a dir soave e piana,
    Con angelica voce in sua favella:
O anima cortese mantovana,
    Di cui la fama ancor nel mondo dura
    E durerà quanto 'l mondo lontana,   60
L' amico mio, e non della ventura,
    Nella deserta piaggia è impedito
    Sì nel cammin, che vôlto è per paura;
E temo che non sia già sì smarrito,
    Ch' io mi sia tardi al soccorso levata,   65
    Per quel ch' i' ho di lui nel cielo udito.
Or muovi, e con la tua parola ornata,
    E con ciò ch' è mestieri al suo campare,
    L' aiuta sì, ch' io ne sia consolata.
I' son Beatrice, che ti faccio andare: 70
    Vengo di loco, ove tornar disio:
    Amor mi mosse, che mi fa parlare.

' Such ever was Love's Way : to rise, it stoops.'

———————————— (VI) ————————

THE Pilgrim is convicted of Cowardice in doubting of his Enterprise, and is encouraged to press onwards by the description of the Love that had sought out a Messenger and Guide to bring him on his way.

Nothing is too hard for Love—there is no distance, no possibility of separation where Love unites.

In Heaven, the Home of Love, there must be immediate knowledge when the Beloved lingers or turns back from his homeward path. By any means, a way must be devised to restore him.

' Yet do we still persist as we began,
  And so should perish, but that nothing can,
  Though it be cold, hard, foul, from loving man withhold
    Thee !'—GEO. HERBERT.

Virgil makes further appeal to Dante's courage, reminding him again of the three blessed Ladies in Heaven who care for him.

———————— (VII) ————————

INFERNO, CANTO II. 115-126.

POSCIA che m' ebbe ragionato questo,   115
Gli occhi lucenti, lagrimando, volse:
Per che mi fece del venir più presto.
E venni a te così, com' ella volse:
Dinanzi a quella fiera ti levai,
Che del bel monte il corto andar ti tolse.   120
Dunque che è? perchè, perchè ristai?
Perchè tanta viltà nel cuore allette?
Perchè ardire e franchezza non hai?
Poscia che tai tre donne benedette
Curan di te nella corte del cielo,   125
E 'l mio parlar tanto ben t' impromette?

What can awaken the sleeping Soul but Love?

(VII)

THE Heaven-sent Guide continues to plead with the half-hearted, delaying Pilgrim, and again pictures before him the weeping eyes of One whom he had loved on Earth, who is so much caring for his salvation. Shall not the memory, nay, the present knowledge of this abiding love and solicitude turn out all baseness from his heart?

Divine Love, Clemency, and Wisdom in the Courts of Heaven are caring for all, and perhaps have been interpreted to some of us by one who has yearned for our highest good, and dowered us with great love (born of the heart that loves, and not of our love worthiness); One who has now passed from our sight into the 'great cloud of witnesses that encompasseth us.' Amongst these, our 'Friend in God,' in his truest essential being, is surely more loving and more potent than when burdened by the flesh.

This blessed faith, even should it be built in part on memories that give us pain, will stimulate us to run with patience the race that is set before us.

Quickened by Virgil's words, Dante's courage revives, and his will is at one with Virgil's.

———————— (VIII) ————————

INFERNO, CANTO II. 127-142.

Quale i fioretti dal notturno gielo
   Chinati e chiusi, poi che 'l Sol gl' imbianca,
   Si drizzan tutti aperti in loro stelo;
Tal mi fec' io di mia virtude stanca,   130
   E tanto buono ardire al cor mi corse,
   Ch' io cominciai, come persona franca:
O pietosa colei che mi soccorse,
   E tu cortese, ch' ubbidisti tosto
   Alle vere parole che ti porse!   135
Tu m' hai con desiderio il cor disposto
   Sì al venir con le parole tue,
   Ch' io son tornato nel primo proposto.
Or va', chè un sol volere è d' ambedue:
   Tu duca, tu signore, e tu maestro.   140
   Così gli dissi; e poichè mosso fue,
Entrai per lo cammino alto e silvestro.

'Our wills are ours to make them Thine.'

(VIII)

AT last the Pilgrim's heart is kindled to the venture of Faith. Love has given power to the faint. The Will is inwilled by the Supreme Will, and, in union with that, all things *seem* possible, even as, indeed, they *are* possible.

> 'But, above all, the Victory is most sure
> For him, who, seeking faith by virtue, strives
> To yield entire submission to the law
> Of Conscience—Conscience reverenced and obeyed,
> As God's most intimate presence in the soul,
> And His most perfect image in the world.
> 'The Excursion,' Book IV.

'Let the weak say, I am strong.—Joel iii. 10.

'Transformed by the renewing of your mind.'—Rom. xii. 2.

> 'Who would have thought my shrivel'd heart
>   Could have recovered greenness? It was gone
> Quite underground; as flowers depart
>   To see their mother-root, when they have blown;
>   Where they together,
>   All the hard weather,
>   Dead to the world keep house unknown.
> These are Thy wonders, Lord of power,
>   Killing and quick'ning, bringing down to hell
> And up to heaven in an hour,
>   Making a chiming of a passing bell.
>   We say amiss,
>   This or that is:
> Thy word is all if we could spell.'—G. HERBERT.

The words inscribed over the Gates of Hell.

— (IX) —

INFERNO, CANTO III. 1-9.

PER ME SI VA NELLA CITTÀ DOLENTE ;
   PER ME SI VA NELL' ETERNO DOLORE ;
   PER ME SI VA TRA LA PERDUTA GENTE.
GIUSTIZIA MOSSE 'L MIO ALTO FATTORE :
   FECEMI LA DIVINA POTESTATE,   5
   LA SOMMA SAPÏENZA, E 'L PRIMO AMORE.
DINANZI A ME NON FUR COSE CREATE,
   SE NON ETERNE, ED IO ETERNO DURO :
   LASCIATE OGNI SPERANZA, VOI CH' ENTRATE.

> '*Far deeper than all and mortally wounded is the innermost heart.*'—JER. xvii. 9 (Septuagint).

(IX)

JUSTICE, Omnipotence, Wisdom, and Love cannot give His Children life and peace apart from Himself, for these, God's essential forces, cause and maintain the true Order of the Universe, of which man is a part; and, as depicted within these Gates, he makes

> 'An impious warfare with the very life
> Of his own soul.'

Well would it be for us if we could read this 'handwriting on the wall' of any ante-chamber to Evil, which we are entering with the hope of finding there some promised good—

> 'ALL HOPE ABANDON, YE WHO ENTER HERE.'

'Man in this world is already in Heaven or Hell. If his spirit is in harmony with God, he is then spiritually in Heaven. If he dwells here in the Wrath, he is already in Hell, and in the company of all the evil spirits.'—JACOB BOEHME.

Line 7.—It has been believed by other Seers than Dante that the Chaos from which Creation was evolved originated from the Fall of the Angels, who are deemed 'Eterne.'

The Chaos, from which the Cosmos is to be evolved, is repeated in each human heart.

The dolorous people who have lost the primal good of Reason.

(X)

INFERNO, CANTO III. 10-21.

Q UESTE parole di colore oscuro 10
    Vid' io scritte al sommo d' una porta ;
    Perch' io: Maestro, il senso lor m' è duro.
Ed egli a me, come persona accorta :
    Qui si convien lasciare ogni sospetto ;
    Ogni viltà convien che qui sia morta. 15
Noi sem venuti al luogo ov' io t' ho detto
    Che vederai le genti dolorose,
    C' hanno perduto 'l ben dell' intelletto.
E poi che la sua mano alla mia pose
    Con lieto volto, ond' io mi confortai, 20
    Mi mise dentro alle segrete cose.

'*Darkness was upon the face of the Deep, and the Spirit of God was brooding upon the face of the Water.*'—GEN. i. 2.

———————— (X) ————————

'BEFORE God's word is heard, the creature is void and formless, with an unknown deep within. In this deep all is darkness, yet God's Spirit is breathing there; the creature is helpless, but God is very near.'—ANDREW JUKES.

'Those who tarry in darkness apart from the Light that lighteneth every man have lost the supreme good of mind, or the intuition of God as the Truth that can alone satisfy its cravings.'—DEAN PLUMPTRE.

Who shall dare look into the darker depths of his own heart without the presence of One who knows it better, and who inspires Hope (lines 19, 20).

The 'glad Countenance' and the 'Hand that leads into the secret things' speak to us of One who has conquered and is conquering.

Perhaps the 'Evangelizing power' of both the 'glad Countenance' and the 'Hand' must be seen and felt through human fellowship before the Word can be effectively heard. 'He took hold of the blind man by the hand.'—Mark viii. 23.

Dante's question answered: 'Were any led forth through those Gates by the Mighty One with Victory crowned?'

(XI)

INFERNO, CANTO IV. 46-61.

Dimmi, maestro mio, dimmi, signore,
    Comincia' io, per voler esser certo
    Di quella fede che vince ogni errore:
Uscinne mai alcuno, o per suo merto,
    O per altrui, che poi fosse beato?   50
    E quei che intese 'l mio parlar coverto,
Rispose: Io era nuovo in questo stato,
    Quando ci vidi venire un Possente,
    Con segno di vittoria incoronato.
Trasseci l' ombra del primo Parente,   55
    D' Abel suo figlio, e quella di Noè,
    Di Moisè legista, e l' ubbidiente
Abraàm patriarca, e David Re;
    Israel con suo padre e co' suoi nati,
    E con Rachele per cui tanto fe;   60
Ed altri molti; e fecegli beati.

'He descended into Hell.'

(XI)

THOSE Eternal adamantine Gates inclosing the Prisoners of dark despair, bound hand and foot by the chains of their enslaving sins, cannot be opened by these paralyzed Wills from within; but shall those gates prevail in strength against the entrance of the 'crowned Mighty King of Love' and His Church?

'Who went and preached to the spirits in prison which aforetime were disobedient.'—1 Pet. iii. 18.

'I have the keys of Death and of Hell.'—Rev. iii. 18.

'Upon this Rock I will build My Church, and the Gates of Hell shall not prevail against it.'—Matt. iii. 18.

'O Israel, thou hast destroyed thyself, but in Me is thy help.'—Hosea xiii. 9.

The ignominious Souls mixed with the Caitiff Angels, who were neither faithful to God nor to His Enemies, but were for Self.

(XII)

INFERNO, CANTO III. 31-51.

ED io, ch' avea d' error la testa cinta,
    Dissi : Maestro, che è quel ch' i' odo ?
    E che gent' è, che par nel duol sì vinta ?
Ed egli a me : Questo misero modo
    Tengon l' anime triste di coloro,   35
    Che visser senza infamia e senza lodo.
Mischiate sono a quel cattivo coro
    Degli angeli, che non furon ribelli,
    Nè fur fedeli a Dio, ma per sè foro.
Cacciârli i Ciel per non esser men belli ;   40
    Nè lo profondo inferno gli riceve,
    Ch' alcuna gloria i rei avrebber d' elli.
Ed io : Maestro, che è tanto greve
    A lor, che lamentar gli fa sì forte ?
    Rispose : Dicerolti molto breve.   45
Questi non hanno speranza di morte ;
    E la lor cieca vita è tanto bassa,
    Che invidïosi son d' ogni altra sorte.
Fama di loro il mondo esser non lassa :
    Misericordia e Giustizia gli sdegna ;   50
    Non ragioniam di lor, ma guarda e passa.

' I would thou wert either hot or cold.'—REV. iii. 15.

(XII)

THE Pilgrim, who has been led within the dark portals, is first shown, just within the threshold, that life for Self alone is the initiation into the 'blind life'—the beginning of Death.

These miserable souls, too petty for praise or blame, are here seen only as germs, as it were, of the Monster that we shall in the end behold as the 'powerful worm that undermines the whole world,' who is also ' Emperor of the dolorous people.'

> ' To give away yourself keeps yourself still.'
> Shakespeare's ' Sonnets.'

In learning that Christ *is* the Centre of all life, the renewed man finds his higher self liberated, baptized, and renamed. He has lost his life to find it.

*The Crowds who 'never were alive,' who follow the
Banner that whirls round.*

INFERNO, CANTO III. 52-65.

E D io, che riguardai, vidi una insegna,
    Che, girando, correva tanto ratta,
    Che d'ogni posa mi pareva indegna:
E dietro le venía sì lunga tratta   55
    Di gente, ch'io non avrei mai creduto,
    Che morte tanta n' avesse disfatta.
Poscia ch'io v' ebbi alcun riconosciuto,
    Guardai, e vidi l' ombra di colui
    Che fece per viltate il gran rifiuto.   60
Incontanente intesi, e certo fui,
    Che quest' era la setta de' cattivi,
    A Dio spiacenti ed a' nemici sui.
Questi sciaurati, che mai non fur vivi,
    Erano ignudi, e stimolati molto.   65

'No man can serve two masters.'—MATT. vi. 24.

(XIII)

THE coward Neutrals had followed public opinion, the watchwords and banners that were for the moment popular, and can but follow such through all the vicissitudes of their ever-changing vacillations,* for they have forfeited their moral force and their power of discerning and choosing a true Cause. These Trimmers and Waverers would refuse any post of responsible action, lest it should compromise their own personal safety.

'He that loveth his life shall lose it.'

The live fish swim against the stream, the dead drift with it. While we drift, we are the thing we cannot help; but in willing and working in God's will we become men.

My soul, beware, even in thy day of small things, lest by selfish cowardice thou art preparing thyself to make some 'great refusal' (line 60).

'We prepare ourselves for sudden deeds by the reiterated choice of good and evil, which gradually determines character.'—GEORGE ELIOT.

---

* See Dean Plumptre's note.

The description of those who sigh without hope, and live in desire, not having been baptized into Faith.

———————————— (XIV) ————————

INFERNO, CANTO IV. 22-45.

ANDIAM, chè la via lunga ne sospigne.
   Così si mise, e così mi fe entrare
   Nel primo cerchio che l'abisso cigne.
Quivi, secondo ch'io pote' ascoltare,   25
   Non avea pianto, ma che di sospiri,
   Che l'aura eterna facevan tremare.
E ciò avvenia di duol senza martiri,
   Ch'avean le turbe, ch'eran molte e grandi,
   E d'infanti e di femmine e di viri.   30
Lo buon Maestro a me : Tu non dimandi
   Che spiriti son questi che tu vedi?
   Or vo' che sappi, innanzi che più andi,
Ch'ei non peccaro : e s'egli hanno mercedi,
   Non basta, perch'e' non ebber battesmo,   35
   Ch'è porta della Fede che tu credi.
E se furon dinanzi al Cristianesmo,
   Non adorâr debitamente Dio :
   E di questi cotai son io medesmo.
Per tai difetti, e non per altro rio,   40
   Semo perduti, e sol di tanto offesi,
   Che sanza speme vivemo in disio.
Gran duol mi prese al cor quando lo intesi ;
   Perocchè gente di molto valore
   Conobbi che in quel Limbo eran sospesi.   45

Desire unquickened by Hope is impotent.

(XIV)

THE atmosphere of trembling and sighs must be breathed by the defective, though noble and innocent souls, whose inner perceptions and faculties are unopened to behold the relationship of God to man. Till we know Him as our Father, through initiation into the Christian Faith, we find ourselves, unsupported by Hope, at the mercy of fears and of desires.

'All the world is as one Orphanage so long as its children know not God as their Father.'—Ruskin.

> '. . . Lost in a gloom of uninspired research,
> Meanwhile, the heart within the heart, the seat
> Where Peace and happy consciousness should dwell,
> On its own axis restlessly revolving,
> Seeks, yet can nowhere find, the light of truth.'
> 'The Excursion.'

The Temple of Philosophy with its Seven Walls and Gates, and the mighty spirits who dwelt there.

──────────── (XV) ────────────

INFERNO, CANTO IV. 106-120.

VENIMMO al piè d' un nobile castello,
    Sette volte cerchiato d' alte mura,
    Difeso intorno da un bel fiumicello.
Questo passammo come terra dura:
    Per sette porte entrai con questi savi;   110
    Giugnemmo in prato di fresca verdura:
Genti v' eran con occhi tardi e gravi,
    Di grand' autorità ne' lor sembianti:
    Parlavan rado, con voci soavi.
Traemmoci così dall' un de' canti,   115
    In luogo aperto, luminoso ed alto,
    Sì che veder si potean tutti quanti.
Colà diritto, sopra 'l verde smalto,
    Mi fur mostrati gli spiriti magni,
    Che di vederli in me stesso m' esalto.   120

The Grand Temple awaiting Consecration.

──────── (XV) ────────

IT is not enough to enter through the Seven Gates of earthly knowledge into the Temple of Philosophy, or to become acquainted with the grand beings 'whom to have known ennobles the Pilgrim' without the Divine Wisdom that inspires Faith, Hope, and Love.

> 'What hath not man sought out and found
>   But his deare God?   Who yet His glorious law
> Embosoms in us, mellowing the ground
>   With showres and frosts, with love and aw,
> So that we need not say, "Where's this command?"
>   Poore man, thou searchest round
> To find out *death*, but missest *life* at hand.'
>
>   GEO. HERBERT.

'Philosophy is the middle state between Science or Knowledge, and Sofia or Wisdom.'—COLERIDGE.

'For in the place wherein the Highest beginneth to show His City there can no man's building be able to stand.'—2 Esdras x. 54.

'. . . Whether there be knowledge it shall be done away, for we know in part . . . but when that which is perfect is come, then that which is in part shall be done away.'—1 Cor. xiii. 9, 10 (N.V.).

'These . . . received not the promise, God having provided some better thing for us, *that apart from us* they should not be made perfect.' —New Version, Heb. xi. 40.

*The hurricane that gives no rest to those whose appetites
made a prey of their right reason.*

(XVI)

INFERNO, CANTO V. 26-45.

. . . . . . or son venuto
Là dove molto pianto mi percuote.
Io venni in luogo d'ogni luce muto,
   Che mugghia come fa mar per tempesta,
   Se da contrari venti è combattuto.   30
La bufera infernal, che mai non resta,
   Mena gli spirti con la sua rapina;
   Voltando e percotendo gli molesta.
Quando giungon davanti alla ruina,
   Quivi le strida, il compianto e 'l lamento;   35
   Bestemmian quivi la Virtù divina.
Intesi ch'a così fatto tormento
   Eran dannati i peccator carnali,
   Che la ragion sommettono al talento.
E come gli stornei ne portan l'ali,   40
   Nel freddo tempo, a schiera larga e piena;
   Così quel fiato gli spiriti mali
Di qua, di là, di giù, di su gli mena:
   Nulla speranza gli conforta mai,
   Non che di posa, ma di minor pena.   45

' I feel the weight of chance desires.'

———————————— (XVI) — ————————

AFTER the stillness and stately gravity of the Temple of the Seven Gates, and of the People of great Authority—Poets, Heroes, and Philosophers (whose benefaction to their race, it is intimated, had obtained for them the grace of this resting-place), the Pilgrim has to pass forth from the quiet to the air that trembles and to a place 'where nothing shines.' It is the Second Circle of the Inferno. The First Circle is analogous to the Ante-Purgatorio; also to the Eden-restored at the threshold of the Celestial Paradise. Each stage in this symmetrical Poem has its counterpart or its antithesis.

In this Circle the dim light and the bellowing, never-resting hurricane fearfully tell of the darkened reason and the tempestuous passion and impulse that characterize those who find here 'their own place.'

They are the carnally-minded and self-indulgent, who are thus tossed about as the chaff by the wind, seeking repose in vain.

It is in this Circle that Francesca da Rimini tells her heart-rending story, and that Dante in pity falls as one dead.

The Will must be lord over the desire, and rule the life of the desire and use it as *It* pleases.

'Evil desires enter the heart of a man silently and wormlike until the soul becomes entangled therein as in the folds of a Serpent.'—Hartmann's 'Jacob Boehme.'

INFERNO, CANTO VII. 25-35, 49-66.

Qui vid' io gente, più ch' altrove troppa,   25
    E d' una parte e d' altra, con grand' urli
    Voltando pesi, per forza di poppa :
Percotevansi incontro, e poscia pur lì
    Si rivolgea ciascun, voltando a retro,
    Gridando : Perchè tieni ? e : Perchè burli ?   30
Così tornavan per lo cerchio tetro,
    Da ogni mano all' opposito punto,
    Gridando sempre loro ontoso metro ;
Poi si volgea ciascun, quand' era giunto,
    Per lo suo mezzo cerchio, all' altra giostra.   35

      *   *   *   *   *

Ed io : Maestro, tra questi cotali
    Dovre' io ben riconoscere alcuni,   50
    Che furo immondi di cotesti mali.
Ed egli a me : Vano pensiero aduni :
    La sconoscente vita, che i fe sozzi,
    Ad ogni conoscenza or gli fa bruni.
In eterno verranno agli duo cozzi :   55
    Questi risurgeranno del sepulcro
    Col pugno chiuso, e quelli co' crin mozzi.
Mal dare e mal tener lo mondo pulcro
    Ha tolto loro, e posto a questa zuffa :
    Qual ella sia, parole non ci appulcro.   60
Or puoi, figliuol, veder la corta buffa
    De' ben, che son commessi alla Fortuna,
    Per che l' umana gente si rabbuffa.
Chè tutto l' oro, ch' è sotto la luna,
    E che già fu, di quest' anime stanche   65
    Non poterebbe farne posar una.

'*Make thy gold thy vassal, not thy King.*'

(XVII)

THE Avaricious and the Squanderers, through unfaithfulness in the 'unrighteous Mammon' (Luke xviii. 11) —'the price put into their hands to get Wisdom,' are both equally suffering in soul, for they have lost the sense of all true worth, and can discern nothing beyond the heavy loads which some would keep and some would throw away. Dante thinks he might recognise some amongst them, but is told by Virgil that they cannot now be distinguished, through having lost their own discernment. They have lavished their powers on sordid things, and in these have submerged their own distinctive personality.

The unsatisfying nature of all that is dispensed by Fortune, for which things men vainly scramble, is pointed out; and he is told that all the gold beneath the Moon could never give repose to one of these weary souls.

*The Angry Souls who tear one another, and the Sullen
immersed in the Mud.*

(XVIII)

INFERNO, CANTO VII. 109-126.

ED io, che a rimirar mi stava inteso,
    Vidi genti fangose in quel pantano,   110
    Ignude tutte, e con sembiante offeso.
Queste si percotean, non pur con mano,
    Ma con la testa e col petto e co' piedi,
    Troncandosi co' denti a brano a brano.
Lo buon Maestro disse: Figlio, or vedi   115
    L' anime di color cui vinse l' ira:
    Ed anche vo' che tu per certo credi
Che sotto l' acqua ha gente che sospira,
    E fanno pullular quest' acqua al summo,
    Come l' occhio ti dice u' che s' aggira.   120
Fitti nel limo dicon: Tristi fummo
    Nell' aer dolce che dal sol s' allegra,
    Portando dentro accidïoso fummo;
Or ci attristiam nella belletta negra.
    Quest' inno si gorgoglian nella strozza,   125
    Chè dir nol posson con parola integra.

'Neither murmer ye, as some of them murmured, and perished by the Destroyer.'—1 COR. x. 10.

──────── (XVIII) ────────

THE murmuring of gloomy temper is considered an off-shoot from the angry, violent heart. This spirit, encouraged within, consumes our life in sullen broodings over wrongs and grievances; and less account is taken of the elements of gladness, which may be discovered on all sides. The Sullen can perceive these elements only when in the past, or in the lives of others, and seldom rejoice in their present personal mercies.

Murmurers carry within themselves the dull mists of discontent, which always intensify as time goes on, and at length stifle and blind those who harbour them. '. . . Thou servedst not the Lord thy God with joyfulness and gladness of heart for the abundance of all things' (Deut. xxviii. 47).

'Put sadness away from thee, for truly sadness is the sister of half-heartedness and bitterness. . . . He that is sad doth always wickedly; first, because he maketh sad the Holy Spirit that hath been given to man for joy; and, secondly, he worketh lawlessness, because he neither prays to God nor gives Him thanks. Therefore cleanse thyself from this wicked sadness, and thou shalt live unto God, "Yea, unto God shall all they live who have cast out sadness from themselves and arrayed themselves in all joy."'

Quotation from the 'Shepherd of Hermas' in Dean Paget's preface to 'The Spirit of Discipline.'

'. . . He that hides a dark soul and foul thoughts,
Benighted walks under the mid-day Sun;
Himself is his own dungeon.'—'Comus.'

The fen-encompassed red City of Dis, the Erinnys on its Battlements, and their call for Medusa.

───────────────── (XIX) ─────────────────

INFERNO, CANTO IX. 31-33, 45-63.

Q UESTA palude, che 'l gran puzzo spira,
    Cinge d' intorno la città dolente,
    U' non potemo entrare omai senz' ira.
         *   *   *   *   *
Guarda, mi disse, le feroci Erine.   45
Quest' è Megera, dal sinistro canto:
    Quella, che piange dal destro, è Aletto:
    Tisifone è nel mezzo; e tacque a tanto.
Con l' unghie si fendea ciascuna il petto;
    Batteansi a palme; e gridavan sì alto,   50
    Ch' io mi strinsi al Poeta per sospetto.
Venga Medusa, e sì 'l farem di smalto,
    Gridavan tutte, riguardando in giuso:
    Mal non vengiammo in Teseo l' assalto.
Volgiti indietro, e tien lo viso chiuso: 55
    Chè se 'l Gorgon si mostra, e tu il vedessi,
    Nulla sarebbe del tornar mai suso.
Così disse 'l Maestro; ed egli stessi
    Mi volse, e non si tenne alle mie mani,
    Che con le sue ancor non mi chiudessi.   60
O voi, ch' avete gl' intelletti sani,
    Mirate la dottrina, che s' asconde
    Sotto 'l velame degli versi strani.

The Sorrow that worketh Death.

(XIX)

IN this fiery City the infidel and the heretic find their home. Here the Pilgrim is brought into contact with union in the midst of disunion, a union for evil, used against one who travels to the City of Peace.

The three terrible Erinnys (like Conscience unenlightened gone mad with remorse) would urge their prey to take refuge in callous indifference through gazing into the face of Unbelief (Medusa's stony spell); but blessed intervention from above hides the eyes of the Pilgrim from beholding the perilous depth of Doubt, and the consequent petrification of all life. 'There is a point at which the contemplation of evil becomes fatal.' Victory in this struggle can be obtained only by Divine Grace.

The City of Dis* is the Antithesis to the City of the living God. Its turreted walls and Sepulchres keep in Death, and shut out Life. The Heavenly Jerusalem has no confines but Light and Love.

* The Greek name for Pluto.

*The Violent who use force against God, themselves,
and their neighbour.*

———————————— (XX) ————————————

INFERNO, CANTO XI. 28-32, 40-56.

D E' vïolenti il primo cerchio è tutto ;
    Ma perchè si fa forza a tre persone,
    In tre gironi è distinto e costrutto.   30
A Dio, a sè, al prossimo si puone
    Far forza ; dico in loro ed in lor cose :
    *   *   *   *   *
Puote uomo avere in sè man vïolenta,   40
    E ne' suoi beni : e però nel secondo
    Giron convien che sanza pro si penta
Qualunque priva sè del vostro mondo,
    Biscazza, e fonde la sua facultade,
    E piange là dove esser dee giocondo.   45
Puossi far forza nella Deïtade,
    Col cuor negando e bestemmiando quella,
    E spregiando natura e sua bontade :
E però lo minor giron suggella
    Del segno suo e Soddoma e Caorsa,   50
    E chi, spregiando Dio, col cuor favella.
La frode, ond' ogni coscïenza è morsa,
    Può l' uomo usare in colui che si fida,
    E in quello che fidanza non imborsa.
Questo modo di retro par ch' uccida   55
    Pur lo vincol d' amor, che fa natura.

The Cords of Love which man would violently sever.

(XX)

THE Supreme Love and Wisdom has bound man to His own Heart in the bonds of Love, 'the cords of a man.' He has set certain bounds to man's habitation with laws that necessitate his obedience to them—or he must be crushed by them. He has bound him also with the necessities and interdependence of love to his fellow creatures. These three bonds may be each and all, in more or less degree, wilfully broken by the headstrong and violent spirit. How is it possible that such disruption can produce anything but chaos and self-destruction? misery at the same time must be brought into the realm in which others are involved.

It is a remarkable suggestion that violence towards ourselves through dissipation of our own property is considered reprehensible, in that it causes 'weeping where we should be jocund'; it is a wasting of the means lent to us for joy and helpfulness; and the disdain of Nature and her bounty is, in Dante's eyes, blasphemy against God.

The dusky thornbearing Wood of the Suicides.

INFERNO, CANTO XIII. 1-10, 70-72, 94-102.

NON era ancor di là Nesso arrivato,
    Quando noi ci mettemmo per un bosco,
    Che da nessun sentiero era segnato.
Non frondi verdi, ma di color fosco;
    Non rami schietti, ma nodosi e involti;   5
    Non pomi v' eran, ma stecchi con tosco.
Non han sì aspri sterpi, nè sì folti
    Quelle fiere selvagge, che in odio hanno,
    Tra Cecina e Corneto, i luoghi colti.
Quivi le brutte Arpie lor nido fanno.   10
    *   *   *   *   *
*L' animo mio, per disdegnoso gusto,   70
    Credendo col morir fuggir disdegno,
    Ingiusto fece me contra me giusto.
    *   *   *   *   *
Quando si parte l' anima feroce   94
    Dal corpo, ond' ella stessa s' è disvelta,
    Minòs la manda alla settima foce.
Cade in la selva, e non l' è parte scelta;
    Ma là dove fortuna la balestra,
    Quivi germoglia come gran di spelta.
Surge in vermena, ed in pianta silvestra: 100
    L' Arpie, pascendo poi delle sue foglie,
    Fanno dolore, ed al dolor finestra.

---

* The suicide, Pier delle Vigne, recounts his own endeavour to escape his misery; and later describes the fate of souls so dying, who fall like chance seeds into unprepared ground, and their consequent suffering.

'Trees whose fruit withereth, without fruit, twice dead.'
JUDE 12.

──────────── (XXI) ────────────

THOSE who outrage with suicidal hands the bonds of their nature forfeit their true humanity and sink into a lower Kingdom, taking with them into it their consciousness of pain and remorse. Contrast this distorted, thorn-bearing, poisonous thicket, infested by cruel Harpies, with the natural woods and orchards, vocal with birds, in which we have reposed and rejoiced from childhood upwards—a Picture, in the Vegetable Kingdom, of Man unreplenished with the Sap of God. Are we not suicidal when we sever ourselves from our true, divinely human nature in Christ Jesus? It is in the strength of the Divine Man that instead of flying before evil, 'thinking by dying to escape disdain,' we may meet and overcome it.

'If a man abide not in Me, he is cast forth as a branch and is withered; and men gather them, and cast them into the fire, and they are burned.' —John xv. 6.

'Blessed is the man . . . (whose) delight is in the law of the Lord. . . . He shall be like a tree planted by the rivers of water, that bringeth forth his fruit in his season; his leaf also shall not wither, and whatsoever he doeth shall prosper.'—Psalm i. 3.

Nature speaks to us in Parables, and we also see reflected in her our own moods. 'We have the choice,' as Ruskin says, ' of turning all the voices of Nature into one song of rejoicing, and all her lifeless creatures into a glad company, whereof the meanest shall be beautiful in our eyes by its kind message; or of quenching her sympathy into a fearful withdrawn silence of condemnation, or into a crying out of her stones and a shaking of her dust against us.'

*The arrogance and rage of Capaneus are sufficient
torment to him.*

——————————— (XXII) ———————————

INFERNO, CANTO XIV. 43-51, 61-66.

IO cominciai : Maestro, tu che vinci
   Tutte le cose, fuor che i dimon duri,
   Ch' all' entrar della porta incontro uscinci ;   45
Chi è quel grande, che non par che curi
   L' incendio, e giace dispettoso e torto
   Sì, che la pioggia non par che 'l marturi?
E quel medesmo, che si fue accorto
   Ch' io domandava 'l mio Duca di lui,   50
   Gridò : Quale i' fui vivo, tal son morto.
   *   *   *   *   *
Allora il Duca mio parlò di forza   61
   Tanto, ch' io non l' avea sì forte udito :
   O Capaneo, in ciò che non s'ammorza
La tua superbia, se' tu più punito :
   Nullo martirio, fuor che la tua rabbia,   65
   Sarebbe al tuo furor dolor compito.

'Such as I was living am I dead.'

(XXII)

'WITHIN the fires the Spirits are,
  Each swathes himself with that wherewith he burns.'—Inferno xxvi. 46, 47.

Here as elsewhere we see the expression of the ruling spirit of the man, and are made to feel that the sin itself punishes the sinner, rather than that the punishment is an arbitrary infliction. Capaneus clings to the fiery pride that consumed him; the rage that he had nourished within now enwraps his whole being. There is a certain grandeur in the picture of his defiance of an external arbitrary force; for he misconceives it to be mere force, and his own spirit, an offspring of the Divine Spirit, cannot be dominated by force alone. The Antithesis to the swathing wherewith each burns in the Inferno is expressed in the Paradiso, as each rayed about with his own gladness, 'like a creature swathed in its own silk.'—Par. viii. 52.

'We are continually fancying that there will be some reversal of the law, that the seed we have sown we must reap. The delusion hangs about us all: we try to persuade ourselves that God's grant of pardon is a warrant for it. God does more than pardon in our poor sense of that word. He gives repentance: it is the grace of turning us from darkness to light, not the impossible mercy of giving us a light which we hate. Good and evil were set before man at the first, they are set before him to the last. As long as there is resistance to good there is misery. There has been no change in the divine order; no conversion of any one thing to its opposite.'—F. D. MAURICE.

INFERNO, CANTO XV. 46-57, 79-87.

E I cominciò : Qual fortuna o destino
    Anzi l' ultimo dì quaggiù ti mena?
        E chi è quel che ti mostra 'l cammino?
Lassù di sopra in la vita serena,
    Rispos' io lui, mi smarrii 'n una valle,   50
        Avanti che l' età mia fosse piena.
Pur ier mattina le volsi le spalle :
    Questi m' apparve, tornand' io in quella ;
        E riducemi a ca' per questo calle.
Ed egli a me : Se tu segui tua stella,   55
    Non puoi fallire a glorïoso porto,
        Se ben m' accorsi nella vita bella.
 * * * * *
Se fosse pieno tutto 'l mio dimando,
    Risposi lui, voi non sareste ancora   80
        Dell' umana natura posto in bando :
Chè in la mente m' è fitta, ed or m' accuora
    La cara e buona imagine paterna
        Di voi, quando nel mondo ad ora ad ora
M' insegnavate come l' uom s' eterna :   85
    E quant' io l' abbo in grado, mentr' io vivo
        Convien che nella mia lingua si scerna.

'For man there is but one great misfortune: to receive an idea that exerts no influence on his active life.'

──────── (XXIII) ────────

DANTE finds Brunetto Latini still his Friend and Teacher—yet in banishment from human nature, having failed to be one in deed and in truth with that which he had so ably taught, 'How man should eternize himself.' Perhaps the greatest peril to our own spiritual life lies in the attitude assumed by us, or it may be the vocation laid upon us of teaching others. The divergence between the intellectually perceived truth taught, and the truth lived up to, insidiously undermines character and blinds the conscience. Note the expression, Rom. i. 18 (N. V.), 'Who hold down the truth in unrighteousness.' The Truth pleads within, but is 'held down' by the predominance of the lower nature.

On one side this friendship has fructified; on the other, it has had no redeeming power. Yet with what a relieving gleam this converse of friends seems to penetrate the awful tints which paint hell for us—a faint flicker of unity in the midst of the dislocation of all human bonds!

The fulfilment of our Lord's last prayer, 'That they may be perfected in one'—the Communion of Saints—lies enfolded in promise and embryo in each true friendship, a heavenly treasure peculiarly subjected to all the chills and blights of Earth; for does it not lie nearest, perhaps, of all such treasures to the shadow of Self-love and jealousy, and though indestructible, as we hope, may it not in that shadow lose all the potent fragrance of its own clime?

The Monster Geryon, Fraud.

(XXIV)

INFERNO, CANTO XVII. 1-18.

ECCO la fiera con la coda aguzza,
 Che passa monti, e rompe muri ed armi:
 Ecco colei che tutto il mondo appuzza.
Sì cominciò lo mio Duca a parlarmi;
 Ed accennolle che venisse a proda,   5
 Vicino al fin de' passeggiati marmi.
E quella sozza imagine di froda
 Sen venne, ed arrivò la testa e 'l busto;
 Ma in su la riva non trasse la coda.
La faccia sua era faccia d' uom giusto,   10
 Tanto benigna avea di fuor la pelle;
 E d' un serpente tutto l' altro fusto.
Duo branche avea pilose infin l' ascelle;
 Lo dosso e 'l petto ed ambedue le coste
 Dipinte avea di nodi e di rotelle.   15
Con più color sommesse e soprapposte
 Non fêr mai in drappo Tartari nè Turchi,
 Nè fur tai tele per Aracne imposte.

The Subtleties of the beguiling Serpent.

———————— (XXIV) ————————

'THE Monster which infecteth all the world,' Deceit, whose root is hidden in each heart, is here brought to view full grown and personalized. We see the benign face of a just man, a serpent body with hairy paws and arms, the skin as though painted and wondrously embroidered, and hung with spider-web tissues—all without organic unity, all taken on from others. We see, reflected as in a mirror, our desires to look better than we are, self-interested motives hidden under specious actions or words, divers colouring given to match divers objects, nooses to entrap others, or even our own consciences, and the subtle tissues of flatteries that entangle with sophistries and plausibilities. Through the agency of this Monster Geryon (Fraud) the lowest Hell is entered; the descent is made from the region of animal impulse to that of the calculating, conscious disregard of the Divine and the social bond.

> 'Farewell, remorse; all good to me is lost;
> Evil, be thou my good.'—MILTON.

Dante, terrified by the imagined grip of the Malebranche demons, is rescued by Virgil.

INFERNO, CANTO XXIII. 19-33, 37-51.

Già mi sentia tutti arricciar li peli
   Dalla paura; e stava indietro intento,   20
   Quand' io dissi: Maestro, se non celi
Te e me tostamente, i' ho pavento
   De' Malebranche; noi gli avem già dietro:
   Io gl' immagino sì, che già li sento.
E quei: S' io fossi d' impiombato vetro,   25
   L' imagine di fuor tua non trarrei
   Più tosto a me, che quella dentro impetro.
Pur mo venieno i tuoi pensier tra i miei,
   Con simile atto, e con simile faccia,
   Sì che d' entrambi un sol consiglio fei.   30
S' egli è, che sì la destra costa giaccia,
   Che noi possiam nell' altra bolgia scendere,
   Noi fuggirem l' immaginata caccia.

*   *   *   *   *

Lo Duca mio di subito mi prese,
   Come la madre, ch' al romore è desta,
   E vede presso a sè le fiamme accese,
Che prende il figlio, e fugge, e non s' arresta,   40
   Avendo più di lui che di sè cura,
   Tanto che solo una camicia vesta.
E giù dal collo della ripa dura
   Supin si diede alla pendente roccia,
   Che l' un de' lati all' altra bolgia tura.   45
Non corse mai sì tosto acqua per doccia
   A volger ruota di mulin terragno,
   Quando ella più verso le pale approccia;
Come 'l Maestro mio per quel vivagno,
   Portandosene me sovra 'l suo petto,   50
   Come suo figlio, e non come compagno.

'As one whom his Mother comforteth.'

(XXV)

THE terror of Dante at the ghastly pranks of the demons in 'the Pantomime of Hell,' as this Circle of it has been called, brings out the interior relationship between the Pilgrim and his divinely enlightened Guide. As here revealed to us, the indwelling Word portrayed in Virgil seems the very personification of Love, who reads the thoughts of his beloved 'long before,' in whom these thoughts are blent and imaged in unity with his own; who enfolds the Pilgrim in his arms, swiftly fleeing with him in perfect sympathy with *his* fears, even as a Mother with her child, losing herself completely in him, having more care of him than of herself.

Dante more than once brings be.... strength and efficient action of a mother, as well as her self-forgetting tenderness. Her comforting to him would imply strengthening, even as the derivation of that word teaches us. 'I will not leave you comfortless.'

Note the wonderful intimacy of spiritual communion described in lines 25 to 30, reminding us of the experience of the Psalmist.

'O Lord, Thou hast searched me, and known me. Thou knowest my downsitting and mine uprising, Thou understandest my thought afar off.'—Ps. cxxxix.

> 'Not youngest thought in me doth grow,
> No, not one word I cast to talk
> But yet unuttered Thou dost know.'—SIR PHILIP SIDNEY.

The heavily-clad Hypocrites.

———————————— (XXVI) ————————

INFERNO, CANTO XXIII. 58-72.

LAGGIÙ trovammo una gente dipinta,
   Che giva intorno assai con lenti passi,
   Piangendo, e nel sembiante stanca e vinta.   60
Egli avean cappe, con cappucci bassi
   Dinanzi agli occhi, fatte della taglia
   Che in Cologna per li monaci fassi.
Di fuor dorate son, sì che egli abbaglia,
   Ma dentro tutte piombo; e gravi tanto,   65
   Che Federigo le mettea di paglia.
O in eterno faticoso manto!
   Noi ci volgemmo ancor pure a man manca
   Con loro insieme intenti al tristo pianto:
Ma per lo peso quella gente stanca   70
   Venia sì pian, che noi eravam nuovi
   Di compagnia ad ogni muover d'anca.

'Take heed that ye do not your righteousness before men, to be seen of them.'—MATT. vi. 1.

(XXVI)

THE painted, weary folk have been weaving themselves these eternally-heavy mantles under which their natural characters, with all play of spontaneity, have withered away. It needs special effort to live an eternal 'make-believe,' to make a continual endeavour to seem. They are not only tired but vanquished, for they have not succeeded in imposing much on others; as it has been said, 'If we say we have no sin, we deceive *ourselves*' (*rarely others*). Contrast the self-made, crushing clothes of these 'oppressed people' with the clothing God makes to express, not to conceal, the true life.

'Consider the Lilies, how they grow; they toil not, neither do they spin; yet I say unto you, that Solomon in all his glory was not arrayed like one of these.'—Matt. vi. 28.

Contrast with this Matt. xxiii. 27, 'For ye are like unto whited Sepulchres, which indeed appear beautiful outwardly, but are within full of dead men's bones, and of all uncleanness.'

Again, God's clothing is shown to us in Rev. xix. 8—His clothing in which the clothed participate by working out what He works within. 'And to her was granted that she should be arrayed in fine linen, clean and white: for the fine linen is the righteousness of the Saints.'

'The King's daughter is all glorious *within*.'

'Nothing that has not become living experience can become living expression.'—LOWELL.

'*The True*, that is the soul's natural state. The false is the abnormal monstrous state. We feel it by the infinite sweetness, the expanding of our whole being, when surrounded with persons who are true and straightforward. We feel it by the dreadful discomfort which we experience through the contact of dissemblers.'—MADAME QUINET.

Virgil urges Dante to put off Sloth, lest he leave no fame behind him.

(XXVII)

INFERNO, CANTO XXIV. 46-60.

OMAI convien che tu così ti spoltre,
    Disse 'l Maestro; chè, seggendo in piuma,
    In fama non si vien, nè sotto coltre:
Sanza la qual, chi sua vita consuma,
    Cotal vestigio in terra di sè lascia,   50
    Qual fummo in aere, od in acqua la schiuma.
E però leva su; vinci l' ambascia
    Con l' animo che vince ogni battaglia,
    Se col suo grave corpo non s' accascia.
Più lunga scala convien che si saglia;   55
    Non basta da costoro esser partito:
    Se tu m' intendi, or fa' sì che ti vaglia.
Levaimi allor, mostrandomi fornito
    Meglio di lena, ch' i' non mi sentia;
    E dissi: Va', ch' io son forte ed ardito.   60

'Be of good courage, for I am with thee.'

(XXVII)

THE Pilgrim on his awful way comes from time to time to such straits and passes as call for more courage than he can summon; happy for him, then, if he have a friendly voice by his side, as well as the Monitor within, to adjure him not to sink with hands folded under downy coverlid, leaving no trace behind him of his part in the great conflict; and to remind him that the Spirit may overcome all things, if it sink not under the weight of the flesh. The literal word 'impossible' is not in the language of Spirit. 'Overcome in My might,' must obliterate it. And as it has been said, 'It is the impossible only that is worth anything.'

'Be not dismayed' (not because there is nothing to dismay, but), 'for I am thy God.' Such a word may command a venture for which there is no felt strength; then a courage must be, apparently to one's self, even feigned in order to go forward. Emmanuel is our Watchword.

'Claim for your own the morally best. Act on Christ's promise as if it were true, and you find it is. This is faith, to act on what transcends experience, to act on what you do not feel possible, to act in faith on a promised strength, and to find it in the using. Faith involves the recognition of our own weakness, the surrender of our own independence into the hands of God: it gains as its reward the promised help; it sets free the "virtue" which goes out of Christ. It can yield up to higher forces than it has yet known. Only when the forces have become in experience thoroughly familiar can they be subjected to the analysis of reason.'—From Gore's Preface to Edition x. of 'Lux Mundi.'

Virgil reproves Dante for lingering to hear an unworthy dispute.

(XXVIII)

INFERNO, CANTOS XXX. 130-148, XXXI. 1-6.

AD ascoltarli er' io del tutto fisso, 130
   Quando 'l Maestro mi disse: Or pur mira;
   Chè per poco è che teco non mi risso.
Quand' io 'l senti' a me parlar con ira,
   Volsimi verso lui con tal vergogna,
   Ch' ancor per la memoria mi si gira. 135
E quale è quei che suo dannaggio sogna,
   Che sognando desidera sognare,
   Sì che quel ch' è, come non fosse, agogna;
Tal mi fec' io, non potendo parlare;
   Chè disiava scusarmi, e scusava 140
   Me tuttavia, e nol mi credea fare.
Maggior difetto men vergogna lava,
   Disse 'l Maestro, che 'l tuo non è stato;
   Però d' ogni tristizia ti disgrava.
E fa' ragion ch' io ti sia sempre allato, 145
   Se più avvien che fortuna t' accoglia
   Dove sien genti in simigliante piato;
Chè voler ciò udire è bassa voglia.

*   *   *   *   *

Una medesma lingua pria mi morse, 1
   Sì che mi tinse l' una e l' altra guancia,
   E poi la medicina mi riporse.
Così od' io, che soleva la lancia
   D' Achille e del suo padre esser cagione 5
   Prima di trista, e poi di buona mancia.

'*They judge all Nature from her feet of clay.*'

(XXVIII)

AS the Pilgrim tastes more and more of the fruit of the knowledge of evil, though he be of a lofty nature, he lingers on his way, through curiosity to hear an unworthy and spiteful quarrel. We are told sometimes that we should look at the actual human being as he really is (apart from any ideal concerning him) in his baseness and corruption ; to reproduce this debased portrait is deemed frank and real; but can this be done loyally by the Christian who 'divinely through all hindrance finds *the man*,' believing the real manhood to be in Christ—the true nature in man? Further, how shall our limited capacities for hearing and seeing retain their subtler powers of perceiving that better and nobler side of each human heart, if we blunt these capacities by lingering needlessly amidst the discords of contradicting sounds and sights?

'Love taketh not account of evil.'—1 Cor. xiii. 5 (N.V.).

'For it is a shame even to speak of those things which are done of them in secret.'—Ephes. v. 12.

'Finally, whatsoever things are true, whatsoever things are honourable, whatsoever things are just, whatsoever things are pure, whatsoever things are lovely, whatsoever things are of good report ; if there be any virtue, and if there be any praise, think on these things.'—Phil. iv. 8.

Note the function of Conscience, as distinguished from that of the Accuser of the brethren in the last lines of Canto XXX. and first lines of Canto XXXI.

'The cause first of a sad and then a gracious boon.'

The Convincer of Sin and the Comforter are One.

'Teach me with quick-ear'd spirit to rejoice
In admonitions of thy softest voice !'—'The Excursion.'

Another language needed to speak of the dark world.

──────────── (XXIX) ────────────

INFERNO, CANTO XXXII. 1-9.

S' IO avessi le rime ed aspre e chiocce,
   Come si converrebbe al tristo buco,
   Sovra 'l qual pontan tutte l' altre rocce,
Io premerei di mio concetto il suco
   Più pienamente; ma perch' io non l' abbo,   5
   Non senza tema a dicer mi conduco.
Chè non è impresa da pigliare a gabbo
   Descriver fondo a tutto l' universo,
   Nè da lingua che chiami mamma e babbo.

'Doth a Fountain send forth at the same place sweet water and bitter?'—JAMES iii. 1.

(XXIX)

THE heights and depths of our experience need new language; indeed, in the many worlds within our world various languages are spoken and needed. The Word is broken to pieces amongst us, and only those in full affinity with one another who can *divine* the thing signified can receive real transference of spiritual thought from each other; between the less related there must be still clumsier signalling. In the lines that lead our meditation to-day nothing could, by contrast, more forcibly flash upon us a lurid gleam from hell than the three last—another language needed to describe it than the one used in which the familiar and tender cries of 'Mamma' and 'Dadda' proceed from innocent infant lips! Alas! this contrast was felt the other day in a London street, and never can be forgotten, when a little boy of hardly four was seen trotting after a half-drunken man, and catching at his hand with his little fingers as he cried 'Father!' The little hand was repulsed, and a savage oath was the answer to the blessed name; yet the child clung to the man's coat and smiled and babbled on with his baby language. Surely one of those was at that moment in hell, the other in heaven, and neither could pass from one world to the other. Yet heaven there stretched further towards the one dwelling in hell, than he then could stretch towards heaven. God grant us deafness and dumbness to the dark world of unlove within ourselves, and open our ears and lips to the tones and language of the Heavenly City.

The demon-possessed body on Earth while the Soul is already in Hell.

──────────────── (XXX) ────────────────

INFERNO, CANTO XXXIII. 121-123, 129-147.

OH, dissi lui, or se' tu ancor morto?
    Ed egli a me: Come il mio corpo stea
Nel mondo su, nulla scïenzia porto.
   *   *   *   *   *
Sappi che tosto che l' anima trade,
Come fec' io, lo corpo suo l' è tolto   130
    Da un dimonio, che poscia il governa,
    Mentre che 'l tempo suo tutto sia vôlto.
Ella ruina in sì fatta cisterna:
    E forse pare ancor lo corpo suso
    Dell' ombra, che di qua dietro mi verna.   135
Tu 'l dèi saper, se tu vien pur mo giuso.
    Egli è ser Branca d' Oria; e son più anni
    Poscia passati ch' ei fu sì racchiuso.
Io credo, dissi lui, che tu m' inganni;
    Chè Branca d' Oria non morì unquanche,   140
    E mangia e bee e dorme e veste panni.
Nel fosso su, diss' ei, di Malebranche,
    Là dove bolle la tenace pece,
    Non era giunto ancora Michel Zanche,
Che quegli lasciò un diavol in sua vece   145
    Nel corpo suo, e d' un suo prossimano,
    Che 'l tradimento insieme con lui fece.

> '*The soul grows clotted by contagion,*
> *Imbodies and imbrutes, till she quite lose*
> *The divine property of her first being.*'

(XXX)

THE consummation of the death of the soul, before the death of the body takes place, is here brought before us. One is described who 'eats and drinks and sleeps and puts on clothes,' as usual in the body, while his spirit has migrated to the evil spirits in the lower hell. He has betrayed another, and is betrayed in his own betrayal—cast out from his own habitation, which another takes possession of, to a lower place for which he has fitted himself.

> '*The mind is its own place, and in itself*
> *Can make a heav'n of hell, a hell of heav'n.*'

'The heart liveth where it loveth.' We are happily more familiar with this thought when applied to the blessed, of whom it has often been said that they seem to live in heaven before their time—'whose conversation or citizenship is in heaven.'

The ghastly picture of the bodily presence still carrying on the semblance of the man's personality, whilst a devil is its only motive power, adds terrible emphasis to the conception of alliance with 'spiritual wickedness in high places,' and gives depth to the cry, Deliver us from Evil!

'For we must know that the wicked man may truly be called dead—of such an one some might say how is he dead and yet goes about? I answer that the man is dead, and the beast remains.'—'Convito,' Tr. IV., c. 7.

Lucifer, the Son of the Morning, fallen, and the Three Supreme Traitors.

(XXXI)

INFERNO, CANTO XXXIV. 1-9, 16-27.

VEXILLA regis prodeunt Inferni
   Verso di noi : però dinanzi mira,
   Disse 'l Maestro mio, se tu 'l discerni.
Come quando una grossa nebbia spira,
   O quando l' emisperio nostro annotta,   5
   Par da lungi un mulin, che il vento gira ;
Veder mi parve un tal dificio allotta :
   Poi, per lo vento, mi ristrinsi retro
   Al Duca mio ; chè non v' era altra grotta.

    *   *   *   *   *

Quando noi fummo fatti tanto avante,
   Ch' al mio Maestro piacque di mostrarmi
   La creatura ch' ebbe il bel sembiante,
Dinanzi mi si tolse, e fe ristarmi ;
   Ecco Dite, dicendo, ed ecco il loco,   20
   Ove convien che di fortezza t' armi,
Com' io divenni allor gelato e fioco,
   Nol domandar, lettor ; ch' io non lo scrivo,
   Però ch' ogni parlar sarebbe poco.
Io non mori', e non rimasi vivo :   25
   Pensa oramai per te, s' hai fior d' ingegno,
   Qual io divenni, d' uno e d' altro privo.

*'*The infernal Banners forward go*' *of the Creature who once had the beautiful semblance.*

──────── (XXXI) ────────

THROUGH all the Circles of Fraud and Deceit the Pilgrim has descended step by step even to this last stagnant, frozen pool of Treachery and Betrayal, wherein are welded in Eternal Ice the Supreme Traitors of their Lords and Benefactors. There he is bidden to gaze on the wreck and travesty of Angelhood, 'the Creature that once had the beautiful semblance.' We are told to conceive that which Dante found unspeakable, the terror and paralysis produced by the vision of the essence and root of all evil.

The Church and the Empire (always recognised by Dante as the Channels of Divine Government) were betrayed by the three Traitors seen in the nethermost Hell.

'The entire Circle of Treachery is covered with Ice to symbolize the isolating and freezing character of the crime of Treachery, the daughter of Pride. This sin alone completely isolates each man from every other. Pride is consistent selfishness, because it makes itself sole end and sole means. It is frozen, and it freezes all others.'— W. T. HARRIS.

---

* A travesty of the Church's hymn :
     'The Royal banners forward go,
     The Cross shines forth in mystic glow.'

The Monster with three faces, from whose Wings proceeded the icy blasts.

(XXXII)

INFERNO, CANTO XXXIV. 28, 29, 34-38, 46-52.

L'IMPERADOR del doloroso regno
   Da mezzo 'l petto uscia fuor della ghiaccia:
*   *   *   *   *
S'ei fu sì bel com' egli è ora brutto,
   E contra 'l suo Fattore alzò le ciglia,   35
   Ben dee da lui procedere ogni lutto.
O quanto parve a me gran meraviglia,
   Quando vidi tre facce alla sua testa!
*   *   *   *   *
Sotto ciascuna uscivan duo grand' ali,
   Quanto si conveniva a tant' uccello:
   Vele di mar non vid' io mai cotali.
Non avean penne, ma di vipistrello
   Era lor modo; e quelle svolazzava,   50
   Sì che tre venti si movean da ello.
Quindi Cocito tutto s'aggelava.

'*The Source of all Tribulation.*'

(XXXII)

NO further descent can be made—no deeper gaze into the negation of all good and all life is possible, for the spectacle is presented of the brow ever lifted against his Maker. Supreme Pride, and supreme Self-worshipping Isolation.

We confess our pride with less difficulty than other sins, sometimes in half-caressing tones; yet we find it here represented, probably truly, as the father of the basest and most universally despised of crimes, Treachery and Betrayal.

We may well shudder at the piercing phantasy of those six huge bat-like pinions ever waving, the only motion in the ice-bound region, ever sending forth their freezing blast; the fatal wind from which the Pilgrim would fain have screened himself has been noticed more than once during the descent; he knows now whence it blows.

Mockery of goodness or of love, cynicism, whispered hints of suspicion, chill questioning of all noble enthusiasms, these such Pilgrims as Dante will not fail to detect as effects (though but faint breezes) of the Bat-like pinions, and they will seek to shut the door of their hearts against them. What an antithesis we have to such in the Breath of the Spirit, genial, fructifying, imparting one Life, one Love throughout the whole Family of Heaven and Earth!

Line 38.—There is a certain absurdity in the view of any creature struggling to maintain itself in opposition to the laws of its own being. The vision of this self-stultifying revolt gives play to a grotesque irony in Dante's imagery, which is, however, always in deepest, direst earnest; such passages have been generally omitted, as they can only be read in this age with any sympathy when the mind is penetrated with Dante's work as a whole.

'The three faces have been taken as a symbol of a Trinity of Evil, the antithesis of Power, Wisdom, and Charity.'

The Climb upwards and the Centre of Gravity passed.

(XXXIII)

INFERNO, CANTO XXXIV. 82-84, 91-93, 97-111.

ATTIENTI ben : chè per cotali scale,
 Disse 'l Maestro ansando com' uom lasso,
 Conviensi dipartir da tanto male.
 *   *   *   *   *
E s' io divenni allora travagliato,
 La gente grossa il pensi, che non vede
 Qual è quel punto ch' io avea passato.
 *   *   *   *   *
Non era camminata di palagio,
 Là 'v' eravam ; ma natural burella,
 Ch' avea mal suolo, e di lume disagio.
Prima ch' io dell' abisso mi divella,   100
 Maestro mio, diss' io quando fui dritto,
 A trarmi d' erro un poco mi favella.
Ov' è la ghiaccia ? e questi com' è fitto
 Sì sottosopra ? e come in sì poc' ora
 Da sera a mane ha fatto il Sol tragitto ?   105
Ed egli a me : Tu immagini ancora
 D' esser di là dal centro, ov' io m' appresi
 Al pel del vermo reo che 'l mondo fóra.
Di là fosti cotanto, quant' io scesi :
 Quando mi volsi, tu passasti il punto,   110
 Al qual si traggon d' ogni parte i pesi.

'*We have passed from Death unto Life.*'

(XXXIII)

BARELY kept alive in the Sepulchre of Death, the Pilgrim is, after a certain point, carried upwards, as he imagines, by the same way that he had descended; but it is explained to him that he has passed the centre of Gravity, and is in another Hemisphere. He is puzzled and bewildered; what was above is now beneath, everything is reversed; he is in a new relationship to the Centre. Is not this turning-point Conversion? the passing from the sway of Self to that of Christ?

Our planetary system was once supposed to be Geocentric; we know now it is Helio centric, and each one has to learn for himself that it is Christo-centric. For a time the Pilgrim's steps must be taken with difficulty ' over floor uneven and with un-ease of light,' for he knows not how to adjust himself to the sway of the newly-recognised power of attraction.

' Death is the condition of Resurrection. There is indeed a continuity through Death, but a form of severance from the past must be the prelude to the New Birth.'—WESTCOTT.

' Suppose a planet gifted with intelligence and volition on the strength of this gift emancipating itself from the law of gravitation; it would soon find that all its sweet order and harmony were gone, and that its independent efforts to perform its revolution could not do the work of a centre of gravity. Its completeness consists in the maintenance of its relation to this Centre, without which all goes wrong.'—' The Spiritual Order,' by T. Erskine.

INFERNO, CANTO XXXIV. 127-139.

Luogo è laggiù da Belzebù rimoto
   Tanto, quanto la tomba si distende,
   Che non per vista, ma per suono è noto
D' un ruscelletto, che quivi discende   130
   Per la buca d' un sasso, ch' egli ha roso
   Col corso ch' egli avvolge; e poco pende.
Lo Duca ed io per quel cammino ascoso
   Entrammo, per tornar nel chiaro mondo;
   E senza cura aver d' alcun riposo   135
Salimmo su, ei primo ed io secondo,
   Tanto ch' io vidi delle cose belle,
   Che porta 'l ciel, per un pertugio tondo:
E quindi uscimmo a riveder le stelle.

The dark passage from the Sepulchre to the shining of the Stars.

———————————— (XXXIV) ————

WHAT can be the meaning of the little rivulet unseen in the darkness, that had issued from the very jaws of stony Death, boring for itself through the hard rock a winding way towards the light, a way of Escape for the Pilgrim's willing feet? Its small voice must indeed have seemed musical after the fiery circles of harsh din and the ice-bound silence of Despair in the lowest hell. Was it Hope? Was it Prayer?

> 'A stream which from the fountain of the Heart
> Issuing, however feebly, nowhere flows
> Without access of unexpected strength.'

The aperture of the dark tunnel comes at length into sight, and the blissful vision of some of the 'beautiful things that Heaven doth bear' beyond it. Again the Pilgrim beholds the stars! Nature is restored to him with a far deeper significance than she had before; and not Nature alone—for to this Pilgrim '*the stars*' meant the divine witnesses to God's orderly and spiritual rule of His Universe, and the channels of His Providential influences on the minds and circumstances of men.

PURGATORIO.

THE UPHILL WAY OF THE PURGATORIO.

'Be saluted by the air
Of meek repentance, wafting wall-flower scents
From out the crumbling ruins of fallen Pride.'
'Excursion,' Book IV.

'After some hard fights with the powers of darkness, my spirit broke through the doors of Hell and penetrated even into the innermost essence of the newly-born Divinity; where it was received with great love, such as is offered by a Bridegroom welcoming a beloved Bride.

'I cannot compare the gladness to anything except to a state in which life is born in the midst of the dead.

'While in this state my spirit immediately saw through everything, and recognised God in all things, even in herbs and grasses, and it knew what is God and what is His will.'—JACOB BOEHME, 'Aurora,' xix. 4.

PURGATORY is often thought of as a modified Hell—only less painful because it is supposed to be a temporary process, rather than an everlasting condition. We are taught here to regard this 'Second Kingdom,' 'wherein the human spirit doth purge itself,' as the very antipodes of Hell (indeed, so it is placed in the external imagery of the allegory)—the very vestibule of Heaven. The soul at its portals knows itself to be no longer the defiant victim of a cruel fate, but the beloved and loving child under the welcomed discipline of Love; and by that

The Uphill Way of the Purgatorio.

(2)

discipline being made meet for its home, and for the ardently desired vision of God.

In the Inferno, as we have seen, the controlling Power was regarded as arbitrary and cruel in its antagonism to those who had 'lost the good of reason.'

In Sir Philip Sidney's words, the Divine Creator was deemed 'the Outward Maker's force' and not 'an inward Father.' His love-life, drawing each of His offspring into unity with Himself and with every other member of His family, cannot be recognised by those who deny and exclude it, isolating themselves in the strongholds of Self and Pride. When the soul, as we have seen the Pilgrim's, is emancipated from this incarceration, it issues into the new sphere of God's attractive power. When we say, when we mean, 'I repent, I have sinned,' we are in the second Kingdom; not by getting our passport arbitrarily signed for permission to enter this Kingdom, but by the birth of the soul into it. There must be a death to one world before we can be born into another.

The gulf that divides the two worlds of the Inferno and Purgatorio, as shown to us by the Poet, seems, it is true, but inadequate to mark the wide separation between the two states; a moment's Repentance, one act of forgiveness, 'one little tearlet' as the demon complains (Canto v. 107)— such slight tokens, we find, rescue souls from the angels of darkness and set them on their way heavenward. But such slight tokens mark life; they indicate the moment of separation from the death of self-assertion. The soul has found its true element. 'The little tear' was the first trembling emotion of the 'poor in spirit' to whom the Kingdom of Heaven belongs; it showed the door opened by the Will towards the reception of all Heaven's gifts and all earth's ministries.

The Uphill Way of the Purgatorio.

(3)

The Ascent of the Mount thenceforth lies before the home-returning affections. The journey has begun; not merely the journey through this life to the Home beyond the skies; it is rather the heart's restoration to sanity—a restoration like that of the naked demoniac, from his abode among the tombs, to his right mind, his clothing, and his rest at the feet of Jesus, while learning of Him the Way, the Truth, and the Life (Mark v. 15-19; Luke viii. 35, 39).

To follow Dante's imagery, the Way is long and difficult before the Pilgrim, but he is in the way of Life. The growth of Life, its efforts, its perplexities even, are before him; in the way of Death he has gravitated downwards. On the ascending Way, Humility and Repentance are throughout the watchwords.

The seven deadly Sins, which reign throughout the Ten Circles of the dark pit with their complex subdivisions, are here made manifest by confession; they are marked as open wounds on the brow of the Pilgrim, to be cleansed away and closed one by one in the seven circles appointed for the discipline of each sin or *Peccato*. These sins are spoken of as the Seven P's. The Pilgrim's steps in the hard climb become freer and easier as he mounts, and as he is delivered from the wound of each P, through the light shed on the nature of the sin by its consequences, and through the fanning of an Angel's wing (heaven's refreshing Grace).

In the lowest Circles of Purgatorio he finds the sins of the lowest Hell—Pride, Envy, and Anger—repented of and cleansed; the Slothful and the Avaricious are seen in the fourth and fifth Circles; and, lastly, the sins of the flesh are purified in flames more terrible than those of molten glass. Yet the souls 'are content in the flames,' for their longing for the heavenly vision is more intense than their suffering.

and they 'listen to the singing on the other side.' Those who ascend the Mount of Purification have learnt so to hate the corruptions of the first kingdom, that linger as scales before their eyes, preventing their vision of God, that they welcome with joy any pain, even, that shall deliver them from these hindrances. When their longing for the beatific vision, or perfect union with their true Lord and Country, overmasters their personal sense of defilement and unfitness for His Presence, they rise upwards to their Goal, for they find no prison-walls or barriers to keep them in any school of discipline.

Virgil continues the Guide and Mentor of the Pilgrim, conducting him by philosophical, moral, and intellectual virtues, aided by heavenly ministrations of grace, till the summit of the Mount of Purification has been attained. There the renewed man finds the Paradise of Earth recovered. All his powers as Man are developed, and there he meets again the beloved Beatrice, who had first awakened his soul to the new Life. In her glorified condition he beholds her as the personification of the Celestial Wisdom, who not only instructs him with regard to his own past life, and concerning the condition of the Church Militant, but prepares him for a further ascent into more spiritual Truth, into which She is to lead him in the Paradise beyond.

'Light such as we see it and recognise it, the light of the morning and evening growing and fading, takes off from the unearthliness of the Purgatorio; peopled as it is by the undying, who through suffering for sin can sin no more; it is thus made like our familiar world, made to touch our sympathies as an image of our own purification in the flesh.'—
DEAN CHURCH.

'Like our familiar world'—and like the experience of the human heart here, in its progressive dissociation from false conceptions of God and of man's true end. Like our own world, in that there remains still some perplexity concerning the Way; in the necessity also there, as here, for counsels, both from brethren and from heavenly ministrations of grace. Like our world in the intercommunion of friends and neighbours, and in the witnessing of Nature's Sacramental teaching to the Invisible; but unlike it, in the absence of temptation, in the perfect comprehension and acceptance of its discipline, in the absolute certainty of the attainment of an ardently desired Goal. Unlike it also, alas! in the unfailing mutual aid and meek courtesies of each to each, and in the fulness of joy of its united organism (and even of Nature herself) when any member advances in the upward way. It seems the Ideal of the Church Expectant, in blessed consciousness of the realities within the Holy City, of the Communion of Saints and of Ministering Angels.

> 'As men from men
> Do, in the constitution of their souls,
> Differ, by mystery not to be explained;
> And as we fall by various ways, and sink
> One deeper than another, self-condemned,
> Through manifold degrees of guilt and shame;
> So manifold and various are the ways
> Of restoration, fashioned to the steps
> Of all infirmity, and tending all
> To the same point, attainable by all—
> Peace in ourselves, and union with our God.'
>
> 'The Excursion,' Book IV.

From the Dank air of the Sepulchre Dante escapes under the Sapphire Sky and Morning Star into the Second Realm.

───────── (I) ─────────

PURGATORIO.

CANTO I. 1-6, 13-18.

PER correr miglior acqua alza le vele
   Omai la navicella del mio ingegno,
   Che lascia dietro a sè mar sì crudele :
E canterò di quel secondo regno,
   Ove l' umano spirito si purga,   5
   E di salire al ciel diventa degno.
   *   *   *   *   *
Dolce color d' orïental zaffiro,
   Che s' accoglieva nel sereno aspetto
   Dell' aer puro infino al primo giro,   15
Agli occhi miei ricominciò diletto,
   Tosto ch' io fuori usci' dell' aura morta,
   Che m' avea contristato gli occhi e 'l petto.

*'Sorrow may endure for a night,
But joy cometh in the morning.'*

(I)

ONLY after a night of anguish and dark distress, dispelled by the morning hour, can we enter into the miracle of such a Dawn as these lines suggest to us. The beauty, the perfume, and the radiant purity of the Dawn behind all dawns, seems awakened within us.

For the Pilgrim, whose footsteps we follow, it is Life from the Dead.

This New Day contains an unspeakable wonder and promise—a fulfilling, rather, of the promise of all preceding dawns.

'The Star that strengthens to love' presides in the East over the first unfolding of the 'Second Kingdom,' the realm of Purification; that star had been wholly forgotten in the Inferno; the 'dead air' there could not carry its rays to the weighted eyes and the oppressed heart.

At the Southern Pole beamed the four stars, beheld by the ancient people who had been inspired by their virtues—Prudence, Justice, Strength, and Temperance. The heavens were rejoicing in these lights as of old, though one hemisphere had been widowed of their rays; this expresses, perhaps, the discontent of Dante with the degenerate people whose eyes, he thought, were blind to the formerly esteemed and practised cardinal virtues.

The Pilgrim beholds the four Stars of the Cardinal virtues.

——— (I) ———

(*Continued from last page.*)

PURGATORIO, CANTO I. 19-27.

L O bel pianeta, ch' ad amar conforta,
    Faceva tutto rider l' oriente,   20
    Velando i Pesci, ch' erano in sua scorta.
Io mi volsi a man destra, e posi mente
    All' altro polo, e vidi quattro stelle
    Non viste mai, fuor ch' alla prima gente.
Goder pareva 'l ciel di lor fiammelle.   25
    O settentrïonal vedovo sito,
    Poichè privato se' di mirar quelle !

' All my fresh Springs are in Thee.'

(I)

We experience sundry kinds of death and of night seasons, and surely also sundry kinds of dawn.

In our sense of Nature's beautiful morning hours, of Spring-tides, of fresh beginnings,—in the entrance on some new pursuit, in our new friendships, best of all in awakening to new and fuller truths as they open before us, we ourselves seem re-dipt in Hope and Joy.

Our horizon glows and is enlarged in these first hours of new days; they awaken the dulness of our blunted sensibility,—blunted by petty cares, by lethargy, or by the monotony of 'custom with its weight.—Heavy as frost, and deep almost as life.' Our spirit is again 'finely touched to finer issues.'

It has been said that Heaven is made up of first days.

'When I *awake*, I am present with thee.'

Cato, Guardian of the base of the Mount, appears, his countenance illuminated by the splendour of the four Stars.

(II)

PURGATORIO, CANTO I. 28-33, 37-39.

COM' io dal loro sguardo fui partito,
    Un poco me volgendo all' altro polo
    Là, onde 'l Carro già era sparito,   30
Vidi presso di me un veglio solo,
    Degno di tanta reverenza in vista,
    Che più non dee a padre alcun figliuolo.
    *   *   *   *   *
Li raggi delle quattro luci sante   37
    Fregiavan sì la sua faccia di lume,
    Ch' io 'l vedea, come 'l Sol fosse davante.

'*Behold, I make all things New.*'

(II)

ONE who had witnessed to the splendour of the virtues of the Ancient World is to be the Guardian of newly arriving Pilgrims in the Realm of Purification. He is to initiate their early footsteps by the stern lessons he has himself learnt.

The virtues of the old Roman were not to be despised or forgotten, but to be transfused with added beams of light.

Virgil, as enlightened Reason, teaches the Pilgrim to reverence the aged man adorned with the effulgence of the four consecrated Stars; and through the love of Liberty, so dear to both, would unite each to each.

The Pilgrim was indeed seeking liberty from the thraldom of corruption, yet the love of liberty in its ordinary sense is appealed to as an actual bond of sympathy.

Every new Dispensation reveals a glory in the preceding one, and gathers it up into its bosom. It 'orbs into the perfect Star' not seen by those who moved therein.

Virgil relates to Cato the rescue of Dante as ordained from Above.

(II)

(*Continued from last page.*)

PURGATORIO, CANTO I. 49-54, 58-75.

LO Duca mio allor mi diè di piglio;
   E con parole e con mani e con cenni,   50
   Reverenti mi fe le gambe e 'l ciglio.
Poscia rispose lui: Da me non venni:
   Donna scese dal ciel, per li cui preghi
   Della mia compagnia costui sovvenni.
   *   *   *   *   *
Questi non vide mai l' ultima sera;
   Ma, per la sua follia, le fu sì presso,
   Che molto poco tempo a volger era.   60
Sì com' io dissi, fui mandato ad esso
   Per lui campare; e non c' era altra via
   Che questa, per la quale io mi son messo.
Mostrat' ho lui tutta la gente ria;
   Ed ora intendo mostrar quegli spirti,   65
   Che purgan sè sotto la tua balía.
Com' io l' ho tratto, saria lungo a dirti:
   Dall' alto scende virtù, che m' aiuta
   Conducerlo a vederti ed a udirti.
Or ti piaccia gradir la sua venuta: 70
   Libertà va cercando, ch' è sì cara,
   Come sa chi per lei vita rifiuta.
Tu 'l sai; chè non ti fu per lei amara
   In Utica la morte, ove lasciasti
   La veste, ch' al gran dì sarà sì chiara.   75

(II)

ST. PAUL recognised that the ministration of death, 'written and engraven *in stones*,' was glorious, when he pronounced the ministration of the Spirit to be more glorious (2 Cor. iii. 7, 8).

We want added Life, fuller, more abundant. Not the obliteration of the Past because the Present is better; not new things instead of old, so much as old things quickened, 'made new,' expanded to meet growing capacities. We want the enlarging, deepening stream of Time, enriched by all its affluents, to carry us on into the Ocean of the fulness of Life in God.

'Think not I am come to destroy the Law or the Prophets; I am not come to destroy but to fulfil,' says the Life of men.

The Pilgrim's Guide recounts to Cato that he came not of his own choice, but under a commission from Heaven to rescue One, on the very verge of death through his own folly. He has led him through the 'dead world' to this realm of Purification on his way towards the liberty which he is seeking from Corruption, and he reminds Cato of his own love of Liberty, who for her sake had refused life.

Cato gives directions for Dante's due preparation for the Ascent of the Mountain.

─────────────── (III) ───────────────

PURGATORIO, CANTO I. 86, 91-99.

(diss' egli allora)
*   *   *   *   *
Ma se donna del ciel ti muove e regge,
   Come tu di', non c' è mestier lusinga :
   Basta ben che per lei tu mi richegge.
Va' dunque, e fa' che tu costui ricinga
   D' un giunco schietto, e che gli lavi 'l viso,   95
   Sì ch' ogni sucidume quindi stinga :
Chè non si converria, l' occhio sorpriso
   D' alcuna nebbia, andar davanti al primo
   Ministro, ch' è di quei di Paradiso.

The Pilgrim is to receive cleansing from the stains of the 'far country' and to be clothed with Humility.

(III)

PREPARATIONS are ordained for the Pilgrim's reception of the graces of Cleansing and Humility.

He must have the stains on his face washed away, and its true colour must be made visible. He must also be girded about with the smooth rush that grows low down at the Water's Edge. No other plant could grow there, for none other would be so pliable to the waves that beat upon it.

How much this symbolism says to us! It needs no interpreter, but it needs taking to our 'indurate' hearts!

Equipped thus, the scales would fall from his eyes, and he would be fitted for beholding the first Angel that should descend from Paradise.

The rising Sun, always the image of the Divine Presence, was to direct the right Ascent of the Mount. As it had been said at the first awakening of the Pilgrim, 'That Planet's rays lead others right by every road.'

The wave-beaten shore where the rushes grow and no other plant.

(III)

(*Continued from last page.*)

PURGATORIO, CANTO I. 100-114.

QUESTA isoletta intorno ad imo ad imo 100
 Laggiù, colà dove la batte l' onda,
 Porta de' giunchi sovra 'l molle limo.
Null' altra pianta, che facesse fronda,
 O che indurasse, vi puote aver vita,
 Perocchè alle percosse non seconda. 105
Poscia non sia di qua vostra redíta:
 Lo Sol vi mostrerà, che surge omai,
 Prendere 'l monte a più lieve salita.
Così sparì. Ed io su mi levai
 Sanza parlare; e tutto mi ritrassi 110
 Al Duca mio, e gli occhi a lui drizzai.
Ei cominciò: Figliuol, segui i miei passi:
 Volgiamci indietro; chè di qua dichina
 Questa pianura a' suoi termini bassi.

The Valley of Humiliation.

(III)

'This Valley of Humiliation is the best and most fruitful piece of ground in all those parts. It is a fat ground and consisteth much in meadows. . . . Behold how green this Valley is, also how beautiful with Lilies! . . . Now, as they were going along and talking, they espied a boy feeding his father's sheep. The boy was in very mean clothes, but of a very fresh and well-favoured countenance; and as he sat by himself, he sung. "Hark!" said Mr. Greatheart, "to what the Shepherd's boy saith." So they hearkened, and he said:

> '"He that is down need fear no fall,
> He that is low no Pride;
> He that is humble ever shall
> Have God to be his Guide."

'Then said their Guide, "Do you hear him? I will dare to say that this boy lives a merrier life, and wears more of the Heart's Ease in his bosom, than he that is clad in silk and velvet."

'In this Valley our Lord formerly had His country house; He loved much to be here. . . . Here a man shall be free from the hurryings of this life. All states are full of noise and confusion, only the Valley of Humiliation is that empty and solitary place. This is a valley that nobody walks in, but those that love a Pilgrim's life.'—BUNYAN'S PILGRIM'S PROGRESS.

Dante is cleansed and girded for the upward Way.

(IV)

PURGATORIO, CANTO I. 115-129.

L'ALBA vinceva l' ôra mattutina
    Che fuggia innanzi, sì che di lontano
    Conobbi il tremolar della marina.
Noi andavam per lo solingo piano,
    Com' uom che torna alla smarrita strada,
    Che infino ad essa gli pare ire invano.   120
Quando noi fummo dove la rugiada
    Pugna col Sole, e, per essere in parte
    Ove adorezza, poco si dirada;
Ambo le mani in su l' erbetta sparte
    Soavemente 'l mio Maestro pose :   125
    Ond' io che fui accorto di sua arte,
Pòrsi vêr lui le guancie lagrimose :
    Quivi mi fece tutto discoverto
    Quel color, che l' Inferno mi nascose.

'The dew of thy birth is of the Womb of the morning.'

(IV)

A VISION opens before us to-day of God's wonderful gift of Water.

We see it, if we can follow the Seer's eye, trembling into light reflecting the growing Dawn; and again as the early dew on the shadowed grass, or glistening where the Sunbeams have but just made the shadows to flee away. These waters of heaven and earth are mingled with the precious tears of the penitent man. Beyond these visible tokens our thoughts are led to the 'untraversed' Waters of the Spirit whence 'none return.'

> 'O useful Element and clear!
> My sacred wash and cleanser here;
> My first consigner unto those
> Fountains of life, where the Lamb goes!
> What sublime truths and wholesome themes,
> Lodge in thy mystical, deep streams!
> Such as dull man can never finde,
> Unless that Spirit lead his minde,
> Which first upon thy face did move,
> And hatch'd all with his quick'ning love.'
>   HENRY VAUGHAN.

The Pilgrim and his Guide seek along this solitary shore that lost Way of which we read in the first Canto of the Poem; *the Way* which the newly-awakened Pilgrim had abandoned, he knew not when or how, so profound had been his slumber. Till he find it again, it seems to him that he walks in vain.

The moment of initiation into the new life which is to lead him into the lost, or perhaps only dreamt-of, Way, has arrived. The directions of the Guardian of the base of the Ascending Way are tenderly carried out by the Guide. This is the first of many baptisms of Water and of Spirit.

(IV)

(*Continued from last page.*)

PURGATORIO, CANTO I. 130-136.

<pre>
Venimmo poi in sul lito diserto,   130
   Che mai non vide navigar sue acque
   Uom, che di ritornar sia poscia esperto.
Quivi mi cinse, sì com' altrui piacque.
   O maraviglia ! chè qual egli scelse
   L' umile pianta, cotal si rinacque   135
Subitamente là, ond' ei la svelse.
</pre>

Be clothed with Humility.

(IV)

The morning dew from the grass is gathered by the gentle outspread hands of Love's Minister, and mixing with the tears on the face of the willing disciple, the stains, which he had contracted during his sojourn in the 'dead air' of Wrath and Death, are removed.

The true colour of the 'human face divine' is discovered.

Then they descend to the Mystic Water's edge, and the Pilgrim is girt with the humble plant which springs up at once again wherever it is wounded, with the soft persistency of the poor in spirit who lack self-love.

'No plant which bears leaves, or hardens its bark, can live on that shore, because it does not yield to the chastisement of its waves.' How deep and harmonious a significance runs through all these words of Dante! Each word the more we penetrate its meaning becomes a seed of further thought! For follow up this image of the girding with the reed, under trial, and see to whose feet it will lead us. As the grass of the Earth, thought of as the herb yielding seed, leads us to the place where the Lord commanded the multitude to sit down by companies upon the grass; so the grass of the waters, thought of as sustaining itself among the waters of affliction, leads us to the place where a stem of it was put into our Lord's hand for His Sceptre; and in the crown of thorns, and the rod of reed, was foreshown the everlasting truth of the Christian ages—that all glory was to be begun in suffering, and all power in humility.'— RUSKIN's 'Modern Painters,' Vol. III. 233.

Dante beholds a light swiftly approach across the Sea; its whiteness increases, and wings appear unfolded.

———— (V) ————

PURGATORIO, CANTO II. 10-36.

NOI eravam lunghesso 'l mare ancora,
   Come gente che pensa a suo cammino,
   Che va col cuore, e col corpo dimora:
Ed ecco qual, sul presso del mattino,
   Per gli grossi vapor Marte rosseggia
   Giù nel ponente sovra 'l suol marino;   15
Cotal m' apparve, sì ancor lo veggia,
   Un lume per lo mar venir sì ratto,
   Che 'l muover suo nessun volar pareggia.
Dal qual com' io un poco ebbi ritratto
   L' occhio, per dimandar lo Duca mio,   20
   Rividil più lucente e maggior fatto.
Poi d' ogni lato ad esso m' appario
   Un non sapea che bianco; ed al di sotto
   A poco a poco un altro a lui n' uscío.
Lo mio Maestro ancor non fece motto   25
   Mentre che i primi bianchi apparser ali:
   Ma allor che ben conobbe 'l galeotto,
Gridò: Fa' fa' che le ginocchia cali:
   Ecco l' angel di Dio; piega le mani:
   Oma' vedrai di sì fatti officiali.   30
Vedi che sdegna gli argomenti umani,
   Sì che remo non vuol, nè altro velo
   Che l' ali sue, tra liti sì lontani.
Vedi come l' ha dritte verso 'l cielo,
   Trattando l' aere con l' eterne penne,   35
   Che non si mutan come mortal pelo.

*'Then kneel, my soul and body, kneel and bow;
If Saints and Angels fall down, much more thou.'*

(V)

STILL, the constant question is concerning the Way; the uncertainty causing thoughts to be busy and movement slow. See the use of the expression 'the Way' with its capital letter in New Version (Acts ix. 2; xix. 9; xix. 23; xxii. 4; xxiv. 14, 22).

Dean Church reminds us that this Poem is the work of a Wanderer, and says: 'The very form into which it is cast is that of a journey difficult, toilsome, perilous, and full of change. It is more than a working out of that touching phraseology of the Middle Ages in which "the Way" was the technical expression for this mortal life; and *Viator* meant man in his state of trial, as "*Comprehensor*" meant man made perfect as having attained to his heavenly country.'

Across the waters a white light flashes towards the wanderers along the solitary Shore, and is discerned by the lowly and attentive Soul to be an Angel-piloted Vessel with newly arriving spirits. Deep reverence is enjoined on the Pilgrim as he awaits the arrival of the first Angel of Paradise. In silence they watch the white light growing into the Angel's unfolding wings, and the attitude of body as well as soul is to betoken reverent expectation from above.

> 'Irreverence everywhere is blindness, not sight; you can know nothing which you do not reverence. . . . All of the mystery which surrounds life and pervades life is really one mystery. It is God. . . . It is Love. And of this personal mystery of love—of God—it is supremely true that only by reverence, only by the hiding of the eyes, can He be seen. One who thinks to look God full in the face and question Him, blinds himself thereby, and cannot see God; he sees something, but what he sees is not God, but himself.'—PHILLIPS BROOKS, 'The Wings of the Seraphim.'

The blessed Spirits brought across the Waters by the Celestial Pilot.

PURGATORIO, CANTO II. 37-54.

POI, come più e più verso noi venne
   L' uccel divino, più chiaro appariva:
   Per che l' occhio da presso nol sostenne;
Ma chinail giuso. E quei sen venne a riva   40
   Con un vassello snelletto e leggiero,
   Tanto che l' acqua nulla ne inghiottiva.
Da poppa stava 'l celestial nocchiero,
   Tal che parea beato per iscritto;
   E più di cento spirti entro sediero.   45
In exitu Israël de Ægypto
   Cantavan tutti insieme ad una voce,
   Con quanto di quel salmo è poscia scritto.
Poi fece 'l segno lor di santa croce;
   Ond' ei si gittâr tutti in su la piaggia: 50
   Ed ei sen gio, come venne veloce.
La turba, che rimase lì, selvaggia
   Parea del loco, rimirando intorno,
   Come colui che nuove cose assaggia.

The chorus of Man, Earth, and Heaven.

(VI)

WE must read every word of this joyful Song of Deliverance (Psalm cxiv.), not in cold blood, but with the blessed spirits just set free from mortality and from the perils of moral death. It is the Jubilate of the Realm whose watchwords are Humility and Penitence.

Some of Dante's words with regard to its interpretation (as a pattern for the interpretation also of his own Poem) have been cited in the Preface; they may be quoted here at more length. He says: 'If we view it in the letter, we see it describes the Exodus of the Children of Israel from Egypt in the time of Moses; if allegorically, we see signified our redemption by Jesus Christ; if we look at its moral sense, we perceive the conversion of the Soul from the plaint and misery of sin to the state of grace; if we regard it mystically, we behold the passage of the blessed Soul from present corruption into the liberty of Eternal Glory.'

These words unlock for us Dante's view of the unfolding life of man. First, under iron rule, labouring without recompense in the midst of people of alien tongues and customs; then breaking these bonds through unity with a Leader sent of God, who over-rules the opposition of the aliens and who dominates Nature;—Herself concurring in joyous, thrilling sympathy with the progressive spirit on its Way to Freedom, Unity, and Glory. With the presence of God —the dividing Sea, the immovable Mountains, the Stony Rock, even the River of Death,—all make for the onward march of the divinely indwelt and divinely led children of God.

Nature and her spiritual Significancies are so blent in this Psalm that we cannot sever them. So also it is with the 'sacred Poem to which Heaven and Earth have lent a hand.' So it is with that Poem's great Theme—Man.

One of the newly-arrived Souls, Casella, came forward to embrace Dante, his love unchanged by death.

— (VII) —

PURGATORIO, CANTO II. 76-90.

IO vidi una di lor traggersi avante,
    Per abbracciarmi, con sì grande affetto,
    Che mosse me a far lo somigliante.
Oh ombre vane, fuor che nell' aspetto !
    Tre volte dietro a lei le mani avvinsi,   80
    E tante mi tornai con esse al petto.
Di maraviglia, credo, mi dipinsi:
    Per che l' ombra sorrise, e si ritrasse;
    Ed io seguendo lei, oltre mi pinsi.
Soavemente disse ch' io posasse: 85
    Allor conobbi chi era, e pregai
    Che per parlarmi un poco s' arrestasse.
Risposemi: Così com' io t' amai
    Nel mortal corpo, così t' amo sciolta;
    Però m' arresto: ma tu perchè vai?   90

> *'Friendship, whence there ever issues forth
> A steady splendour.'*

(VII)

'EVEN as I loved thee in mortal body, so I love thee free.' How much that word 'sciolta' says to us, unswathed, unbound, *freed*—Love unbound, flowing forth unfettered, unchanged, and unchanging.

> 'Rapt from the fickle and the frail,
> With gather'd power yet the same.'

When the reunion, to which our hearts are ever pressing, takes place, shall we not find that we have not been separated except in the consciousness of the fettered one?

'Nous retrouverons ce que nous n'avons point perdu,' said Fénélon; and even the imprisoned in the body have at moments been conscious of the presence of their beloved Saints in Christ, who has said, 'Lo, I am with you all the days.' Yet, till some blessed consummation, there must be an aching sense of the empty arms that, in desiring to renew the former embrace, return unsatisfied to the heart. Our faces must be towards the rising Sun, not 'towards the sunlight that is gone!'

> 'Learn, by a mortal yearning, to ascend
> Seeking a higher object. Love was given,
> Encouraged, sanctioned, chiefly for that end;
> For this the passion to excess was driven—
> That Self might be annulled: her bondage prove
> The fetters of a dream, opposed to love.'
>
>   'Laodamia.'

The converse of Dante and Casella, and the prayed-for singing of Casella entrancing all, till Cato reproves their delay.

(VIII)

PURGATORIO, CANTO II. 91, 92, 106-114.

CASELLA mio, per tornare altra volta
   Là dove i' son, fo io questo viaggio,

*   *   *   *   *

Ed io: Se nuova legge non ti toglie   106
   Memoria, od uso all' amoroso canto,
   Che mi solea quetar tutte mie voglie,
Di ciò ti piaccia consolare alquanto
   L' anima mia, che con la sua persona   110
   Venendo qui, è affannata tanto.
Amor, che nella mente mi ragiona,
   Cominciò egli allor sì dolcemente,
   Che la dolcezza ancor dentro mi suona.

*' Man must pass
From what once seemed good, to what now proves best.'*

──── (VIII) ────

DANTE longs again to be calmed and comforted as in former days on Earth, by the music of Casella; and entreats his Friend, unless some new law of his present condition forbid it, to sing him one of those songs of love which used to fulfil all his longings. His ascent had fatigued his lagging body. Might he again taste the solace of former days? Casella at once pours forth in tones of melody that thrill him with delight one of Dante's own songs. Virgil, also, and the whole company of souls are ravished. Was this natural and innocent delight a looking back to Egypt, when pressing onwards and upwards should have been their sole intention, as Cato's stern reproof implies, and as Virgil's haste and remorse afterwards would seem to confirm? Are there times and seasons in the Pilgrim's life when, though Conscience and Right reason cannot actually condemn, the remembrance of the Stoic virtues should urge to more complete and strenuous endeavour? The Pilgrim has not yet entered the Gate of Purgatory proper—of the actual ascent in the true way of the repentant and aspiring soul; he has escaped the bondage of selfishness and pride, but needs to receive in its fulness the divine gift of persevering repentance. The three stars of Faith, Hope, and Charity have not yet exercised their influences upon him, though he has indeed perceived the morning Star of Love.

The remorse and haste of Virgil.

(VIII)

(*Continued from last page.*)

PURGATORIO, CANTO II. 115-123.

LO mio Maestro, ed io, e quella gente   115
   Ch' eran con lui, parevan sì contenti,
   Com' a nessun toccasse altro la mente.
Noi eravam tutti fissi ed attenti
   Alle sue note: ed ecco 'l veglio onesto
   Gridando: Che è ciò, spiriti lenti?   120
Qual negligenza, quale stare è questo?
   Correte al monte a spogliarvi lo scoglio
   Ch' esser non lascia a voi Dio manifesto.

'Quick to advance and to retreat most slow.'

(VIII)

When Dante enters the Gate of Purgatory proper, one of the injunctions he will receive from the Angel of the Gate is not to venture to look back. He is now in preparation for this decisive epoch.

There are long seasons of transition, long tarryings ere decisions are clenched and thresholds crossed, wondrously true to the experience of life, in Dante's land of 'far distances.' 'Brethren, I count not myself to have apprehended; but this one thing I do, forgetting those things which are behind, and reaching forth unto those things which are before, I press toward the mark for the prize of the high calling of God in Christ Jesus.'—Phil. iii. 13, 14.

In the opening lines of the next Canto, we read that Virgil seemed remorseful. Dante observes, it was a trivia fault that stung this noble and stainless conscience. It is interesting to note the further remark made on his Master's rapid flight under Cato's rebuke — the former lingering necessitated undue, or at any rate undignified haste, so the disciple thought. Dante speaks of hurry (the Avenger of Delay) as that 'which mars the dignity of every act' (see Canto III. 10, 11). We are often reminded on this Pilgrimage of the dignity and courtesies of outward demeanour, as they pierce through from an inward condition to external expression.

Virgil reminds Dante that Reason without Faith cannot satisfy the Intellect of man.

(IX)

PURGATORIO, CANTO III. 34-54.

MATTO è chi spera che nostra ragione
   Possa trascorrer l' infinita via,   35
   Che tiene una sustanzia in tre persone.
State contenti, umana gente, al *quia* :
   Chè se potuto aveste veder tutto,
   Mestier non era partorir Maria.
E disïar vedeste senza frutto   40
   Tai, che sarebbe il lor disio quietato,
   Ch' eternalmente è dato lor per lutto :
Io dico d' Aristotile e di Plato,
   E di molti altri. E qui chinò la fronte,
   E più non disse ; e rimase turbato.   45
Noi divenimmo intanto appiè del monte :
   Quivi trovammo la roccia sì erta,
   Che indarno vi sarien le gambe pronte.
Tra Lerici e Turbía, la più diserta,
   La più ruinata via è una scala,   50
   Verso di quella, agevole ed aperta.
Or chi sa da qual man la costa cala,
   Disse 'l Maestro mio, fermando 'l passo,
   Sì che possa salir chi va senz' ala ?

The Mystery of the Shadow and of the Infinite One.

─────────────── (IX)

A WORD of explanation is necessary to link the fragment of to-day with a passage preceding it, which introduces it and accounts for Virgil's utterance.

The red morning Sun is behind Dante and Virgil, and Dante sees before him but one Shadow—his own ; he turns, frightened lest he should find his Guide had forsaken him, but is reassured by Virgil, who explains that 'the body within which he cast a shadow' lies at Naples. He then speaks of the mystery of the spiritual substance, that should be capable of feeling heat and cold, and yet is not material as one that casts a shadow. From this mystery he is led on to speak of the mystery of mysteries—the Three in One and His ways, before which human reasonings must be dumb ; and alludes pathetically to those great spirits whom they had seen in Limbo, himself amongst them, whose fruitless desires for Truth have never been satisfied, for lack of Faith. He reminds the Pilgrim that there would have been no necessity for the Incarnation, if man's intellect had been sufficient to penetrate the mysteries of the Universe.

The little Child who is the model for one who would enter the Kingdom of Heaven, is ever asking questions, trusting in an Answerer and the possibility of an answer.

We need divine teaching to know when and where to question, and when and where to wait in silence and trust for an answer, ever reposing in the Answerer, even if it be till our last day on Earth, and beyond.

The steepness of the Ascent perplexes Virgil. *He asks the way of a band of timid souls, astonished at Dante's shadow.*

(X)

PURGATORIO, CANTO III. 73-99.

O BEN finiti, o già spiriti eletti,
   Virgilio incominciò, per quella pace,
   Ch' io credo che per voi tutti s' aspetti,   75
Ditene dove la montagna giace,
   Sì che possibil sia l' andare in suso :
   Chè 'l perder tempo, a chi più sa, più spiace.
Come le pecorelle escon del chiuso
   Ad una, a due, a tre, e l' altre stanno   80
   Timidette atterrando l' occhio e 'l muso ;
E ciò che fa la prima, e l' altre fanno,
   Addossandosi a lei, s' ella s' arresta,
   Semplici e quete, e lo perchè non sanno ;
Sì vid' io muovere, a venir, la testa   85
   Di quella mandra fortunata allotta,
   Pudica in faccia e nell' andare onesta.
Come color dinanzi vider rotta
   La luce in terra dal mio destro canto,
   Sì che l' ombr' era da me alla grotta,   90
Ristaro, e trasser sè indietro alquanto ;
   E tutti gli altri, che venieno appresso,
   Non sapendo 'l perchè, fero altrettanto.
Senza vostra dimanda io vi confesso
   Che questo è corpo uman che voi vedete ;   95
   Per che 'l lume del Sole in terra è fesso.
Non vi maravigliate ; ma credete,
   Che non sanza virtù, che dal ciel vegna,
   Cerca di soverchiar questa parete.

'*The Paradisaical man is clear as transparent glass, and he is fully penetrated by the light of the Divine Sun.*'

———————— (X) ————————

IN the lines that precede the quotation on the opposite page uncertainty about the Way still oppresses the Pilgrim and his Guide. The thought expressed in lines 34-44 seems manifested here by the perplexity of the Guide. His reason tells him that he himself is not sufficient for this perplexity, without recourse to the fuller Christian light in others.

The path up the mountain is seen to be so steep that Virgil thinks they would need wings to mount on that side. A throng of souls is at last seen advancing in the same direction, and Virgil addresses them in the passage selected. His invocation of their aid is beautiful in its courtesy and encouragement—'by that Peace which I believe is waiting for you all.' The demeanour of these souls befits those who have been lately delivered from the snare of the enemy, who are setting their faces heavenwards—meek, diffident, and looking for counsel. They have been startled by observing the wonder of Dante's shadow ; this is several times brought before us, and is of special significance. In the Inferno he was recognised as a mortal man by his breathing ; in the Purgatorio by his Shadow ; in Paradise he is revealed as he is, without such signs, to the all-piercing vision of the glorified Saints. Does the Shadow cast by him 'who is within the body' (remark the expression—not simply cast *by* the body) symbolize the self-hood or perhaps *the flesh*, as St. Paul uses the word when he says, 'in my flesh dwelleth no good thing'?

'If thine eye be single, thy whole body shall be full of light.' The Souls in Purgatory are delivered from all temptations of the flesh, and their eye is single. Some such meaning may possibly have been latent in Dante's mind.

The Shadow.

— (X) —

A few lines of a forcible poem of Victor Hugo's, perhaps suggested by Dante's mention of the Shadow, connects it with the apparent evil in materiality.

'CE QUE DIT LA BOUCHE D'OMBRE.'

* * * * *

' Ne réfléchis-tu pas lorsque tu vois ton ombre?
Cette forme de toi, rampante, horrible, sombre,
Qui liée à tes pas comme un spectre vivant,
Va tantôt en arrière et tantôt en avant ;
Qui se mêle à la nuit, sa grande sœur funeste,
Et qui contre le jour, noire et dure, proteste ;
D'où vient elle? De toi, de ta chair, du limon
Dont l'esprit se revêt en devenant démon ;
De ce corps qui, créé par ta faute première ;
Ayant rejeté Dieu, résiste à la lumière ;
De ta matière, hélas ! de ton iniquité.
Cette ombre dit : " Je suis l'être d'infirmité ;
Je suis tombé déjà, je puis tomber encore."
L'ange laisse passer à travers lui l'aurore ;
Nul simulacre obscur ne suit l'être anormal ;
Homme, tout ce qui fait de l'ombre a fait le mal !'

VICTOR HUGO.

The steep and exhausting climb of the Cliff at the base of the Mountain, and Virgil's exhortations to perseverance.

———————— (XI) ————————

PURGATORIO, CANTO IV. 25-51.

VASSI in Sanleo, e discendesi in Noli: 25
   Montasi su Bismantova in cacume
   Con esso i piè; ma qui convien ch' uom voli:
Dico con l' ale snelle e con le piume
   Del gran disio, diretro a Quel condotto,
   Che speranza mi dava e facea lume.   30
Noi salivam per entro 'l sasso rotto;
   E d' ogni lato ne stringea lo stremo,
   E piedi e man voleva 'l suol di sotto.
Quando noi fummo in su l' orlo supremo
   Dell' alta ripa, alla scoverta piaggia,   35
   Maestro mio, diss' io, che via faremo?
Ed egli a me: Nessun tuo passo caggia.
   Pur suso al monte dietro a me acquista,
   Fin che n' appaia alcuna scorta saggia.
Lo sommo er' alto, che vincea la vista,   40
   E la costa superba più assai,
   Che da mezzo quadrante a centro lista.
Io era lasso, quando cominciai:
   O dolce padre, volgiti e rimira
   Com' io rimango sol, se non ristai.   45
O figliuol, disse, insin quivi ti tira,
   Additandomi un balzo poco in sue,
   Che da quel lato il poggio tutto gira.
Si mi spronaron le parole sue,
   Ch' io mi sforzai, carpando appresso lui,   50
   Tanto che 'l cinghio sotto i piè mi fue.

'*Then welcome* . . .
Each sting that bids nor sit nor stand, but go.'

───────────── (XI) ─────────────

ALL the powers of Body, Soul, and Spirit are needed in some parts of the Pilgrim's most difficult ascent. Body must help Soul, as well as Soul help Body, in the pathway of obedience. Tasks have to be exacted from body and soul by the stronger and more willing Spirit; and during the painful effort imposed, swift Desire from above must be waited for, as David's wing of the dove to lift that which cleaveth to the dust.

'Quicken me, O Lord,' will then be the oft-repeated cry.

The difficulty of the arduous way is wonderfully vividly pictured before our mind's eye here. Pilgrims know it.

'Leave me not, my Father, or I remain alone' is the sigh of the jaded Aspirant; and the answering Word is given:

> 'No step of thine descend—still up the Mount
> Behind me, win thy way.'—Line 37.

> 'Yet cease I not to struggle and aspire
> Heavenward; and chide the part of me that flags
> Thro' sinful choice, or dread necessity
> On human nature from above imposed.'
>   WORDSWORTH.

Dante is dismayed at the prospect of the long and steep climb. Virgil encourages him to hope in increasing strength.

──────────── (XII) ────────────

PURGATORIO, CANTO IV. 85-96.

MA, s' a te piace, volentier saprei   85
   Quanto avemo ad andar; chè 'l poggio sale
   Più che salir non posson gli occhi miei.
Ed egli a me: Questa montagna è tale,
   Che sempre al cominciar di sotto è grave;
   E quanto più va su, e men fa male.   90
Però quand' ella ti parrà soave
   Tanto, che 'l suso andar ti sia leggiero,
   Com' a seconda in giuso andar per nave;
Allor sarai al fin d' esto sentiero:
   Quivi di riposar l' affanno aspetta.   95
   Più non rispondo; e questo so per vero.

> '*Does the road wind uphill all the way?*
> *Yes, to the very end.*'

(XII)

THE Pilgrim, wearied out in nerve and spirit, cannot help asking, How long can I persevere in such effort? Will there be no respite from this endeavour? Is the Way always so difficult? The beautiful dawn has passed into common day, and the prospect is one of an interminable and monotonous ascent.

Relief is rather to be grown up into than to be found at some milestone on the way. Virgil's answer has nothing to do with the computation of Time or distance.

> 'When the going up shall be to thee as easy
> As going down the current in a boat,
> Then at this pathway's ending thou wilt be.'

When thy true nature is attained—when the new man is formed in thee, every spontaneous effort and impulse will carry thee onwards and upwards.

> 'The ultimate Angel's law
> There where law, life, love, impulse are one thing.'

We shall see that this was attained by this Pilgrim on the threshold of the Earthly Paradise. Can it be attained fully on this side of Death? We certainly see that some temptations, at least, utterly lose their power over good men. To those who have persevered in Truth, Honesty, and Temperance, the opposite vices pull in vain against their whole nature. Such as these are now carried along as in a boat on a descending current. We may have seen some few, at the prow of whose vessel Faith, Hope, and Charity so steer and propel that the Voyager within seems meanwhile at rest.

> 'For a work to be perfect it must be wrought in us, without our co-operation as principal agents; it must be God's work, done in God, and man must not in any way take the lead.'—ST. CATHARINE OF GENOA.

*Dante, listening to whispering comments, is adjured by
Virgil to stand firm like a Tower.*

──────────────── (XIII) ────────────────

PURGATORIO, CANTO V. 7-24.

G LI occhi rivolsi al suon di questo motto,
   E vidile guardar per maraviglia
   Pur me, pur me, e 'l lume ch' era rotto.
Perchè l' animo tuo tanto s' impiglia,   10
   Disse 'l Maestro, che l' andare allenti?
   Che ti fa ciò che quivi si pispiglia?
Vien dietro a me, e lascia dir le genti;
   Sta, come torre, fermo, che non crolla
   Giammai la cima per soffiar de' venti.   15
Chè sempre l' uomo, in cui pensier rampolla
   Sovra pensier, da sè dilunga il segno,
   Perchè la foga l' un dell' altro insolla.
Che potev' io più dir, se non: I' vegno?
   Dissilo, alquanto del color consperso,   20
   Che fa l' uom di perdon talvolta degno.
Intanto per la costa di traverso
   Venivan genti, innanzi a noi un poco,
   Cantando *Miserere* a verso a verso.

'They saie; Quhat saie thei? Lette them saie.'

(XIII)

THE Pilgrim finds himself in another throng of spirits. As he passes through them, they, as others before them have done, point out to one another the puzzling shadow cast by Dante. He listens to their words, and is self-occupied by the suggestions they cause; and without knowing it he slackens his pace. Then follows the well-known counsel, so especially needed in a world like our own. 'Come after me,' says the Wisdom of Conscience, 'and let the people talk'—'Lascia dir le genti.' He is also instructed concerning the waste of energy that arises from letting one thought spring up after another, removing the Thinker from his aim (16-18).

Concentration of purpose in the innermost thoughts, and disregard of whisperings behind, seem the lesson of the day.

'God works unstayed, untroubled, in the soul that has been trained to think in all its leisure times, true and high and gentle thoughts. He enters in and stays there, not as a Wayfaring Man, but as a willing welcome Guest in a house that has been prepared and decked and furnished. There the voice of God is clearly heard. There is no knowing whither God might call us, if only we would keep our minds, by His help, free and true to hear His bidding when it comes, and on the drift and tone which our minds are now acquiring it may depend whether, when the time comes, we recognise our work or not; whether we press forward with the host of God, or dully fall away, it may be, into the misery of a listless, aimless life.'—PAGET'S 'Spirit of Discipline.'

The violently slain, but repenting and pardoning souls, who ask prayers from their friends on earth, and long to see God.

─────────────── (XIV) ─── ─────── ──

PURGATORIO, CANTO V. 46-72.

O ANIMA, che vai, per esser lieta,
 Con quelle membra con le quai nascesti,
 Venian gridando, un poco 'l passo queta.
Guarda s' alcun di noi unque vedesti;
 Sì che di lui di là novelle porti.   50
 Deh perchè vai? deh perchè non t' arresti?
Noi fummo tutti già per forza morti,
 E peccatori infino all' ultim' ora:
 Quivi lume del ciel ne fece accorti,
Sì che, pentendo e perdonando, fuora   55
 Di vita uscimmo a Dio pacificati,
 Che del disio di sè veder n' accuora.
Ed io: Per che ne' vostri visi guati,
 Non riconosco alcun: ma s' a voi piace
 Cosa ch' io possa, spiriti ben nati,   60
Voi dite; ed io 'l farò per quella pace,
 Che dietro a' passi di sì fatta guida
 Di mondo in mondo cercar mi si face.
Ed uno incominciò: Ciascun si fida
 Del benefizio tuo senza giurarlo,   65
 Pur che 'l voler nonpossa non ricida.
Ond' io, che solo, innanzi agli altri, parlo,
 Ti prego, se mai vedi quel paese
 Che siede tra Romagna e quel di Carlo,
Che tu mi sie de' tuoi prieghi cortese   70
 In Fano sì, che ben per me s' adori,
 Perch' io possa purgar le gravi offese.

*'Thro' the Gates that bar the distance
Comes a gleam of what is higher.'*

──────── (XIV) ────────

ONE detaches himself from the crowd of spirits through which Dante has passed, entreating him to stop that he may speak with him; he declares that he and the company with him have all died sudden and violent deaths, and were sinners even to their latest hour; but that through light from Heaven they issued forth from the body, pardoning and repenting and reconciled to God, with great longing to see His face. He then begs Dante, on his return to Earth, to pray for him, and to ask his friends at Fano, where he had lived, to pray for him. This request is continually made to the Pilgrim who is to return to Earth, and we shall see later the grave question it awakens in his mind.

Dante, though so stern a moralist, shows us here his belief that one moment of true repentance is the turning-point of a soul from death to life. Forgiveness of those who had inflicted the sudden death manifested in this Circle the reality of this repentance. Recognition '*in the light of Heaven*' (54) of our own need of forgiveness must unlock our power of forgiving others. The claim made upon us to forgive must at times be a severe test of our own state of heart. To ask our Father for the measure of forgiveness that we mete to others is a strangely searching prayer.

> 'Make my forgiveness downright, such as I
> Should perish if I did not have from Thee!'
> GEORGE MACDONALD.

(XV)

PURGATORIO, CANTO V. 88-108.

IO fui di Montefeltro; io son Buonconte:
   Giovanna ed altri non han di me cura;
   Per ch' io vo tra costor con bassa fronte.   90
Ed io a lui: Qual forza, o qual ventura
   Ti traviò sì fuor di Campaldino,
   Che non si seppe mai tua sepoltura?
Oh, rispos' egli, appiè del Casentino
   Traversa un' acqua c' ha nome l' Archiano,   95
   Che sovra l' Ermo nasce in Appennino.
Là, dove il nome suo diventa vano,
   Arriva' io, forato nella gola,
   Fuggendo a piede e insanguinando 'l piano.
Quivi perdei la vista; e la parola   100
   Nel nome di Maria finìo, e quivi
   Caddi, e rimase la mia carne sola.
Io dirò 'l vero, e tu 'l ridi' tra i vivi:
   L' angel di Dio mi prese, e quel d' Inferno
   Gridava: O tu dal ciel, perchè mi privi?   105
Tu te ne porti di costui l' eterno,
   Per una lagrimetta che 'l mi toglie;
   Ma io farò dell' altro altro governo.

' Prayer, from a living source within the will,
And beating up thro' all the bitter world,
Kept him a living soul.'

———————— (XV) ————— ——

WE are constantly being reminded throughout this Poem of the knitting together of the whole human family, and of the interdependence of its members. It is most touchingly brought before us in the story of Buonconte; one of those who had suffered a violent death, and who had set out on his climb up the lofty mountain, knowing that Giovanna cares not for him, nor does any other care, and therefore 'he goes with downcast face.' He is poverty-stricken without love, lonely and sick at heart for this new Enterprise. If he might but get the prayers of some who knew him in his life on Earth! some of those loving aspirations that he would probably have despised before the late-accepted light had dawned that sent him forth at last repentant and forgiving! Such affectionate desires for his ascending steps would give his drooping courage wings. He recounts that he was but just saved from the clutches of a Minister of Hell, by 'one little tearlet,' as the demon himself had complained, and he thinks, if those he left behind knew his story and its sequel, their prayers would follow and aid him.

Virgil affirms that prayer for another, warmed with love and in God, does avail; but directs Dante to fuller Truth through Beatrice.

(XVI)

PURGATORIO, CANTO VI. 34-57.

ED egli a me: La mia scrittura è piana;
   E la speranza di costor non falla,   35
   Se ben si guarda con la mente sana;
Chè cima di giudicio non s'avvalla,
   Perchè fuoco d'amor compia in un punto
   Ciò che dee soddisfar chi qui s'astalla.
E là, dov'io fermai cotesto punto,   40
   Non s'ammendava, per pregar, difetto,
   Perchè 'l prego da Dio era disgiunto.
Veramente a così alto sospetto
   Non ti fermar, se quella nol ti dice,
   Che lume fia tra 'l vero e l'intelletto.   45
Non so se intendi; io dico di Beatrice:
   Tu la vedrai di sopra, in su la vetta
   Di questo monte, ridente e felice.
Ed io: Buon Duca, andiamo a maggior fretta;
   Chè già non m'affatico come dianzi: 50
   E vedi omai che 'l poggio l'ombra getta.
Noi anderem con questo giorno innanzi,
   Rispose, quanto più potremo omai:
   Ma 'l fatto è d'altra forma che non stanzi.
Prima che siam lassù, tornar vedrai   55
   Colui che già si cuopre della costa,
   Sì che i suoi raggi tu romper non fai.

'*Whether one member suffer, all the members suffer with it; or one member be honoured, all are honoured with it.*'—1 Cor. xii. 26.

(XVI)

THE Spirits in numbers pressed around Dante, asking that prayers should be made for them 'so as to hasten their becoming holy'; and he, pondering the matter, appeals to Virgil, and asks whether in some text of his, he has not affirmed that no orison can bend aside a decree of Heaven. Are then, he asks, the hopes of these spirits vain? This universe would indeed be chaotic if the Will of Heaven permitted itself to be over-ruled and twisted by our ignorant, short-sighted multiplicity of Wills!

Virgil reiterates his affirmation; but says that he had spoken of prayer separate from God: not of prayer inbreathed by His Spirit. The Teacher adds that the expectations of those who looked for help through prayers offered for them were not vain. The translation given by Longfellow is rather obscure. In Dean Plumptre's, the meaning of the Original seems more definitely conveyed.

'My text is clearly taught.
And yet that hope of theirs leads not astray,
If to discernment reason should be brought.
For height of Justice doth not fall away
Because Love's fire doth in an hour complete
The debt which he who dwells here needs must pay.'

The foot-note adds further explanation.

'When a Christian prays fervently for the soul of one whom he has loved, that fervent Charity is accepted by the Divine Justice as a satisfaction, and so the prayer can be granted without any abatement from the strict law of retribution. In the teaching of the Schoolmen, it did not matter whether the satisfaction were given by the sinner himself, or by others on his behalf. Virgil, the representative of human Wisdom, speaks, however, with a conscious diffidence. The true solution of all such difficulties was to come from Beatrice as the representative of Theology, as Divine Wisdom in its highest aspect.'

'We are very members incorporate in the mystical body of Thy Son.'

---(XVI)---

Meditating on the words of St. Paul in Rom. xii. 5, 'we, being many, are one body in Christ, and every one members one of another;' and in 1 Cor. xii. 12 and Ephes. iv. 16, we are led to realize the power within this mystical Organism of taking hold of the unseen forces proceeding from its Divine Head; each member receiving or giving forth as it may lack or abound. We see how the ardour of Love may be increased and sent forth in swifter circulation through a benumbed member by the prayers of another member in more active relationship with the Head, and in this way the Divine requirements of Righteousness and Love (which rule ever undivided) would be satisfied.

As men have learnt more of the laws of Nature, submitting to these laws and so learning to use them, what wonders in that realm have been accomplished! What, then, may be accomplished in the realm of Spirit where soul touches soul, where 'all things are in common, none saying aught that he has is his own.' What, then, may be the growth of the Body when each member becomes inwilled by the Divine Wisdom and the Divine Love? None, then, will have to go with downcast brow because nor Giovanna, nor any other, cares for him!

'Till we all come . . . unto a perfect man.'

(XVI)

'For as we have many members in one body, and all members have not the same office:

'So we, being many, are one body in Christ, and every one members one of another.'—Rom. xii. 4, 5.

'For as the body is one, and hath many members, and all the members of that one body, being many, are one body: so also is Christ.

'For by one Spirit are we all baptized into one body, whether we be Jews or Gentiles, whether we be bond or free; and have been all made to drink into one Spirit.

'For the body is not one member, but many.

'If the foot shall say, Because I am not the hand, I am not of the body; is it therefore not of the body?

'And if the ear shall say, Because I am not the eye, I am not of the body; is it therefore not of the body?

'If the whole body were an eye, where were the hearing? If the whole were hearing, where were the smelling?

'But now hath God set the members every one of them in the body, as it hath pleased Him.

'And if they were all one member, where were the body?

'But now are they many members, yet but one body.

'And the eye cannot say unto the hand, I have no need of thee: nor again the head to the feet, I have no need of you.

'Nay, much more those members of the body, which seem to be more feeble, are necessary:

'And those members of the body, which we think to be less honourable, upon these we bestow more abundant honour; and our uncomely parts have more abundant comeliness.

'For our comely parts have no need: but God hath tempered the body together, having given more abundant honour to that part which lacked:

'That there should be no schism in the body; but that the members should have the same care one for another.

'And whether one member suffer, all the members suffer with it; or one member be honoured, all the members rejoice with it.

'Now ye are the body of Christ, and members in particular.'—1 Cor. xii. 12-27.

Virgil asks Sordello if they may continue their ascent by night.

———————— (XVII) ————————

PURGATORIO, CANTO VII. 37-57.

MA se tu sai e puoi, alcuno indizio
  Da' noi, perchè venir possiam più tosto
  Là, dove 'l Purgatorio ha dritto inizio.
Rispose: Luogo certo non c'è posto; 40
  Licito m'è andar suso ed intorno:
  Per quanto ir posso, a guida mi t'accosto.
Ma vedi già come dichina 'l giorno,
  Ed andar su di notte non si puote:
  Però è buon pensar d'un bel soggiorno. 45
Anime sono a destra qua remote:
  Se 'l mi consenti, menerotti ad esse,
  E non senza diletto ti fien note.
Com' è ciò? fu risposto; chi volesse
  Salir di notte, fora egli impedito 50
  D' altrui? ovver saria ch' e' non potesse?
E 'l buon Sordello in terra fregò 'l dito,
  Dicendo: Vedi, sola questa riga
  Non varcheresti dopo 'l Sol partito:
Non però ch' altra cosa desse briga, 55
  Che la notturna tenebra, ad ir suso:
  Quella col non poter la voglia intriga.

'Walk in the Light.'

(XVII)

THE Pilgrim's Guide, but partially illumined, has to learn through the experience of another (Sordello), whom he has accosted, some of the laws of the new Realm.

Sordello says, in answer to inquiries from Virgil, that he may accompany him through these outer precincts of Purgatory, for no one is restrained by fixed bounds or by authority. All are free to go up as long as the Sun illuminates their path; they might wander without hindrance to the base of the Mount at night, but cannot take even one step upwards without that divine Light. Virgil wonders what should hinder, and is told that darkness perplexes the Will and renders it impotent.

This law prevails not only outside the true beginning of the Way, but all through its ascending Circles. Pilgrims have to wait at the step they have attained, directly the Sun sets.

For progress there must be further light to dispel the ignorance that bewilders. Waiting for light is part of the discipline of our pathway. Perhaps there are ebbs and tides and seasons in the Spiritual as well as in the Natural world, and these have to be watched for. When the Celestial City itself is reached, we are told that we shall find that the Sun goes not down. 'I must work the works of Him that sent Me while it is day; the night cometh when no man can work.'—John ix. 4. Did our Lord mean that He Himself came under some such limitations? See John xi. 9, 10; xii. 35, 36: 'These things spake Jesus and departed, and did hide Himself from them.' Was this a Sunset to them, and a season to Him when He could not work in that sphere, even as in one city He could do no mighty work because of their unbelief?

The beautiful dell for the first night's repose in the Realm of Purification.

(XVIII)

PURGATORIO, CANTO VII. 61-84.

ALLORA 'l mio Signor, quasi ammirando,
   Menane, disse, dunque là 've dici
   Ch' aver si può diletto dimorando.
Poco allungati c' eravam di lici,
   Quand' io m' accorsi che 'l monte era scemo,   65
   A guisa che i valloni sceman quici.
Colà, disse quell' ombra, n' anderemo,
   Dove la costa face di sè grembo;
   E colà il nuovo giorno attenderemo.
Tra erto e piano er' un sentiero sghembo,   70
   Che ne condusse in fianco della lacca
   Là, dove più ch' a mezzo muore il lembo.
Oro ed argento fino e cocco e biacca
   Indico legno lucido e sereno,
   Fresco smeraldo allorachè si fiacca,   75
Dall' erba e dalli fior, dentro a quel seno
   Posti, ciascun saria di color vinto,
   Come dal suo maggiore è vinto 'l meno.
Non avea pur natura ivi dipinto,
   Ma di soavità di mille odori   80
   Vi faceva un incognito indistinto.
Salve, Regina, in sul verde, e in su' fiori
   Quivi seder, cantando, anime vidi,
   Che per la valle non parean di fuori.

> *'Thy glorious household-stuff did me entwine*
> *And 'tice me unto Thee.'*

---(XVIII)---

IT seems strange to find this Dell prepared, as it would seem, for luxurious repose, with flowers of richest and most brilliant hues, and an atmosphere of mingled odours—new and indescribably blended, and with sounds of tender music ascending from it. It seems the sweet childhood stage of Purgatory, though in the ante-courts of Penitence at the threshold of the stern and solemn Gates. We find nothing like it all the way up the Mount of Purification till at the summit the terrestrial Paradise is attained. A very few Palm-shaded halting-places were appointed in the sandy burning Desert for Israel coming out of Egypt. Our English 'Pilgrim's Progress' has its House Beautiful on the King's Highway for the refreshment of Pilgrims. Such stations have been found, on the threshold, perhaps, of some especially trying times of discipline.

The first Dawn and the first Evening in the repentant Pilgrim's pathway, here represented to us, seem as though they had flowed forth from that 'Prodigal Father's' heart—as the Parable we all know so well has been newly named—the Father who flew to meet his home-returning son, welcoming him with music and dancing, good cheer, the best robe, and his own ring. No doubt that son found discipline afterwards unsparcd to him by the wise Parent who had found it meet in his welcome to make merry and be glad, for the son 'who was dead and is alive, who was lost and is found.' Needed discipline the Squanderer of half the Father's living would certainly find through the elder Brother, on whose bounty he would have to live, as the Father had divided to each the half of his own living.

The Evening-hour of the Pilgrim's farewell-day to home.

──────────── (XIX) ────────────

PURGATORIO, CANTO VIII. 1-6.

E RA già l' ora che volge 'l disio
    A' naviganti e intenerisce il cuore,
        Lo dì c' han detto a' dolci amici addio;
E che lo nuovo peregrin d' amore
    Punge, se ode squilla di lontano,   5
        Che paia 'l giorno pianger che si muore.

> *'Sweet Hesper-Phosphor! double name*
> *For what is one—the first, the last.'*

───────────── (XIX) ─────────────

THE spirit of the Dawn with its promise, and its fresh beauty unstained by disappointment and failure, was revealed to us in the description of the first Morning at the entrance of the Second Kingdom. The first Evening hour is here given to us in like perfection, with the tender regrets and pathos that belong to the dying day.

These six first lines of Canto VIII. are so well known that they would have been omitted from these selections had it not been felt that the significance of Morning and Evening, in relation to the Pilgrim's life, should be a subject of fruitful meditation. Dante repeatedly alludes to these seasons in the Purgatorio. He feels them to be fraught with messages to the Traveller, as he passes through the revolution of the Heavens and the scenery of the Earth. We are most of us but half alive to these Voices, and need the Poet's inward ear and eye to transmit them to our duller apprehensions.

Morning and Evening 'outgoings' are each important for our teaching, even as Childhood and Old Age for the rounding of our disciplinary life in this stage of our being. We learn with Tennyson ('In Mem.,' CXX.) to watch the dimming glory of the finished day, and to listen to the pathetic sound of the closing door, as well as to the cheerful notes of the wakeful bird and the newly stirring energies of busy man. He teaches us to find the same star presiding over Past and Present.

Memory and Hope become one as we trust in God, and we recognise the low dark verge of life as

'The twilight of Eternal Day.'

The Evening Hymn in the flowery dell and the descent of the Guardian Angels.

(XX)

PURGATORIO, CANTO VIII. 7-33.

Quand' io incominciai a render vano
  L' udire, ed a mirar una dell' alme
  Surta, che l' ascoltar chiedea con mano.
Ella giunse e levò ambe le palme,   10
  Ficcando gli occhi verso l' oriente,
  Come dicesse a Dio : D' altro non calme.
Te lucis ante sì devotamente
  Le uscì di bocca, e con sì dolci note,
  Che fece me a me uscir di mente.   15
E l' altre poi dolcemente e devote
  Seguitâr lei per tutto l' inno intero,
  Avendo gli occhi alle superne ruote.
Aguzza qui, lettor, ben gli occhi al vero ;
  Chè 'l velo è ora ben tanto sottile,   20
  Certo che 'l trapassar dentro è leggiero.
Io vidi quello esercito gentile
  Tacito poscia riguardare in sùe,
  Quasi aspettando, pavido ed umile :
E vidi uscir dall' alto, e scender giùe   25
  Due angeli con due spade affocate,
  Tronche e private delle punte sue.
Verdi, come fogliette pur mo nate,
  Erano in veste, che da verdi penne
  Percosse traean dietro e ventilate.   30
L' un poco sovra noi a star si venne,
  E l' altro scese all' opposita sponda :
  Sì che la gente in mezzo si contenne.

> '*Ah, Lord ! do not withdraw,*
> *Lest want of awe make sin appear.*'

(XX)

THE colour and interweaving of the 'subtle veil' (line 19) is here so very beautiful that the Poet's invitation to gaze through it, rather than on it, is hard to comply with. He gave us the like advice in Inferno IX. 60, just after the terrible Erinnys on the walls of Dis had called on Medusa to come and petrify with her gaze the terrified Pilgrim, when the hands of the Guide were immediately protectingly placed over his eyes. A heaven-sent messenger at the same time approached through the marshy Styx. At the present juncture in the flowery Vale, so contrasted with the murky walls of Dis, an approach of the Adversary is, as before, expected; the Spirits await protection in prayer, and 'in expectation, pale and humble,' and they wait not in vain. Two Angels descend clothed in the green of Spring's Promise, and, proceeding to either side of the dell, they guard and enclose the blessed Company. The attitude of the Spirit in the inner Sanctuary of the heart is perfectly imaged in lines 10 to 16 by the Leader of the Evening hymn—'Te lucis ante terminum.'

In the Roman Breviary the hymn 'Te lucis' is followed, after the 'Nunc Dimittis' and versicle, by a Collect 'Visit, O God, we beseech Thee, this habitation and drive from it all snares of the enemy ; let Thy holy Angels dwell in it. . . .'

The Angels seem to have been sent in answer to this Prayer.

Silence, Humility, Expectation, form a fructifying soil for the seeds of Prayer.

Three brilliant stars now rule the hemisphere where four had appeared in the morning. At the same moment the Adversary glides onwards.

──────────────── (XXI) ────────────

PURGATORIO, CANTO VIII. 85-108.

GLI occhi miei ghiotti andavan pure al cielo, 85
   Pur là dove le stelle son più tarde,
      Sì come ruota più presso allo stelo.
E 'l Duca mio: Figliuol, che lassù guarde?
   Ed io a lui: A quelle tre facelle,
      Di che 'l polo di qua tutto quanto arde. 90
Ed egli a me: Le quattro chiare stelle,
   Che vedemmo staman, son di là basse;
      E queste son salite ov' eran quelle.
Com' ei parlava, e Sordello a sè 'l trasse,
   Dicendo: Vedi là il nostr' avversaro: 95
      E drizzò 'l dito, perchè in là guatasse.
Da quella parte, onde non ha riparo
   La picciola valletta, era una biscia,
      Forse qual diede ad Eva il cibo amaro.
Tra l' erba e i fior venía la mala striscia, 100
   Volgendo ad or ad or la testa, e 'l dosso
      Leccando, come bestia che si liscia.
Io nol vidi, e però dicer nol posso,
   Come mosser gli astor celestïali;
      Ma vidi bene l' uno e l' altro mosso. 105
Sentendo fender l' aere alle verdi ali,
   Fuggío 'l serpente; e gli angeli dier volta
      Suso alle poste rivolando eguali.

The transition state between the Old and New Dispensation.

(XXI)

THE dusk of Evening increases as Dante converses with the Friend who has recognised him (Judge Nino) in the flowery Vale.

The spirits of Kings and others are reposing here during the hours of darkness. When Dante looks upwards he finds the Heavens aflame with the splendours of three Stars where, in the early morning, four had ruled.

The three represent the especially Christian graces of Faith, Hope, and Charity. These Three are the mother-souls— the veiled springs of the four Cardinal Virtues. In the earthly Paradise we shall find again the Four and the Three, not as stars, but as Nymphs in attendance on Beatrice. There the seven are seen in their true relative positions, and in their more perfect embodiment.

It seems significant that at the very moment of the Pilgrim's discovery of the disappearance of the four signs of a former Dispensation and the dominance of a more glorious one, the Adversary should have drawn near. May this hint to us that an advance into the perception of fuller light has in the transition period its peril for the Pilgrim? Is it an insidious temptation to continue in carelessness where grace abounds?

> 'For I say this is death and the sole death,
> When a man's loss comes to him from his gain,
> Darkness from light, from knowledge ignorance,
> And lack of love from love made manifest.'—BROWNING.

The Adversary approached on that side of the Valley that had no barrier, and he came through the innocent delights of beautiful nature. The self complacency depicted in his movements may perhaps intimate some corresponding disposition in the Pilgrim whereby the Tempter sought to gain access; his sly approach is, however, at once turned back by the mere sound of the angel's verdant wings.

*The morning dream of the Eagle who snatched up Dante
and bore him into the Fire above.*

────────── (XXII) ──────────

PURGATORIO, CANTO IX. 10-33.

Q UAND' io, che meco avea di quel d' Adamo,   10
    Vinto dal sonno, in su l' erba inchinai
  Là, 've già tutti e cinque sedevamo.
Nell' ora, che comincia i tristi lai
  La rondinelli presso alla mattina,
  Forse a memoria de' suoi primi guai;   15
E che la mente nostra, pellegrina
  Più dalla carne, e men da' pensier presa,
  Alle sue visïon quasi è divina;
In sogno mi parea veder sospesa
  Un' aquila nel ciel con penne d' oro,   20
  Con l' ale aperte, ed a calare intesa:
Ed esser mi parea là, dove fôro
  Abbandonati i suoi da Ganimede,
  Quando fu ratto al sommo concistoro.
Fra me pensava: Forse questa fiede   25
  Pur qui per uso; e forse d' altro loco
  Disdegna di portarne suso in piede.
Poi mi parea che, più rotata un poco,
  Terribil come folgor discendesse,
  E me rapisse suso infino al foco.   30
Ivi pareva ch' ella ed io ardesse:
  E sì l' incendio immaginato cosse,
  Che convenne che 'l sonno si rompesse.

> '*August anticipations, symbols, types*
> *Of a dim splendour ever on before.*'

(XXII)

THE Pilgrim in his Adam-body, wearied with his wonderful Way and high converse, had slept for some hours. In the early morning, when Dante tells us that the soul is further from the flesh and less imprisoned by the intellect (or by reasoning, perhaps), his prophetic soul dreamed a dream of terror, yet of rapture. It was of high import on the very threshold of the Gates of Purgatory proper.

The ardent Eagle, as of St. John or of Ezekiel, snatched him from the Earth and bore him upwards even into the consuming Fire; the flames so scorched him and the wings that carried him, that the imagined burning awakened him from the terrible vision.

He will indeed have to pass through flames more burning than 'molten glass,' and will experience the terrible demands of a revelation of blinding Light and Purity, beyond the powers of one in the flesh to sustain; but he will find himself prepared for ascent after ascent and brought into unity with the unfolding revelation of this prevision, by such fine gradations that its shock and terror will not be repeated. Such Eagle wings are sent but for the few elect souls who are fitted for the vision, and fitted also for its communication, in some measure, to others; yet all may count upon One who beareth up His children even as an Eagle on her wings—Deut. xxxii. 11. And the promise remains sure for each pilgrim who will by faith and patience inherit it:

'They that wait upon the Lord shall renew their strength, they shall mount up with wings as Eagles, they shall run and not be weary, and they shall walk and not faint.'—Isa. xl. 31.

Dante is carried in his morning sleep by Lucia to the Entrance of Purgatory.

(XXIII)

PURGATORIO, CANTO IX. 40-63.

CHE mi scoss' io, siccome dalla faccia 40
   Mi fuggío 'l sonno; e diventai smorto,
   Come fa l' uom che spaventato agghiaccia.
Dallato m' era solo il mio Conforto;
   E 'l Sole er' alto già più di du' ore;
   E 'l viso m' era alla marina torto. 45
Non aver tema, disse il mio Signore:
   Fátti sicur, chè noi siamo a buon punto:
   Non stringer, ma rallarga ogni vigore.
Tu se' omai al Purgatorio giunto:
   Vedi là il balzo, che 'l chiude d' intorno; 50
   Vedi l' entrata là 've par disgiunto.
Dianzi, nell' alba che precede al giorno,
   Quando l' anima tua dentro dormia,
   Sopra li fiori, onde laggiù è adorno,
Venne una donna, e disse: Io son Lucia. 55
   Lasciatemi pigliar colui che dorme;
   Sì l' agevolerò per la sua via.
Sordel rimase, e l' altre gentil forme:
   Ella ti tolse; e come 'l dì fu chiaro,
   Sen venne suso, ed io per le su' orme. 60
Qui ti posò: e pria mi dimostraro
   Gli occhi suoi belli quell' entrata aperta;
   Poi ella e 'l sonno ad una se n' andaro.

*'And from a dream
Straightway a waking vision it became!'*

─────────── (XXIII) ───────────

E VEN while, in dream-vision, Dante felt the scorching fires, he was being carried tenderly upwards over the last difficult steps to the entrance of the rugged Way.

So it is at times when we least expect it; rough places are made plain and crooked paths straight, and Love has wafted us through dreaded places without effort of our own.

The Pilgrim awakens, and is astonished at his new surroundings; his guide encourages and warns him at the same time. He has attained so far by sweet Mercy's lifting arms during his sleep; but he is to relax no effort and to summon all his powers, for the straight Gate and narrow Way are just before him. Uncertainty and perplexity have vanished. The next momentous step must be taken, having been clearly indicated by Lucia's enlightening eyes.

'O send out thy light and thy truth : let them lead me :
Let them bring me unto thy holy hill.'—Ps. xliii. 3.

'I will guide thee with mine Eye.'—Ps. xxxii. 8.

PURGATORIO, CANTO IX. 73-93.

NOI ci appressammo; ed eravamo in parte,
    Che là, dove pareami in prima un rotto,
    Pur com' un fesso ch' un muro diparte,   75
Vidi una porta, e tre gradi di sotto,
    Per gire ad essa, di color diversi,
    Ed un portier, ch' ancor non facea motto.
E come l' occhio più e più v' apersi,
    Vidil seder sopra 'l grado soprano,   80
    Tal nella faccia ch' io non lo soffersi:
Ed una spada nuda aveva in mano,
    Che rifletteva i raggi sì vêr noi,
    Ch' io dirizzava spesso il viso invano.
Ditel costinci, che volete voi?   85
    Cominciò egli a dire: Ov' è la scorta?
    Guardate che 'l venir su non vi nôi.
Donna del ciel, di queste cose accorta,
    Rispose 'l mio Maestro a lui, pur dianzi
    Ne disse: Andate là, quivi è la porta.   90
Ed ella i passi vostri in bene avanzi,
    Ricominciò 'l cortese portinaio:
    Venite dunque a' nostri gradi innanzi.

> *'That sight of the most Fair*
> *Will gladden thee, but it will pierce thee, too.'*

(XXIV)

AS we ponder this stern parable of Judgment, each line brings us into a deeper sense of its solemn meaning.

We feel the cessation of all the fellowship that has been present before; the rocky wall with its narrow fissure shutting out the horizon in front; the long ascent of breathless expectation terminating at the threshold of an unknown life; and the soul brought face to face with that single Spiritual Presence—silent and with a countenance too penetrating to be endured. His naked sword was in his hand 'quick and powerful, piercing even to the dividing asunder of soul and spirit,' making manifest by the dazzling light it reflected every thought and intent of the heart.

The Angel breaks silence with a question and a warning. To approach that judgment more closely may injure the unprepared and the uncalled soul, he says, but the Guide having named the directions of Lucia, the Pilgrim is bidden to come nearer to the Three Steps.

The Three Steps: of white polished Marble, of dark and broken Stone, and of crimson Porphyry.

———————————— (XXV) ————————————

PURGATORIO, CANTO IX. 94-105.

LÀ ne venimmo: e lo scaglion primaio
   Bianco marmo era sì pulito e terso,   95
   Ch' io mi specchiava in esso quale i' paio.
Era 'l secondo, tinto più che perso,
   D' una petrina ruvida ed arsiccia,
   Crepata per lo lungo e per traverso.
Lo terzo, che di sopra s' ammassiccia,   100
   Porfido mi parea sì fiammeggiante,
   Come sangue che fuor di vena spiccia.
Sopra questo teneva ambo le piante
   L' angel di Dio, sedendo in su la soglia,
   Che mi sembiava pietra di diamante.   105

Ideal Innocence: the Cross and Self-Sacrifice.

(XXV)

WHAT do these three Steps symbolize as initiation in the narrow way? 'Shortly,' as defined by the Schoolmen, 'Contrition, Confession, Satisfaction, as the three elements of Penitence.'

Those three great blocks of marble by which the Pilgrim had to mount seem to speak as Nature speaks, and to rivet our attention by their silent voices. The first, of white polished marble, mirroring the downcast face of the Pilgrim. In that spotless surface, did he recall the ideal of his early life and see himself as he now appeared in contrast to that whiteness? Later, in the Earthly Paradise, we shall find him ashamed at his own reflection in a clear stream.

In mounting the second step of dark, rugged, dark-tinctured stone, cracked lengthwise and crosswise, he must become aware of the destruction that sin and death have wrought in him, and accept the condemnation of the Cross. Having thenceforth no hope in himself, he can only plant his next step on that Rock of Ages 'crimson* like living blood gushing from the veins,' in the Knowledge of the Love that loved and forgave even unto death and of the Life blood that is the Source and Substance of the New Life of Self-Sacrifice.

The Angel of the Gate at the summit of the three steps, the Representative and Minister of the gifts of Contrition, was seated at the threshold of the Gate. His seat was a stone of Adamant or Diamond, symbolizing the Foundation Stone on which the Church is built. Its Minister held the Keys, tokens of the Source of his authority. His feet were both firmly planted on the Crimson rock-step below.

---

* Dante calls crimson, in which he saw Beatrice clothed in the Vita Nuova, 'that noble colour of Love'; and the third Grace, Charity, in the Earthly Paradise was seen 'so very red, that in the fire she hardly had been noted.'

The Angel of Penitence makes manifest on the Pilgrim's forehead the Wounds of the seven deadly Sins, and opens the Gate.

───────── (XXVI) ─────────

PURGATORIO, CANTO IX. 106-129.

PER li tre gradi su di buona voglia
    Mi trasse 'l Duca mio, dicendo: Chiedi
    Umilemente che 'l serrame scioglia.
Divoto mi gittai a' santi piedi ;
    Misericordia chiesi, e ch' e' m' aprisse :   110
    Ma pria nel petto tre fiate mi diedi.
Sette P nella fronte mi descrisse
    Col punton della spada ; e : Fa' che lavi,
    Quando se' dentro, queste piaghe, disse.
Cenere, o terra, che secca si cavi,   115
    D' un color fora col suo vestimento :
    E di sotto da quel trasse duo chiavi.
L' una era d' oro, e l' altra era d' argento :
    Pria con la bianca, e poscia con la gialla
    Fece alla porta sì ch' io fui contento.   120
Quandunque l' una d' este chiavi falla,
    Che non si volga dritta per la toppa,
    Diss' egli a noi, non s' apre questa calla.
Più cara è l' una ; ma l' altra vuol troppa
    D' arte e d' ingegno, avanti che disserri,   125
    Perch' ell' è quella che 'l nodo disgroppa.
Da Pier le tengo : e dissemi ch' i' erri
    Anzi ad aprir ch' a tenerla serrata,
    Purchè la gente a' piedi mi s' atterri.

'If we confess our sins, He is faithful and just to forgive us our sins, and to cleanse us from all unrighteousness.'

(XXVI)

THE Pilgrim was drawn up those three steps of mystic import by his Guide, and bidden to ask humbly for admittance through the Gate. Casting himself down on that crimson Rock before the feet that were planted there, three times he smote upon his breast, thus fully acknowledging the ruined condition witnessed to by the previous step, and besought entrance for Mercy's sake.

The sharp and piercing Spirit-Sword was then in the Angel's hand to do its work; inscribing on his forehead, bringing into full manifestation the seven P's (peccati) or wounds of the seven deadly sins, hitherto speciously concealed within the Pilgrim's heart. He is told he must cleanse those wounds when he has passed within the Portal. The Angel is clothed in colour of dust and ashes, and brings forth from under that garb of the penitence he personifies and teaches the two Keys of the Entrance Gate. He holds them from St. Peter; one is of silver, the other of gold. The more precious one is supposed to signify the Authority from whence its power is derived—the Commission of the Head of the Church. The silver key, which is used first, betokens the adaptive power of the Spirit-anointed Minister to discern and deal with each heart. Here the work of the Church on Earth seems so blent in description with that of the more interior Spirit-world of Purgatory that the two can hardly be separated; the possibility of error through human mists in using the keys is contemplated, and the part of Mercy in opening, rather than that of Justice (or severity) in closing, is said to have been counselled by St. Peter, if only marks of true penitence may be discerned.

Dante is bidden to enter the solemn Gates of Purgatory, and warned not to look back. Within he hears the singing of the Te Deum.

———————— (XXVII) ————————

PURGATORIO, CANTO IX. 131-145.

INTRATE; ma facciovi accorti,
   Che di fuor torna chi indietro si guata.
E quando fur ne' cardini distorti
   Gli spigoli di quella regge sacra,
   Che di metallo son sonanti e forti,   135
Non ruggìo sì, nè si mostrò sì acra
   Tarpeia, come tolto le fu 'l buono
   Metello, per che poi rimase macra.
Io mi rivolsi attento al primo tuono,
   E *Te Deum laudamus* mi parea   140
   Udire in voce mista al dolce suono.
Tale imagine appunto mi rendea
   Ciò ch' i' udiva, qual prender si suole
   Quando a cantar con organi si stea;
Ch' or sì or no s' intendon le parole.   145

'*Search me, O God, and know my heart; see if there be any wicked way in me, and lead me in the Way Everlasting.*'

——————————— (XXVII) - ———————————

THE solemn Gates open with harsh and discordant roaring, as though their hinges were seldom turned. Their grating sound suggests imprisonment, rather than the opening of the Way to liberty; and the Angel's voice, commanding no looks backward, echoes the stern words of like import from the Master's voice: 'Strait is the Gate and narrow is the Way that leadeth unto Life;' and, 'He that putteth his hand to the plough and looketh back, is not fit for the Kingdom of GOD.'

There seems no tenderness here. There is nothing like the Father's large-hearted welcome in this parable of the Entrance Gate. There could be no compromise in such a severance from evil, acknowledged to be evil. The Pilgrim shudders, and makes us shudder, as he recounts his initiation into the realm of purification. Directly these grating sounds have ceased, we are glad to pause with him within the threshold and listen to the voices mingled in sweet melody; the voices of those who give thanks for the enlightened and restored soul in the words of the Te Deum —words sometimes heard, sometimes lost in the music.

Perhaps once for all, perhaps at more than one juncture in many lives, some such heart-searching interview has to take place between the spirit of a man and the Divine Discerner of the thoughts and intents of the heart; a strait and narrow Gate seems to be then set before the Disciple, which apparently to himself will cut him off from all delights. He seems free to enter or to *look back* and endeavour to forget the inexorable and pitiless behest.

The sculptured language by the Wayside, speaking with more force than reality itself.

———————— (XXVIII) ————————

PURGATORIO, CANTO X. 28-33.

L ASSÙ non eran mossi i piè nostri anco,
   Quand' io conobbi quella ripa intorno,
   Che dritto di salita aveva manco,   30
Esser di marmo candido, ed adorno
   D' intagli tai, che non pur Policleto,
   Ma la natura lì avrebbe scorno.

> *'O learn to read what silent Love hath writ,*
> *To hear with eyes belongs to Love's fine wit!'*

―――――――――――― (XXVIII) ――――――――――

A FEW lines must connect the last extract with the one before us to-day.

Within the threshold the Way still mounted, and for some time lay through a dark tunnel within the rock. The footway is as uneven as over petrified waves. Slowly the Pilgrim must wend his way upwards. It is a time of uncertainty and of new adaptation.

When he had proceeded wearily from that 'needle's-eye' of the Gateway (the words again recalling those in Matt. xix. 24) the prospect was lonely and, as far as the eye could reach, monotonous. How often after some new step towards spiritual progress, even after some spiritual victory won, it has seemed so!—a time of human weakness and emptiness which is the condition for the perfecting, divine strength to flow in.

Line 28.—They now reach the cornice of the first encircling of the Mount, and find this to be the region where the root-sin of Pride, which they had seen in fullest development in Hell, had to find its cleansing discipline. In stepping forward on this cornice, the monotonous Embankment, as it had appeared, now dawned upon Dante as of white marble wondrously adorned with sculptures, more living than those of Polycletus, nay, than those of Nature herself, for they appealed not alone to the eye, but with power from Spirit to Spirit.

Let us mark the first object-lesson the Discipline of Love provided for the eyes of the Proud.

Not one of the chastisement of Pride (though such will be seen later), but of the Ideal and Type of Humility.

The heart-moving transcript of the Annunciation.

(XXVIII)

(*Continued from last page.*)

PURGATORIO, CANTO X. 34-45.

L' angel, che venne in terra col decreto
   Della molt' anni lagrimata pace,   35
   Ch' aperse il ciel dal suo lungo divieto,
Dinanzi a noi pareva sì verace,
   Quivi intagliato in un atto soave,
   Che non sembiava immagine che tace.
Giurato si saria ch' ei dicesse *Ave ;*   40
   Però ch' ivi era immaginata quella,
   Ch' ad aprir l' alto amor volse la chiave.
Ed avea in atto impressa esta favella :
   Ecce Ancilla Dei, sì propriamente
   Come figura in cera si suggella.   45

'*This new Guest to her eyes new laws hath given :
'Twas once look up, 'tis now look down to Heaven.*'

(XXVIII)

'The hand-maiden of the Lord' was to be seen in the supreme moment of her election to the Motherhood of Humility's own Essence and Being.

Were not the eyes of Proud Pilgrims bathed and re-opened here as they gazed? for their *hearts* behold the great Reality now, no longer the oft-painted Picture; the very voice of Heaven's tenderness is thrilling through this living presentation, for Gabriel 'did not seem an image that is silent,' and the meek accents of the Hand-maiden of the Lord were within and around her visible presence, and communicated to the beholder. The issuing Life from the Cradle to the Cross could not fail to shine there also. What should prevail to turn out this root-sin of Pride from our hearts, but such a soul-transforming gaze at the central core of our Faith?

Proud Christians are here seen pressed down under heavy weights.

(XXIX)

PURGATORIO, CANTO X. 112-139.

IO cominciai: Maestro, quel ch' io veggio
   Muover a noi, non mi sembran persone,
   E non so che; sì nel veder vaneggio.
Ed egli a me: La grave condizione   115
   Di lor tormento a terra gli rannicchia
   Sì, che i mie' occhi pria n' ebber tenzione.
Ma guarda fisso là, e disviticchia
   Col viso quel che vien sotto a quei sassi:
   Già scorger puoi come ciascun si nicchia.   120
O superbi Cristian, miseri, lassi,
   Che, della vista della mente infermi,
   Fidanza avete ne' ritrosi passi,
Non v' accorgete voi, che noi siam vermi
   Nati a formar l' angelica farfalla   125
   Che vola alla giustizia senza schermi?
Di che l' animo vostro in alto galla?
   Voi siete quasi entomata in difetto,
   Sì come verme, in cui formazion falla?
Come, per sostentar solaio o tetto,   130
   Per mensola talvolta una figura
   Si vede giunger le ginocchia al petto,
La qual fa del non ver vera rancura
   Nascere in chi la vede; così fatti
   Vid' io color, quando posi ben cura.   135
Ver è che più e meno eran contratti,
   Secondo ch' avean più e meno addosso:
   E qual più pazïenza avea negli atti
Piangendo parea dicer: Più non posso.

> '*Quite wingless our desire;*
> *In sense dark-prison'd all that ought to soar;*
> *Prone to the centre, crawling in the dust.*'

──────── (XXIX) ────────

DANTE knew that his besetting sin was Pride. In the next circle he tells the Envious that his soul was even then weighed down by the load that he well knew awaited him after death in this Circle where the proud find their discipline.

Lines 117-119.—In Dean Plumptre's translation the meaning seems more clearly given than in Longfellow's:

> 'Why doth your soul lift up itself on high?
> Ye are as insects yet but half complete,
> As worms in whom their growth fails utterly.'

Dante looks upon the Caterpillar as an unfinished creature at best, and supposes some of these to be without the growing embryo wings within. How can such as these, he says, pretend to float on high with proud looks and words?

'Proud Christians!' Words in conjunction that speak mutual extinction.

The poor weary ones are now bowed to the Earth by the weight of their dominating vice, which had so nearly crushed out of them the Christ-like spirit. The wings that ought to have been formed within are not there to carry them where they fain would be, at the feet of Christ.

'A Parable from Nature,' in a letter from a friend. 'In the Garden last Evening, I suddenly perceived a strange-looking creature struggling about in the grass; it had a long worm-like body and a sort of ugly little frill of attempts at wings round its neck: it looked like a distorted imitation of a butterfly. We felt quite sad, and wondered if some mischance had happened which had hindered its formation, but we did not know enough of such transformations to pronounce whether it was the utter failure it looked or not. Half an hour later we observed it again, and saw that by dint of struggling about, fit neither for crawling nor flight, for earth nor heaven, it had pushed and lengthened out its wings, till they half clothed it, and its worm-like body seemed contracting; the last glimpse we had of it showed it to us almost entirely "clothed upon" with its white plumes, and doubtless by the moonlight hour it was flitting about over the opening Evening Primroses, a happy white moth, and knew what it was meant for.'

The Lord's Prayer as said by the souls in Purgatory.

(XXX)

PURGATORIO, CANTO XI. 1-24.

O PADRE nostro, che ne' cieli stai,
    Non circoscritto, ma per più amore
    Ch' ai primi effetti di lassù tu hai;
Laudato sia 'l tuo nome e 'l tuo valore
    Da ogni creatura, com' è degno   5
    Di render grazie al tuo dolce vapore.
Vegna vêr noi la pace del tuo regno;
    Chè noi ad essa non potem da noi,
    S' ella non vien, con tutto 'l nostro ingegno.
Come del suo voler gli angeli tuoi   10
    Fan sacrificio a te, cantando Osanna,
    Così facciano gli uomini de' suoi.
Da' oggi a noi la cotidiana manna,
    Sanza la qual per questo aspro diserto
    A retro va chi più di gir s' affanna.   15
E come noi lo mal, ch' avem sofferto,
    Perdoniamo a ciascuno, e tu perdona
    Benigno; e non guardare al nostro merto.
Nostra virtù, che di leggier s' adona,
    Non spermentar con l' antico avversaro,   20
    Ma libera da lui, che sì la sprona.
Quest' ultima preghiera, Signor caro,
    Già non si fa per noi, chè non bisogna;
    Ma per color che dietro a noi restaro.

'If the Ideal is never actual, it is always being actualized.'
Christ's Kingdom is ever coming.

──────────── (XXX) ────────────

THE once proud, now evidently most meek, Christians under their crushing burdens, 'unequally in anguish round and round and weary all,' are together saying the Lord's Prayer after their manner.

The variations made in it seem drawn out by their present knowledge of themselves.

> 'Come unto us the Peace of thy dominion,
> For unto it, we cannot of ourselves,
> If it come not, with all our intellect.'

Dante's intellect must often have been occasion to him for placing himself above his fellow-men, and Peace he has often sought in vain. These weary souls of his imagining, that slip back or down under their burdens, see that they cannot expect to reach Peace, with all their efforts of intellect; nor have they strength to go forward in their difficult burdened climb without the gift of the hidden manna to sustain their spirits through the bitter desert path.

They speak their self-distrust in those words, 'Regard not our desert.' They have found out that they must be one and all receivers, and so they are being separated from their proud self-sufficiency. The petition they make (not for themselves, for the Tempter does not enter Purgatory), 'Lead us not into temptation, but deliver us from the Adversary,' expresses with the next sentence the same sense of weakness and failure. They utter this petition for those who remain behind in the world, and they confess their own failure of strength in unison with them. 'Our virtue, which *is easily o'ercome*, put not to proof with the old Adversary.'

The intimate blending of the two worlds is tenderly manifested by this prayer for those below, and by Dante's comment and Virgil's aspiration for these, as he asks of them directions concerning the Way, and again alludes to the Wings they needed, which had hitherto failed them.— Lines 25-40.

Dante is bidden by Virgil to study the sculptured pavement on which they tread. Instances of Pride are livingly portrayed here.

─────────────── (XXXI) ───────────────

PURGATORIO, CANTO XII. 10-15.

<pre>
IO m' era mosso, e seguia volentieri   10
    Del mio Maestro i passi; ed ambedue
  Già mostravam, com' eravam leggieri;
Quando mi disse: Volgi gli occhi in giue:
  Buon ti sarà, per alleggiar la via,
  Veder lo letto delle piante tue.   15
</pre>

> '*When to the Sessions of sweet silent thought
> I summon up remembrance of things past.*'

─────── (XXXI) ───────

DANTE speaks with some Artists and Poets in this Circle, who confess their Pride or their Ambition. They now give honour to one another, as one of them confesses he could not have done on Earth, for then his heart had been too much bent on the great desire of excelling another.

They speak of one succeeding and surpassing another 'through some fresher stamp of the time-bettering days'; they discuss the slight value of this mundane rumour as 'naught but a breath of wind.' With one of these heavy-laden souls Dante walks abreast, in sympathy with him and in the same self-condemnation; he compares himself and this comrade to oxen going together in a yoke; seeming to intimate by using this simile that the heavy-laden Twain had failed in former days to accept the yoke offered by the Blessed Burden-Bearer.

Line 10.—The Pilgrim was now bidden by his Guide as they move onwards to cast down his eyes and read the mystic sculpture beneath his feet, the visible language as he has again called it, 'dear to look upon for its Creator's sake.'

Here instances of Pride were portrayed on the pavement, and were to be trodden on by the Pilgrim's feet as he humbly bent over them. A little beyond the limits of the Extract he says, in describing the wonderfully living power of these representations (or reproductions rather):

> '*Dead seemed the dead, the living seemed alive;
> Better than I, saw not who saw the truth,
> All that I trod upon while bowed I went.*'

The sculptured tombs of the departed which recall tender memories.

(XXXI)

(Continued from last page.)

PURGATORIO, CANTO XII. 16-24.

Come, perchè di lor memoria sia,
   Sovr' a' sepolti le tombe terragne
   Portan segnato quel ch' egli eran pria;
Onde lì molte volte se ne piagne,
   Per la puntura della rimembranza,   20
   Che solo a' pii dà delle calcagne;
Sì vid' io lì, ma di miglior sembianza
   Secondo l' artificio, figurato
   Quanto per via di fuor dal monte avanza.

> *' Yet doth remembrance like a sovereign Prince*
> *For you a stately Gallery maintain*
> *Of gay or tragic pictures.'*

--------------------- (XXXI) ---------------------

Perhaps it is intended here to express Dante's view of God's teaching through Art, and the association with Artists and Poets in this Canto would confirm this view; but lines 15 to 22 would rather lead us to that which is within and point us to the stony heart on which the Lord promises (when it is renewed) to write His laws. It seems at any rate to show us the moving way in which God's speech addresses itself to man apart from words—in present events, or past history. We are often shut through sorrowful memory into our 'chambers of imagery' within.—Lines 19-21.

> *' Whence ofttimes to our weeping comes new birth,*
> *Through the sharp sting of poignant memory*
> *Which spurs on none but souls of loving worth ;'*

or which wounds none but the 'compassionate soul'—the 'anima pia.' Such a soul stands, with the Poet, painfully conscious of that which is passing away, though with his face illumined by the Future's Dawn. Such a one, in his own personal history, as Time takes so much away, must be pierced by this experience as he treads on the monuments of the dead Past.

Memory—in German that beautiful word 'Erinnerung'—is the inner Sanctuary of that which was once outward Often has the 'sound of a voice that is still, and the touch of a vanished hand' in that Sanctuary, been fraught with a divine power, unfelt when palpable to our senses; for quickening is communicated by One whom the Father sends to 'bring all things to our remembrance,' as well as to 'show us things to come.'

Another Angel is reverently welcomed. He comes with the New Day, fans the wounded forehead, and points out an easier ascent.

PURGATORIO, CANTO XII. 73-99.

PIU era già per noi del monte vôlto,
   E del cammin del Sole assai più speso,
   Che non stimava l' animo non sciolto ;   75
Quando colui, che innanzi sempre atteso
   Andava, cominciò : Drizza la testa ;
   Non è più tempo da gir sì sospeso.
Vedi colà un angel, che s' appresta
   Per venir verso noi : vedi che torna   80
   Dal servigio del dì l' ancella sesta.
Di riverenza 'l viso e gli atti adorna,
   Sì che i diletti lo inviarci 'n suso :
   Pensa che questo dì mai non raggiorna.
Io era ben del suo ammonir uso   85
   Pur di non perder tempo ; sì che in quella
   Materia non potea parlarmi chiuso.
A noi venia la creatura bella,
   Bianco vestita, e nella faccia quale
   Par tremolando mattutina stella.   90
Le braccia aperse, ed indi aperse l' ale :
   Disse : Venite ; qui son presso i gradi,
   Ed agevolemente omai si sale.
A questo annunzio vengon molto radi :
   O gente umana, per volar su nata,   95
   Perchè a poco vento così cadi ?
Menocci ove la roccia era tagliata :
   Quivi mi batteo l' ale per la fronte ;
   Poi mi permise sicura l' andata.

'*In the same brook none ever bath'd him twice;
To the same life none ever twice awoke.*'

------------------ (XXXII) ------------------

VIRGIL, who, as Conscience ever watchful and in advance of the Pilgrim, was going forward (76), admonished him that the time for contemplation of the Past was over, and that a Heavenly Messenger was to be prepared for, by reverent expectation and action.

Note concise language of line 84—untranslatable into our tongue :

'Pensa che questo dì mai non raggiorna.'
'*Think that this day* will never dawn again !*'

A reason for observing and preparing to welcome the precious things it, and it alone, can bring to us; for never can we behold its unique light again; never can its jewels be set in the same setting and find us in the same fitted circumstances to receive them.

With the hint of the Sibylline leaves, yet not only with warning of failure to receive, does the new day speak to us, but with the proffered charm of wonder and novelty.

'There is no monotony in living to him who walks even the quietest and tamest paths with open and perceptive eyes. It may be that you think all days alike and grow weary with their sameness, and get none of the stimulus and solemnity which comes from constantly reaching unexpected places and experiences. You cannot think what a different place this world is to a man who goes out every morning into a new world, who is Adam over again every day, who starts each day with the certainty "that he has not passed that way before " . . . the fundamental difference between the two lives lies in the difference of their perception of God.

'It is God and the discovery of Him in life, and the certainty that He has plans for our lives and is doing something with them, that gives us a true deep sense of movement, and lets us feel the power and delight of unknown coming things. Without Him a life must sink into weary monotony, or escape it only by artificial and superficial changes.'—PHILLIPS BROOKS.

* 'Dies' and our word 'Day' are derived from the same root as 'Deus,' thus being literally, as well as figuratively, 'the light of the world.'

The song of Welcome to the new circle:
'Blessed are the Poor in spirit.'

——————— (XXXIII) ———————

PURGATORIO, CANTO XII. 109-126.

NOI volgend' ivi le nostre persone,
   Beati pauperes spiritu, voci   110
   Cantaron sì, che nol diria sermone.
Ahi quanto son diverse quelle foci
   Dall' infernali! chè quivi per canti
   S' entra, e laggiù per lamenti feroci.
Già montavam su per li scaglion santi;   115
   Ed esser mi parea troppo più lieve,
   Che per lo pian non mi parea davanti.
Ond' io: Maestro, di', qual cosa greve
   Levata s'è da me, che nulla quasi
   Per me fatica andando si riceve?   120
Rispose: Quando i P, che son rimasi
   Ancor nel volto tuo presso che stinti,
   Saranno, come l' un, del tutto rasi,
Fien li tuoi piè dal buon voler sì vinti,
   Che non pur non fatica sentiranno,   125
   Ma fia diletto loro esser su pinti.

The crushed soul set free to mount, through Pride removed and Poverty of spirit imparted.

──────────── (XXXIII) ────────────

TO the Pilgrim, this new day was indeed a new era. The divine Messenger, in whose countenance was he appearance of the tremulous morning star, came to h im with a tender direction towards easier ascending steps. He then smote on his forehead with his wings, obliterating the first of the seven P's (Pride), and so setting free his hitherto shackled feet, that hardly any fatigue was felt by him in the arduous ascent. He asks what heavy thing can have been uplifted from him (118). His Guide assures him that when the remaining six P's should be removed, not only should he feel no fatigue, but he would rejoice in springing upwards. An indescribable sweetness of voices singing, 'Blessed are the Poor in spirit' was in the air around them. A Benediction takes the place of the crushing weight of the sin removed, and liberates the soul's own action of blessing.

The process of taking away, or setting free, the sepulchred nature of man, goes on through Purgatory.

Michelangelo* defined Sculpture as 'the Art that works by force of taking away;' he speaks of 'the figure which ever grows the more the stone is hewn away.'

The sculptor seeks and finds within the marble the ideal form his hand sets free.

'As the outward man is perishing' through the changes and chances of Time's terrible mallet and chisel, the Divine Spirit is fashioning and liberating the ideal son of God.

* See 'Life of Michelangelo,' by J. A. Symonds, vol. i., 110.

The second Circle, for the Cleansing Discipline of the Envious. Virgil's invocation of the Sun.

(XXXIV)

PURGATORIO, CANTO XIII. 10-21.

SE qui per dimandar, gente s' aspetta,   10
   Ragionava 'l Poeta, i' temo forse
     Che troppo avrà d' indugio nostra eletta.
Poi fisamente al Sole gli occhi porse ;
   Fece del destro lato al muover centro,
     E la sinistra parte di sè torse.   15
O dolce lume, a cui fidanza i' entro
   Per lo nuovo cammin, tu ne conduci,
     Dicea, come condur si vuol quinc' entro.
Tu scaldi 'l mondo, tu sovr' esso luci ;
   S' altra cagione in contrario non ponta,   20
     Esser den sempre li tuoi raggi duci.

The Blind hear voices in the air.

(XXXIV)

THE Pilgrim is to learn in this second Circle the nature of Envy by its manifested effects; its cleansing is to be through the pain of those effects, through knowledge, and through the opposing grace of Love.

The 'visible language' of the last Circle was no longer to be found. It would be useless here, for the eyes of the Envious could see nothing; the Envious look, the 'evil eye,' had so blinded the true perceptive powers that those who had yielded to this vice must be instructed in another way. For them, Voices are in the air.

Again the Guide was uncertain of his way, and, ever desirous to lead onward and upward, feared the delay of waiting to inquire of some fellow-traveller. He therefore fixes his eyes on the Sun; to him ever the symbol, and, more than that, the presence, of illuminating Reason; and he invokes the shining of those directing rays.

Dante, like our Blake, saw not the Sun as a round disc of fire somewhat like a guinea. 'Oh, no! no!' he says, 'I see an innumerable company of the heavenly Host crying Holy, Holy, Holy is the Lord God Almighty. I question not my corporeal eye, any more than I would question a window concerning a sight; I look through it, not with it.'

The invisible Spirits uttering Love's invitations.

(XXXIV)

(Continued from last page.)

PURGATORIO, CANTO XIII. 22-30.

Quanto di qua per un miglia' si conta,
   Tanto di là eravam noi già iti
   Con poco tempo, per la voglia pronta :
E verso noi volar furon sentiti,   25
   Non però visti, spiriti, parlando
   Alla mensa d' amor cortesi inviti.
La prima voce, che passò volando,
   Vinum non habent, altamente disse ;
   E dietro a noi l' andò reiterando.   30

'Overcome Evil with Good.'

(XXXIV)

As the Pilgrim with ready will (voglia pronta) advances, he hears or feels, but sees not, wings coming to meet him, and 'voices of courteous invitations to Love's Table' are in the air.

Here we have another instance (like that at the entrance of the first Circle) of the method pursued in the Purgatorio of dealing with the sin that needs cleansing. It is by the force of the contrasted Grace, the overcoming of Evil by its opposing Antidote. How striking it is that the first accents that fall on the attentive ears of the blinded ones—of those who had been envious of the goods of others—should be full and free invitations to partake with others of Love's hospitalities! The penetrating cry reiterated around them would recall to their memories the first Miracle at the Marriage Feast—'*They have no wine*'—and would remind them of the motherly commiseration felt at the failure of a Source of joy and hospitality that Love's eyes foresaw. It would also contain the promise of such a joy being renewed in fuller measure and in better quality. The envious could have known but little joy, for they had grudged occasions of it to others, and had therefore neither received it nor given it.

Now that they are awakened to feel their need, they are met by a full tide of assurance, not only of a supply of all their necessities, but even of the overflow of festivities and joyfulness in store for them! Yet, with this revelation of the bounties of Love, they are not to escape the necessity of reaping what they have sown to themselves, or 'the lashes of the scourge that are drawn from Love.' See line 39.

The Envious are seen, clad in miserable Sackcloth, and Blind.

(XXXV)

PURGATORIO, CANTO XIII. 52-75.

NON credo che per terra vada ancoi
    Uomo sì duro, che non fosse punto
    Per compassion di quel ch' i' vidi poi :
Chè quando fui sì presso di lor giunto,   55
    Che gli atti loro a me venivan certi,
    Per gli occhi fui di grave dolor munto.
Di vil cilicio mi parean coperti ;
    E l' un sofferia l' altro con la spalla,
    E tutti dalla ripa eran sofferti.   60
Così li ciechi, a cui la roba falla,
    Stanno a' perdoni a chieder lor bisogna ;
    E l' uno 'l capo sovra l' altro avvalla,
Perchè in altrui pietà tosto si pogna,
    Non pur per lo sonar delle parole,   65
    Ma per la vista che non meno agogna.
E come agli orbi non approda 'l Sole,
    Così all' ombre, di ch' io parlava ora,
    Luce del ciel di sè largir non vuole ;
Ch' a tutte un fil di ferro il ciglio fora   70
    E cuce sì, come a sparvier selvaggio
    Si fa, però che queto non dimora.
A me pareva andando fare oltraggio,
    Vedendo altrui, non essendo veduto :
    Perch' io mi volsi al mio Consiglio saggio.   75

'That severely just vice, which never faileth to punish itself.'

───────────── (XXXV) ─────────────

THE appearance of these helpless, squalid, self-blinded souls is indeed pitiful to imagine. That which was inward has become outward, as is the case, indeed, throughout the whole of the Commedia ; in order that we may read it in the light of Truth, and take it back again into our own hearts. In the Inferno the consequences of the Sin were not acknowledged, as bound together with the Sin like seed and fruit in Nature's necessity ; but the painful consequences of sin were arrogantly defied, as though they were the cruel and despotic acts of an arbitrary Supreme Force. In Humility's Kingdom the righteous law is accepted, and the soul is brought into increasing unity with the Truth, for lack of which it must perforce pine and dwindle into death.

The words 'envy' and 'invidious' point to the perverted use of the eye, and we are taught that our inward vision or power of beholding Truth is injured by the misuse or neglect of that capacity. We are reminded of the message to the Church of Laodicea, who knew not that she was, as these sufferers, 'wretched and miserable and poor and blind,' and was counselled to buy many good things, amongst others 'eye-salve that she might see.' These, in the Circle before us, now know their condition, and the longed-for 'eye-salve' will not be lacking to them.

What a lesson we have in Dante's refined sympathy with the blind ! it seemed to him he did them outrage in seeing them, when they saw not him !

> 'And the darkness of his kind
> Filled him with such endless ruth,
> That the very light of truth
> Pained him, walking with the blind.'
>   LORD HOUGHTON.

Dante asks if any there were fellow-countrymen. He is assured that all are fellow-citizens.

(XXXVI)

PURGATORIO, CANTO XIII. 85-105.

VOLSIMI a loro, ed: O gente sicura,   85
   Incominciai, di veder l'alto lume,
     Che 'l disio vostro solo have in sua cura;
Se tosto grazia risolva le schiume
   Di vostra coscïenza, sì che chiaro
     Per essa scenda della mente il fiume,   90
Ditemi (chè mi fia grazioso e caro)
   S'anima è qui tra voi, che sia latina:
     E forse a lei sarà buon, s'io l'apparo.
O fratel mio, ciascuna è cittadina
   D'una vera città: ma tu vuoi dire,   95
     Che vivesse in Italia peregrina.
Questo mi parve per risposta udire
   Più innanzi alquanto, che là dov'io stava:
     Ond'io mi feci ancor più là sentire.
Tra l'altre vidi un'ombra, ch'aspettava   100
   In vista; e se volesse alcun dir: Come?
     Lo mento, a guisa d'orbo, in su levava.
Spirto, diss'io, che per salir ti dome,
   Se tu se' quegli che mi rispondesti,
     Fammiti conto o per luogo o per nome.   105

Citizens of the City built to Music, 'and therefore built for ever.'

(XXXVI)

IS not this the true way of addressing those who are conscious of any spiritual need? and amongst others we may thus encourage *ourselves;* 'for none can seek a thing but because it is lost and has belonged to him and ought to be his; he was created in it and for it.'—W. LAW.

Note lines 88-90.—Dante speaks of those in the Inferno as having 'lost the good of Reason;' and here he speaks of the scum on the Conscience as preventing the limpid fountain of the mind from flowing through it, and prays that this darkening medium may be removed. He then goes on to ask whether any of the poor sufferers before him were his fellow-countrymen, as he might later be of good use to them. He was answered by a Sienese woman, Sappia, who had been so much under the dominion of Envy that she was actually happier at the misfortune of another than at any good fortune of her own. Her answer to Dante's question shows that she has now so learnt the unity of the human race, and the citizenship of all in the abiding Commonwealth, that addressing her questioner as 'Brother' she speaks of all as belonging to the one true City, whose Builder and Maker is God, seeming scarcely to grasp Dante's allusion to the geographical bond of neighbourhood during the time of pilgrimage.

> 'O Brother mine, each one is Citizen
> Of one true City; but thy meaning is
> Who may have lived in Italy a Pilgrim.'

When the rivalries between the Cities of Siena, Pisa, and Florence were so keen, the conviction of the brotherhood of all in the one abiding Citizenship was much more remarkable than in our day of United Italy and of awakening world-wide sympathies.

Dante asks how possessions are to be shared without diminution for each sharer.

(XXXVII)

PURGATORIO, CANTO XV. 40-57.

LO mio Maestro ed io soli ambodue 40
   Suso andavamo; ed io pensava andando
   Prode acquistar nelle parole sue:
E dirizzaimi a lui sì dimandando:
   Che volle dir lo spirto di Romagna,
   E divieto e consorto menzionando? 45
Per ch' egli a me: Di sua maggior magagna
   Conosce 'l danno; e però non si ammiri
   Se ne riprende, perchè men sen piagna.
Perchè s' appuntano i vostri desiri
   Dove per compagnia parte si scema, 50
   Invidia muove il mantaco a' sospiri.
Ma se l' amor della spera suprema
   Torcesse in suso 'l desiderio vostro,
   Non vi sarebbe al petto quella tema:
Perchè quanto si dice più lì nostro, 55
   Tanto possiede più di ben ciascuno,
   E più di caritate arde in quel chiostro.

> '*Joy flies monopolists; it calls for two.*
> *Rich fruit! heaven planted; never pluckt by one.*'

──────────── (XXXVII) ────────────

AFTER seeing many more souls 'reaping straw from their own sowing,' one of these (line 86 in preceding Canto) exclaims :

> 'O human race ! why dost thou set thy heart
> Where interdict of partnership must be ?'

This is pondered over by Dante and affords a subject for communing with Virgil in our portions for to-day and to-morrow. Before the conversation begins, another dazzling Angel has appeared, almost distressing to the Pilgrim's unaccustomed eyes. He is assured that further on such visitations from the Family of Heaven will become delightful and natural to him. The Angel joyfully points out to them an easier passage upwards towards the third Circle; hearing the Song behind them of the Blessing on the Merciful, and the encouraging words, 'Rejoice, thou that overcomest,' the second P is removed from the Pilgrim's brow and Mercy takes the place of Envy.

Ere they reach the circle of the Angry and Violent, Dante asks explanation of the words alluded to. It seems to have been much on his heart that every possession must be lessened by sharing it with another.

The superiority of the spiritual treasure to merely external loveless partnership is made shining to us in the last three lines of to-day's portion, by the beautiful word 'Our' instead of 'My'; signifying, as it at once does, the doubling of Love and Joy.

> 'For there, as much the more as one says "Our,"
> So much the more of good each one possesses,
> And more of Charity in that cloister burns [94-96].

Doubtless in this knowledge was poured out for the formerly blind and envious some of the Water turned into wine of the Wedding Feast.

Dante craves to understand more concerning the Wealth that is increased to each by its distribution. The Third Circle is reached.

———————— (XXXVIII) ————————

PURGATORIO, CANTO XV. 58-66.

IO son d' esser contento più digiuno,
  Diss' io, che se mi fossi pria taciuto;
  E più di dubbio nella mente aduno.   60
Com' esser puote ch' un ben, distributo
  In più posseditor, faccia più ricchi
  Di sè, che se da pochi è posseduto?
Ed egli a me: Perocchè tu rificchi
  La mente pure alle cose terrene,   65
  Di vera luce tenebre dispicchi.

'*From heart to heart love sinks, it steals, it flows
From these that know Thee, still infecting those.*'

(XXXVIII)

DANTE seems to have so identified himself with the blinded envious folk as to have been puzzled with the paradox that any boon divided and distributed could by that division and distribution increase instead of diminishing the wealth of each possessor. His Guide tells him that his want of comprehension shows that he has fixed his mind so entirely upon earthly things as to pluck darkness from the very light itself. Without implying blame to those who confine their observation to one department of Nature, we remark that, by doing this, they are in danger of losing some of their capacity of vision in other regions of Truth.

Virgil then proceeds, in lines 67 to 72, to unfold and illustrate his meaning. He tells the Pilgrim that even as the Sunbeam flies to any bright object that reflects it, and even as one mirror reflects the light received from another, so increasing and multiplying the strength of light; thus the Infinite and ineffable Goodness above kindles into Love, giving Itself wherever It finds receptive Ardour; increasing as it expends Itself; and the greater the number who love, the better do they love, and the more do they aspire to love.

'If the vision of God constitutes the blessedness of man, then they whose spiritual eye is most enlightened will drink in most of His glory: and, since only like can know like, all advances which are made in Humility, in Holiness, in Love, are a polishing of the Mirror that it may reflect more clearly the Divine glory—an enlarging of the vessel, that it may receive more amply of the Divine fulness.'—ARCHBISHOP TRENCH.

Virgil explains to Dante the secret of increasing Heavenly wealth, and is bidden to expect more light from Beatrice.

(XXXVIII)

(*Continued from last page.*)

PURGATORIO, CANTO XV. 67-84.

Quell' infinito ed ineffabil bene,
   Che lassù è, così corre ad amore,
   Com' a lucido corpo raggio viene.
Tanto si dà, quanto trova d' ardore ;   70
   Sì che quantunque carità si stende,
   Cresce sovr' essa l' eterno valore.
E quanta gente più lassuso intende,
   Più v' è da bene amare, e più vi s' ama ;
   E come specchio l' uno all' altro rende.   75
E se la mia ragion non ti disfama,
   Vedrai Beatrice ; ed ella pienamente
   Ti torrà questa e ciascun' altra brama.
Procaccia pur che tosto siene spente,
   Come son già le due, le cinque piaghe,   80
   Che si richiudon per esser dolente.
Com' io voleva dicer : Tu m' appaghe ;
   Vidimi giunto in su l' altro girone,
   Sì che tacer mi fèr le luci vaghe.

'... *His Father's Name written in their foreheads.*'—
REV. xiv. 1.

'*I ... will give him a white stone, and in the stone a new name.*'—REV. ii. 17.

——————— (XXXVIII) ———————

It seems suggested to us (line 67) that the Infinite and ineffable Divine Goodness passes into Love, or, we might say, becomes personified in meeting with recognition; for Love indeed needs the relationship and interchange of conscious reciprocity in giving and receiving, before it can be in full potency.

It is the sunrise to the Soul when we find that Love knows us by Name. We may venture also perhaps to say that it is through relationship with His offspring that the infinite and ineffable Goodness names Himself, and is no longer the universally diffused impersonal Benevolence alone. In His last prayer our Lord says, 'I have manifested Thy Name.'

The Good Shepherd who loves His sheep calls them by name, though to other eyes, poor things, they look so pitifully alike! The Pilgrim is told that the answer to his questioning will fully satisfy him, when he receives it from his Celestial Beatrice; in the same way the Lord Himself bade His disciples expect the more inward and completing Spirit of Truth to lead them into all Truth.

Dante had already, he was assured, been cleansed from two out of the seven deadly wounds his soul had received (lines 80, 81); which wounds, Virgil tells him, 'close themselves again by being painful.'

'It is the life in the corrupting thing that makes the suffering possible; it is the live part, not the corrupted part, that suffers; it is the redeemable, not the doomed thing, that is subjected to vanity; that subjection is the one hope against the supremacy of corruption.'—GEO. MACDONALD.

Dante is rapt into inner vision regarding the meek and the wrathful in the Third Circle.

(XXXIX)

PURGATORIO, CANTO XV. 85-93.

QUIVI mi parve in una visïone   85
    Estatica di subito esser tratto,
    E vedere in un tempio più persone:
Ed una donna in su l' entrar, con atto
    Dolce di madre, dicer: Figliuol mio,
    Perchè hai tu così verso noi fatto?   90
Ecco, dolenti lo tuo padre ed io
    Ti cercavamo. E come qui si tacque,
    Ciò, che pareva prima, dispario.

The behaviour of the lofty-lowly in their inheritance of the Earth.

(XXXIX)

AS the last words were spoken, the Pilgrim and his Guide entered the third Circle, the School for the Angry.

In the two first Circles they were taught first by God's 'Visible speech,' secondly by 'Voices in the air.' In this circle another advance is made in spiritual perception, and Inward visions are granted.

As they enter this Circle, the Pilgrim's soul becomes rapt in ecstatic contemplation of a Temple, and one who stands at its door with 'the sweet ways of a Mother.' She speaks words of tenderness, though of remonstrance, to the Son whom she could not fully comprehend, for He had caused her and His Father sorrow.

The Proud had been taught, through that same type of Womanly Humility, meekness in reception of a mysterious personal favour.

The Envious had been taught consideration for others in dispensing Love's joy-giving hospitalities.

The Angry are now shown the behaviour of meekness under bewildering personal trial. The lessons are given each time through that same Representative of the womanly element in God's Divine fashioning of His image in Man.

Dante's second vision of Meekness, as opposed to Wrath.

——————————— (XXXIX) ———————————

(*Continued from last page.*)

PURGATORIO, CANTO XV. 106-114.

* * * * *

Poi vidi genti accese in foco d' ira,
   Con pietre un giovinetto ancider, forte
   Gridando a sè pur : Martíra, martíra :
E lui vedea chinarsi, per la morte
   Che l' aggravava già, in vêr la terra ;   110
   Ma degli occhi facea sempre al ciel porte,
Orando all' alto Sire in tanta guerra,
   Che perdonasse a' suoi persecutori,
   Con quell' aspetto che pietà disserra.

> '*Thou, Lord, hast conquered death ; and I aloud
> Should triumph over him with thy saintly crowd
> That, where the Lamb goes, ever followeth.*'

——————— (XXXIX) ———————

The next Biblical vision opened in the Pilgrim's heart is one of the most sublime triumphs of the Kingdom of the overcoming Lamb, in opposition to the outburst of the dark kingdom of violence and rage.

The Pilgrim saw the surging crowd, kindled in the fire of wrath, murdering with stones the young man Stephen; while he, bowed on his knees and 'weighted with death,' ever kept his eyes as portals to Heaven, praying to the Father, 'even midst such a strife,' for pardon for his murderers.

We are told in the Bible narrative that Stephen saw through those opened eyes the opened heavens, with Jesus at the right hand of power. Dante adds the twin-thought, in showing us those eyes as not alone beholding the glorious vision, but as themselves becoming portals for the entrance of the King of Glory within the Martyr's spirit. And did He not enter and take full possession in power of presence and unity of Spirit when the dying voice was 'loud' that cried, 'Lord, lay not this sin to their charge'? making then the full accord with the Divine cry from the Cross, 'Father, forgive them, for they know not what they do.'

> 'To know
> Rather consists in opening out a way
> Whence the imprisoned splendour may escape,
> Than in effecting entry for a light
> Supposed to be without.'
>   PARACELSUS.

In the Circle of the Violent, the atmosphere is dark and smoky; yet voices harmoniously pray for peace to the Lamb of God.

———————————— (XL) ————————————

PURGATORIO, CANTO XVI. 1-21.

B UIO d' Inferno, e di notte privata
  D' ogni pianeta sotto pover cielo,
  Quant' esser può di nuvol tenebrata,
Non fece al viso mio sì grosso velo,
  Come quel fummo ch' ivi ci coperse,   5
  Nè al sentir di così aspro pelo ;
Chè l' occhio stare aperto non sofferse :
  Onde la Scorta mia saputa e fida
  Mi s' accostò, e l' omero m' offerse.
Sì come cieco va dietro a sua guida   10
  Per non smarrirsi, e per non dar di cozzo
  In cosa che 'l molesti o forse ancida ;
M' andava io per l' aere amaro e sozzo,
  Ascoltando 'l mio Duca, che diceva
  Pur : Guarda, che da me tu non sie mozzo. 15
Io sentia voci ; e ciascuna pareva
  Pregar, per pace e per misericordia,
  L' agnel di Dio, che le peccata leva.
Pure *Agnus Dei* eran le loro esordia :
  Una parola in tutte era ed un modo,   20
  Sì che parea tra esse ogni concordia.

The infection of a darkness that may be felt.

(XL)

IN Canto XV. we were shown the increased power of light through the recognition of light by the Children of Light; we also saw the realm of darkness apparently extended through the mad fury of many children of darkness. By their clamour they drowned the voice of truth and meekness, stopping their ears against it and closing their eyes against the face that shone as an Angel's, and against the glory of Heaven.

The Envious were blind, each in separate blindness. In an angry mob the whole atmosphere becomes smoky and rough, and, as represented here, like a 'poor night,' deprived of every star. At such a time the pilgrim must needs fall back on his own conscience (10).

In the midst of this darkness which lingers around the consciences of the formerly wrathful, and still impedes their upward movement, they all draw together by one accord; and one word and one prayer ascends from their lips. It is to the Lamb of God, that taketh away the sin of the world, that they are impelled to address their united cry; the Lamb whose victory was so complete in Stephen's heart over the united strength of the army of darkness and fury.

The Pilgrim enters into the full meaning of those words as proclaiming the removal, not only of the penalty of sin, but of the sins themselves.

'Of all sins, that of anger was perhaps the most difficult for an Italian temper, with its tendencies to the proverbial "Vendetta," to overcome; and Dante's letter to Henry VII. shows how strong a hold it had upon him, even about the time when he was writing this Canto.' DEAN PLUMPTRE.

An illuminating Angel pronounces the blessing on the Peacemakers, removing the third P of Anger from Dante's forehead.

――――――――― (XLI) ―――――――――

PURGATORIO, CANTO XVII. 46-69.

I' MI volgea per veder ov' io fosse,
    Quand' una voce disse : Qui si monta
    Che da ogni altro intento mi rimosse ;
E fece la mia voglia tanto pronta
    Di riguardar chi era che parlava,   50
    Che mai non posa, se non si raffronta.
Ma come al Sol, che nostra vista grava,
    E per soverchio sua figura vela,
    Così la mia virtù quivi mancava.
Questi è divino spirito, che ne la   55
    Via d' andar sua ne drizza senza prego,
    E col suo lume sè medesmo cela.
Sì fa con noi, come l' uom si fa sego :
    Chè quale aspetta prego, e l' uopo vede,
    Malignamente già si mette al nego.   60
Ora accordiamo a tanto invito il piede :
    Procacciam di salir pria che s' abbui ;
    Che poi non si poria, se 'l dì non riede.
Così disse 'l mio Duca ; ed io con lui
    Volgemmo i nostri passi ad una scala :   65
    E tosto ch' io al primo grado fui,
Senti' mi presso quasi un muover d' ala,
    E ventarmi nel volto, e dir : *Beati*
Pacifici, che son sanza ira mala.

A Divine and loving Spirit effaces himself in light.

--- (XLI) ---

VISIONS of instruction have still been pressing in upon the Pilgrim's soul. The last of these was dispelled by an almost blinding effulgence of light, which made his imaginings appear like dreams. Turning round to see where he might be, he heard a voice saying, 'This is the way upwards.' The answer to the desiring soul has sometimes been borne in upon it with an overmastering wave of heavenly illumination, quite beyond all that it has asked or thought, without any discernible channel less Divine than itself. All doubt is dispelled by a voice that seems to be heard saying, 'This is the way, walk ye in it.'

What a high conception of a Divine Messenger is given us here! (55).

> 'This is a Spirit Divine, who in the way
> Of going up directs us without asking,
> And who with his own light *himself conceals*.'

Light, even spiritual light, sometimes proves a temptation to display Self rather than as a veil for concealing self.

This tide of light and grace removed the scar of the third wound, Anger, from the Pilgrim's brow with gentle fanning of wings and with the Divine Benediction 'Blessed are the Peacemakers.'

How shall any sin be uprooted or its scar removed except by a beatitude taking its place? for no soul can remain 'empty, swept and garnished' without further peril.

The fourth Circle, where those languid in Love and Zeal are in process of restoration.

(XLII)

PURGATORIO, CANTO XVII. 82-87.

DOLCE mio Padre, di', quale offensione
   Si purga qui nel giron, dove semo?
   Se i piè si stanno, non stea tuo sermone.
Ed egli a me: L'amor del bene, scemo   85
   Di suo dover, quiritta si ristora;
   Qui si ribatte 'l mal tardato remo.

'... *Do not kill
The spirit of Love with a perpetual dulness.*'

(XLII)

THE fourth Circle is now reached, that stands between the first and second triplets assigned to the discipline of the seven deadly sins.

The first three—Pride, Envy, Anger—seem more nearly allied to the infernal root-spirit of Evil; while Avarice, Greed, and Carnality may be more dependent on external accidents presented by the temptations of sense.

The link between the two series partakes of the character of both; being, perhaps, engendered by the first series, and certainly often engendering the latter.

We read in our selection from Canto VII. of the Inferno of some who were submerged in the slime of the putrid fen of Styx, who had, 'even in the sweet air and sunshine above, carried gloomy smoke within their breasts.' Their sin was called 'Accidia.' Dante and other great spiritual teachers have delineated it as a condition of gloom, sloth, and sullen irritation. Here, amongst the souls saved from its worst development, it is considered as Languid Love; now in process of restoration to true temperature by eager endeavour and aspiration.

We are told in a long and rather difficult discourse that intervenes between our two extracts for to-day that Love is at the root of every movement of the soul, be it good or evil. Love, in true relationship and due temperature, is the Mother of every good thing; perverted, and out of due measure, the parent of all evils.

The eager fervour of the formerly tardy and luke-warm.

(*Continued from last page.*)

PURGATORIO, CANTO XVIII. 94-117.

TALE per quel giron suo passo falca,
    Per quel ch' io vidi, di color, venendo,   95
    Cui buon volere e giusto amor cavalca.
Tosto fur sovra noi, perchè correndo
    Veniva tutta quella turba magna;
    E duo dinanzi gridavan piangendo:
Maria corse con fretta alla montagna;   100
    E: Cesare, per soggiogare Ilerda,
    Punse Marsilia, e poi corse in Ispagna.
Ratto, ratto, chè 'l tempo non si perda
    Per poco amor, gridavan gli altri appresso;
    Chè studio di ben far grazia rinverda.   105
O gente, in cui fervore acuto adesso
    Ricompie forse negligenza e indugio
    Da voi, per tiepidezza, in ben far messo,
Questi che vive (e certo io non vi bugio)
    Vuol andar su, purchè 'l Sol ne riluca: 110
    Però ne dite ond' è presso 'l pertugio.
Parole furon queste del mio Duca:
    Ed un di quegli spirti disse: Vieni
    Diretr' a noi, che troverai la buca.
Noi siam di voglia a muoverci sì pieni,   115
    Che ristar non potem; però perdona,
    Se villania nostra giustizia tieni.

Love fitted for ministry by Order and Measure.

(XLII)

From this Circle of languid Love the voice heard by the Pilgrim comes to each of our too lukewarm hearts, with thrilling appeal (103): 'Quick! quick! so that time may not be lost by little love!'—or by a *poor* love. The formerly tardy souls are now so filled with longing to move upwards and onwards that they cannot linger over directions concerning the Way for which they are asked.

LINES ATTRIBUTED TO S. FRANCIS OF ASSISI.

'Set love in order, thou that lovest Me;
Never was Virtue out of order found,
And though I fill thy heart desirously
By thine own virtue, I must keep My ground;
When to My Love thou dost bring Charity,
Even She must come with order girt and gowned.
All earthly things I had the making of
Were numbered and were measured then by Me;
And each was ordered to its end by Love,
Each kept, through order, clean for ministry.
Charity most of all, when known enough,
Is of her very nature orderly.'
                    Translated by D. G. ROSSETTI.

Dante, thrice called by Virgil from an absorbing vision, follows an Angel upwards.

(XLIII)

PURGATORIO, CANTO XIX. 34-45.

IO volsi gli occhi ; e 'l buon Virgilio : Almen tre
   Voci t' ho messe, dicea : surgi, e vieni ;   35
   Troviam l' aperto, per lo qual tu entre.
Su mi levai : e tutti eran già pieni
   Dell' alto dì i giron del sacro monte ;
   Ed andavam col Sol nuovo alle reni.
Seguendo lui, portava la mia fronte   40
   Come colui che l' ha di pensier carca,
   Che fa di sè un mezzo arco di ponte :
Quand' io udi', Venite, qui si varca,
   Parlare in modo soave e benigno,
   Qual non si sente in questa mortal marca.   45

The temptation of the World and the Senses counteracted by Wisdom.

(XLIII)

THE Pilgrim has seen the many souls who had been too much dominated by the sins of sloth and gloom now permitted to redeem their past negligence by repentance, and restored and quickened through grace of contrition into ardour and zeal.

Darkness and Sleep and an early morning dream of presage followed. Virgil has to awaken the disciple from preoccupation with his dream-vision. It was of the Siren who is dominant in the realm of the senses, in which realm the penitents of the next three Circles had been tempted and had succumbed.

She and her song haunt Dante's memory and imagination, and though on her first appearance his purged eyes perceived her squint and her distorted feet, her false outlook and erring walk, his continued gaze provided her with fresh vitality and some beauty from his own hankerings, and re-awakened her alluring song of fascination. She had derived her power from his own foolishness—a subtle touch which differentiates her from our Bunyan's corresponding picture of Madam Bubble. She is the strange woman of Proverbs vii., who flatters and lures the foolish to their own destruction; her Adversary, 'holy and alert,' is Wisdom described in Proverbs viii. She stands at the other side of the Pilgrim and breaks the spell of the Enchantress by discovering to him her rival's foulness. Her voice sternly calls Virgil twice, as though that Mentor had been negligent in permitting this vision. He awakens Dante, saying that he had already three times called him; Dante follows, bending, perhaps, with some shame, as well as laden with thought.

The Angel delivers Dante from the fourth P of Languid Love, or Sloth.

(XLIII)

(Continued from last page.)

PURGATORIO, CANTO XIX. 46-63.

Con l'ale aperte, che parean di cigno,
   Volseci in su colui che sì parlonne,
   Tra i duo pareti del duro macigno.
Mosse le penne poi e ventilonne,
   Qui lugent affermando esser beati,   50
   *Ch' avran di consolar l' anime donne.
Che hai, che pure in vèr la terra guati?
   La Guida mia incominciò a dirmi,
   Poco ambedue dall' angel sormontati.
Ed io: Con tanta sospicion fa irmi   55
   Novella visïon ch'a sè mi piega,
   Sì ch' io non posso dal pensar partirmi.
Vedesti, disse, quella antica strega,
   †Che sola sovra noi omai si piagne?
   Vedesti come l' uom da lei si slega?   60
Bastiti; e batti a terra le calcagne:
   Gli occhi rivolgi al logoro, che gira
   Lo Rege eterno con le ruote magne.

---

* 'To become mistress-souls of all consolation.' (Benvenuto da Imola's interpretation of this line, given in Vernon's 'Purgatorio.')

† The false pleasure that misleads to the threefold sin disciplined in the circles beyond.

The Lukewarm are transmuted into Mistress-souls of consolation.

(XLIII)

As the Pilgrim climbs on, humbly bowed down, there reaches him the voice of an Angel-like music, more gentle and benign than any voice that can sound in Earth's atmosphere. The Angel affirms those who mourn to be blessed, and to be themselves dispensers of Consolation. Thus, the fourth wound is cleared from the Pilgrim's brow.

It is very noteworthy that the recipients of each of these benedictions is anointed as a Dispenser of the healing blessing imparted. The Envious were not only to find Mercy, but to become merciful. The Angry were not only to find Peace, but to become Peacemakers, and the sullen Mourners were to become 'Mistress-souls of all Consolation.'

It is, indeed, a Divine way of overcoming Evil, not only to heal its wound but to transmute that wound into a fountain of outflowing love!

May there possibly have been some commingling of tender sensitiveness, twin-born with their gloom, in these melancholy, sullen souls, which (though it had added soil for their besetting sin) was now to be gathered up as a fragment of life-substance not to be lost, in their new powers for comforting sufferers?

In the last lines Virgil calls upon Dante to tread under foot the enchantments of the Earth by looking upwards to the lure of Heaven's splendours—the Spheres that the Eternal King 'is turning for us in revolutions vast.'

> 'Why comes Temptation but for man to meet
> And master and make crouch beneath his foot,
> And so be pedestalled in triumph?'
>
> R. BROWNING

The Fifth Circle, where avaricious and prodigal souls are earth-bound and prostrate; Adrian V. is amongst them.

───────── (XLIV) ─────────

PURGATORIO, CANTO XIX. 115-135.

QUEL ch' avarizia fa, qui si dichiara   115
    In purgazion dell' anime converse :
    E nulla pena il monte ha più amara.
Sì come l' occhio nostro non s' aderse
    In alto, fisso alle cose terrene ;
    Così giustizia qui a terra il merse.   120
Come avarizia spense a ciascun bene
    Lo nostro amor, onde operar perdèsi ;
    Così giustizia qui stretti ne tiene
Ne' piedi e nelle man legati e presi :
    E quanto fia piacer del giusto Sire,   125
    Tanto staremo immobili e distesi.
Io m' era inginocchiato, e volea dire ;
    Ma com' io cominciai, ed ei s' accorse
    Solo ascoltando del mio riverire,
Qual cagion, disse, in giù così ti torse ?   130
    Ed io a lui : Per vostra dignitate,
    Mia coscïenza dritta mi rimorse.
Drizza le gambe, e lèvati su, frate,
    Rispose. Non errar : conservo sono
    Teco e con gli altri ad una potestate,   135

'Heart-buried in the rubbish of the World.'

(XLIV)

WHAT Avarice does to the soul is made manifest in this fifth Circle, now reached by the Pilgrim.

> 'People I saw upon it who were weeping,
> Stretched prone upon the ground, all downward turned.'

They were sighing out the words, 'My soul cleaveth to the ground.' They had failed to perceive the true end of property, and knew neither how to give nor how to hold it, being avaricious or prodigal, as impulse directed, 'because their eye did not uplift itself, being fastened upon earthly things.' Dante conversed with Pope Adrian V., who was one of these prostrate people; he humbly confessed his sin, and would not permit any homage from one he called his 'fellow-servant.'

We are reminded of Bunyan's striking picture of such as these, seen in the Interpreter's House:

'Where was a man that could look no way but downwards, with a muck-rake in his hand.

'There stood also One over his head with a celestial crown in his hand, and proffered to give him that crown for his muck-rake; but the man did neither look up nor regard, but raked to himself the straws, the small sticks, and dust of the floor. Then said Christiana, "Oh, deliver me from this muck-rake!" That prayer, said the Interpreter, has lain by till it is almost rusty. Straws and sticks and dust, with most, are the great things now looked after.'

> 'Content to see
> An unseized Heaven dying at his feet!'
>   KEATS.

The trembling of the Mountain freezes Dante with fear. One erect amongst the prostrate (Statius) follows and greets them.

———— (XLV) ————

PURGATORIO, CANTO XX. 124-129, 133-141.

NOI eravam partiti già da esso,
 E brigavam di soverchiar la strada   125
  Tanto, quanto al poter n' era permesso;
Quand' io senti', come cosa che cada,
 Tremar lo monte: onde mi prese un gelo,
  Qual prender suol colui ch' a morte vada.

*   *   *   *   *

Poi cominciò da tutte parti un grido
 Tal, che 'l Maestro in vêr di me si feo,
  Dicendo: Non dubbiar, mentr' io ti guido.   135
Gloria in excelsis, tutti, *Deo*,
 Dicean, per quel ch' io da vicin compresi,
  Onde intender lo grido si poteo.
Noi ci ristemmo immobili e sospesi,
 Come i pastor che prima udir quel canto,   140
  Fin che 'l tremar cessò, ed ei compièsi.

*   *   *   *   *   XXI. 1-13.

LA sete natural, che mai non sazia
 Se non coll' acqua, onde la femminetta
  Samaritana dimandò la grazia,
Mi travagliava; e pungeami la fretta,
 Per la impacciata via, retro al mio Duca;   5
  E condoleami alla giusta vendetta.
Ed ecco, sì come ne scrive Luca
 Che Cristo apparve a' duo ch' erano in via,
  Già surto fuor della sepolcral buca,
Ci apparve un' ombra: e dietro a noi venia,   10
 Dappiè guardando la turba che giace;
  Nè ci addemmo di lei, sin' parlò pria,
Dicendo: Frati miei, Dio vi dea pace.

'Nature seems ever awaiting something.'

(XLV)

THE Pilgrim and his Guide are passing on amongst the prostrate people, victims 'of the old She-wolf' (he says)

> 'That more than all the other beasts has prey
> Because of hunger infinitely hollow,'

when lo! the Mountain trembles so violently that Dante is chilled with fear. Immediately from all sides arose a cry from many voices filling the air; it seemed the utterance of 'Gloria in excelsis Deo.' Perplexed and thoughtful, Dante and his Guide wend their way onwards.

The thirst to know is on the Pilgrim—that universal thirst, he calls it, which nothing can satisfy but the Water of life for which the Woman of Samaria besought the Lord: and behold, even as the Lord appeared to two wayfarers as they reasoned together, One drew nigh erect among the multitude bent to the earth, and greeted them with salutations of Peace.

He was but a Fellow-pilgrim, yet they saw in him, as he walked amongst the prostrate and disabled, the image of the Christ. He was able to minister to them a cup of that cold water from the well of Life, for which the Pilgrim had been so ardently longing.

We shall find later that the trembling of the Mountain was occasioned by sympathy with the resurrection power in this very Soul, who a few moments before was upraised from the crippled people amongst whom he had lain 500 years. 'Tremble, thou Earth, at the presence of the Lord, at the presence of the God of Jacob,' was one of the verses sung at the entrance of Purgatory; as though the dream of the poets of all ages was to be realized that, Man being awakened to a more spiritual condition, Nature also would be thrilled with responsive currents of the new life.

*The question asked, 'Why the Mountain trembled?'
is answered by Statius.*

---------- (XLVI) ----------

PURGATORIO, CANTO XXI. 34-54.

MA dinne, se tu sai, perchè tai crolli
   Diè dianzi 'l monte; e perchè tutti ad una 35
   Parver gridare infino a' suoi piè molli?
Sì mi diè dimandando per la cruna
   Del mio disio, che pur con la speranza
   Si fece la mia sete men digiuna.
Quei cominciò: Cosa non è, che sanza   40
   Ordine senta la religïone
   Della montagna, o che sia fuor d' usanza.
Libero è qui da ogni alterazione:
   Di quel che il cielo in sè da sè riceve,
   Esserci puote, e non d' altro, cagione.   45
Perchè non pioggia, non grando, non neve,
   Non rugiada, non brina più su cade,
   Che la scaletta de' tre gradi breve.
Nuvole spesse non paion nè rade,
   Nè coruscar, nè figlia di Taumante,   50
   Che di là cangia sovente contrade.
Secco vapor non surge più avante,
   Ch' al sommo de' tre gradi ch' or parlai,
   Ov' ha 'l vicario di Pietro le piante.

In the Spiritual Mount the Clime is affected by spiritual causes alone. The three little steps have separated from all physical laws.

(XLVI)

THE erect spirit who had joined Dante and his Guide, even as Christ had appeared to the disciples as they walked to Emmaus, proved to be the poet Statius, who had been led by some words of Virgil into the Christian faith.

He now accompanies Dante and Virgil as far as the Paradise regained on the summit of the Mountain. He can tell them many things, first answering Virgil's question about the trembling of the Mountain, and so satisfying Dante's eager thirst to know its meaning.

He tells them that the *sacred order*, or 'religion' of the Mountain, 'was liable to no changes from physical causes.'

The short stairway of three steps removes our thought from the framework of this world, or indeed of any visible world, into the moral world, where the vicissitudes of the temporal are unknown.

In the realm of Love, of Righteousness, and of Peace the Sun never sets: there is no Night there, no mutability of the Elements.

The Everlasting One, 'and the Blessed Spirits which He includes as the Sea her waves,' move, but are not moved by external causes. Nature herself, and the external part of man, are but as passing blossoms on this Ocean of Life. We can but stammer in tentative figurative words here; but the symbolism presented to us seems suggestive of the thrill of added motion and joy in that deepest Life of Being, when one amongst its multitude moves and is moved to some onward unison with its laws of blessedness.

The Son of Man, who dwelt ever in the Bosom of the Father, could tell us more concerning that Kingdom of Life than any other; and His Words, no doubt, inspired the

The trembling of the Mountain with the liberated Will of Statius.

— (XLVI) —

(Continued from last page.)

PURGATORIO, CANTO XXI. 58-72.

Tremaci quando alcuna anima monda
  Si sente sì, che surga, o che si muova,
  Per salir su ; e tal grido seconda.   60
Della mondizia il sol voler fa pruova,
  Che, tutto libero a mutar convento,
  L' alma sorprende ; ed il voler le giova.
Prima vuol ben ; ma non lascia 'l talento,
  Chè divina giustizia con tal voglia   65
  Come fu al peccar, pone al tormento.
Ed io che son giaciuto a questa doglia
  Cinquecento anni e più, pur mo sentii
  Libera volontà di miglior soglia.
Però sentiste 'l terremoto, e i pii   70
  Spiriti per lo monte render lode
  A quel Signor, che tosto su gl' invii.

thought of the thrilling Mount. 'There is joy in the presence of God and of the holy Angels over one sinner that repenteth.'

Blessed it is to think of that cry of 'Gloria' awakened in the hearts even of those still bound by unready will and slack desire to lower ground, when a Sister-soul is set free. Their song accompanies and helps the freed soul and mingles at once with descending welcomes from above.

Note lines 61-66. The cry 'is raised when the Will of the soul to rise upward is free from all impediments arising out of its own past impurities or the laws of retribution. Till then the Will, which has been turned to sin, is turned to the working out of its appointed sentence, which becomes the object of a new desire. Dante, in this subtle distinction between the will that seeks freedom and that which accepts punishment as the condition of freedom, does but paraphrase the teaching of Aquinas.'—DEAN PLUMPTRE.

We are taught throughout the 'Divina Commedia' that the will-power fails, and impulse contradicts the residue of that will-power, through former habits of yielding to temptation : and this seems to give a reason for the necessity felt that those who are in a freer condition should pray for the renewal of will in those still conscious of their bondage.

Statius had, he says, remained unable to rise for more than 500 years, before he felt his soul 'taken by surprise' and freed to mount.

We are reminded of our Lord's words to bystanders after He had restored Lazarus to life, 'Loose him and let him go.' He is thus calling upon bystanders now to aid in His miracles of restoration.

The Poets proceed and the Pilgrim follows, learning from their discourse. An Apple-tree with tempting yet unattainable fruit is in the midst of the Way.

(XLVII)

PURGATORIO, CANTO XXII. 127-147.

ELLI givan dinanzi, ed io soletto
    Diretro; ed ascoltava i lor sermoni,
    Ch' a poetar mi davano intelletto.
Ma tosto ruppe le dolci ragioni   130
    Un alber, che trovammo in mezza strada,
    Con pomi ad odorar soavi e buoni.
E come abete in alto si digrada
    Di ramo in ramo, così quello in giuso;
    Cred' io perchè persona su non vada.   135
Dal lato, onde 'l cammin nostro era chiuso,
    Cadea dall' alta roccia un liquor chiaro;
    E si spandeva per le foglie suso.
Li duo Poeti all' alber s' appressaro:
    Ed una voce per entro le fronde   140
    Gridò: Di questo cibo avrete caro.
Poi disse: Più pensava Maria, onde
    Fosser le nozze orrevoli ed intere,
    Ch' alla sua bocca, ch' or per voi risponde:
E le Romane antiche per lor bere   145
    Contente furon d' acqua; e Daniello
    Dispregiò cibo, ed acquistò savere.

'*As the Apple-tree among the trees of the Wood.*'—
CANT. ii. 3.

(XLVII)

THE Fifth Circle of the Avaricious and Prodigal (from which latter sin Statius had just been cleansed) had been left behind by the three ascending ones.

The fifth P has been erased from the brow of the Pilgrim, and the ascent has now become easy to him. A strange benediction has been conferred, the benediction of Thirst —the thirst for righteousness, instead of the thirst for riches or for ease which had formerly possessed these souls. The united blessing of hungering and thirsting of St. Matt. v. is here separated into two. The spiritual hunger is reserved for those who in the Sixth Circle (now entered) are disciplined for their earthly greed.

The two Poets walk first and Dante follows, listening to the converse which gives him lessons in the art of song. A mystic Apple-Tree in the midst of the Way arrests their attention. Its fruits are pleasant and odorous, but they are guarded by the form of the Tree and by a warning voice from its foliage, affirming that of such fruit there would be dearth, and citing examples of abstinence. Another such Tree further on, we are told, is a scion from the Tree of Knowledge.

A clear cascade fell from the rock above the Tree, over its green foliage, increasing its refreshing allurement, yet the hungering and thirsting ones were unable to partake of it.

A crowd of famished and emaciated spirits, silent and devout, were seen pressing onwards, and Dante exclaims (xxiii. 34):

> 'Who would believe the odour of an Apple,
> Begetting longing, would consume them so,
> And that of Water.'

Those who yielded to greed on Earth are now the Emaciated, unable to satisfy the spiritual hunger awakened by the Apple-tree.

(XLVIII)

PURGATORIO, CANTO XXIII. 61-66.

ED egli a me: Dall' eterno consiglio
    Cade virtù nell' acqua e nella pianta
    Rimasa addietro, ond' io sì mi sottiglio.
Tutta esta gente, che piangendo canta,
    Per seguitar la gola oltre misura,   65
    In fame e in sete qui si rifà santa.

> *'Yet, Lord, let not the hunger go,*
> *And keep the faintness at my heart.'*

(XLVIII)

IN this Sixth Circle the Victims of greed of all that sense could give in the outward here awaken, to find themselves famine-stricken, emaciated, and squalid. Their unexercised spiritual appetites find nothing with which they can be satisfied. They walk round and round the mystic Tree, craving its scented fruit and the living water that sprinkles its verdure, but they cannot attain its high branches. Their desire is kept alive and their hunger and thirst is unsatisfied. They know the pain they feel should be their solace (line 72), for it is the very condition of their attainment; as it is explained, they are led to that Tree by the same will that led the Christ, rejoicing, to say 'Eli' when he liberated us by His blood. For love's sake He rejoiced to suffer even to the uttermost desolation that forced that cry from Him on the Cross, to win His Bride the Church. Does not this point to a responsive love and longing in these thirsting souls, to be reunited in full fellowship of spousal joy with their Lord? Was not this mystic Tree indeed a scion from the Tree of Life and Love in the midst of the way to the restored Paradise, from which they had debarred themselves through the indulgence of grosser appetites?

The Bridegroom had come, but these poor souls (or representatives of wandering affections) were unready to go in with Him to the Wedding. Through suffering, and continued desire and prayer, these 'foolish Virgins,' while tarrying outside, have to be made meet for the union of perfected Love.

The painful longing to partake of the Tree of Life.

(XLVIII)

(*Continued from last page.*)

PURGATORIO, CANTO XXIII. 67-75.

Di bere e di mangiar n' accende cura
  L' odor, ch' esce del pomo e dello sprazzo,
  Che si distende su per la verdura.
E non pure una volta, questo spazzo   70
  Girando, si rinfresca nostra pena;
  Io dico pena, e dovria dir sollazzo:
Chè quella voglia all' arbore ci mena,
  Che menò Cristo lieto a dire Eli,
  Quando ne liberò con la sua vena   75

'*The Desire of all nations.*'

(XLVIII)

'Nothing works either in God, or Nature, or creature, but Desire. And as God created Angels and men out of eternal Nature, only through a longing Desire of manifesting His own goodness and happiness in them, so every angel and man must find God as a life of happiness and goodness in Him, as soon as Nature, either in Angel or man, is become a hunger after God. For Hunger does all, in all worlds, and finds all that it wants and hungers after. Everything had its beginning in it, and from it, and everything is led by it to all its happiness.'—WM. LAW'S '*Spirit of Prayer.*'

'The souls in Purgatory . . . hope to see that Bread' (of Life) ' and satiate themselves to the full therewith; whence they hunger and suffer pain as great as will be their capacity of enjoying that Bread, which is Jesus Christ the true God, our Saviour and our Love.'—ST. CATHERINE OF GENOA.

> ' Had the refusing
> Tasted but once,
> All would they leave,
> And sit down with us
> To the Table of longing
> Which will never be bare.
> Then would they know Love's
> Infinite fulness,
> And magnify the nourishment
> Of Body and Blood.'
> '*Spiritual Songs of Novalis,*'
> translated by Geo. Macdonald.

An Angel in glowing crimson Light directs the Pilgrim. The breeze that imparted Blessing and Healing, a Harbinger of Morning and of Spring.

———————— (XLIX) ————————

PURGATORIO, CANTO XXIV. 136-154.

D RIZZAI la testa per veder chi fossi ;
 E giammai non si videro in fornace
Vetri o metalli sì lucenti e rossi,
Com' io vidi un che dicea : S' a voi piace
 Montare in su, qui si convien dar volta : 140
Quinci si va chi vuole andar per pace.
L' aspetto suo m' avea la vista tolta :
 Per ch' io mi volsi indietro a' miei Dottori,
Com' uom che va secondo ch' egli ascolta.
E quale, annunziatrice degli albori, 145
 L' aura di maggio muovesi, ed olezza
Tutta impregnata dall' erba e da' fiori ;
Tal mi senti' un vento dar per mezza
 La fronte : e ben senti' muover la piuma,
Che fe sentir d' ambrosia l' orezza. 150
E senti' dir : Beati, cui alluma
 Tanto di grazia, che l' amor del gusto
Nel petto lor troppo disio non fuma,
Esurïendo sempre quanto è giusto.

> '*Still the breath of Love doth move,*
> *And still that breath is Love.*'

(XLIX)

THE Pilgrims are now to leave the Circle of the emaciated spirits below them, with the two Trees still keeping alive their yearnings. The second is described (lines 104 and following) almost as the first, with larger and wider branches above than below; and, as we are told later, it is nourished from above, not from Earth; this was a scion from the Tree of Knowledge. It seems almost as if the two Trees were gradually merging into One in the thought of the Pilgrim. But this Tree also is prohibited at this stage of the Pilgrimage. To forestall a good gift is sometimes a crime. Before either of these Trees can be partaken of, another Baptism, that of Fire, must be submitted to, and two more of Water, for the death of the memory of evil and the renewal of the memory of good.

The Angel of this Circle is of lucent glowing red, most dazzling to the eyes. The Pilgrim's perceptions seem to become more and more sensitive as he mounts upwards, or the Celestial Messengers are more and more enriched with light, colour, and ambrosial perfumes. Note the description of the fanning of this Angel's wings, and the expectation it excited, like that of a Spring Morning's fresh and scented zephyr. The sixth wound is thus cleansed, and the benediction imparted of the renewed Man's rightly adjusted appetite.

Dante, in the Seventh Circle, is questioned by those who are penitent for their sensuality, and questions them again.

──────────── (L.) ────────────

PURGATORIO, CANTO XXVI. 52-75.

    IO, che duo volte avea visto lor grato,
       Incominciai : O anime sicure
         D' aver, quando che sia, di pace stato,
Non son rimase acerbe nè mature   55
    Le membra mie di là, ma son qui meco
       Col sangue suo e con le sue giunture.
Quinci su vo, per non esser più cieco :
    Donna è di sopra che n' acquista grazia,
       Per che 'l mortal pel vostro mondo reco.   60
Ma se la vostra maggior voglia sazia
    Tosto divenga, sì che 'l ciel v' alberghi
       Ch' è pien d' amore e più ampio si spazia,
Ditemi, acciò ch' ancor carte ne verghi,
    Chi siete voi, e chi è quella turba   65
       Che se ne va diretro a' vostri terghi ?
Non altrimenti stupido si turba
    Lo montanaro, e rimirando ammuta,
       Quando rozzo e selvatico s' inurba,
Che ciascun' ombra fece in sua paruta :   70
    Ma poichè furon di stupore scarche,
       Lo qual negli alti cuor tosto s' attuta :
Beato te, che delle nostre marche,
    Ricominciò colei che pria ne chiese,
       Per viver meglio esperïenza imbarche.   75

'Those who are content in the flames.'

— (L) —

THE Pilgrims reach the seventh and last Circle.
A narrow pathway of fearful aspect lies between the steep precipice, on one side, and darting flames on the other. Here they must look well to their footsteps lest they err. Many spirits were seen hurrying past each other in the fires with swift greetings, yet exchanging the kiss of peace. They sang, as they came and went, their songs of warning, or cited examples of encouragement in penitential ardour. In all their suffering they were not self-absorbed, but noted and wondered at the shadow of the mortal man at their side. Even in the consuming flames one described the longing to know this strange phenomenon, as greater thirst than an Ethiop's for cold water. The descriptive lines (14 to 17) of Dante, put into the lips of this spirit, stamp him in swift clear outline on our mind's eye.

> 'O thou who goest, not from being slower,
> But reverent, perhaps, behind the others.'

Though an 'anima sdegnosa,' disdainful of the slight and the mean that surrounded him, his reverence was such as, perhaps, in these days we can hardly understand, for we have scanned everything and said, 'Ce n'est que ça.' Dante read all, great and small, as in the Divine book of Life, with his attentive, searching, wondering eyes.

The Fire must try every man's work of what sort it is.

──────────────── (L) ────────────────

Dante now saw some others intent to listen, and addresses them at the opening of to-day's Extract as 'Souls secure in the possession of Peace,' though that Peace was not yet attained. He tells them that 'he goes upward to be no longer blind'; and the spirit with whom he converses, and whom he in his turn questions, understands that he is passing through those borderlands ' to freight his bark with experience.' The two lines 58 and 75 might well be taken as the Pilgrim's mottoes as he passes along his way.

It is Guido Guinicelli who converses with him and confesses his fault; he was one who 'ever practised the sweet and gracious rhymes of love,' dear to Dante, and praised by him to their Author, who modestly points to another behind him as more worthy. Dante silently considered his words as the penitent, vanishing in the flames, asked him for his prayers, when it should be granted to him to reach the inner Sanctuary of Christ. A Provençal poet 'weeping and singing' was the other pointed out by Guinicelli, who 'contrite sees the folly of the past, and joyous sees the hoped-for day before.'

No regrets are expressed by these poets as to their modes of exercising their gifts, yet one divines by their self-detachment in speaking of these that not only themselves, but their work, is being tried in the fire, ' of what sort it is.'

At some stages of the Pilgrim's way, his *work* is more precious to him than himself; it has become so subtly blent with his more spiritual self, that to see it tried by fire is like seeing his ideal, or his faith, trembling in the balances between life and death.

The Fire must try every man's work of what sort it is.

—— (L.) ——

'For other Foundation can no man lay than that is laid, which is Jesus Christ.

'Now if any man build upon this foundation gold, silver, precious stones, wood, hay, stubble; Every man's work shall be made manifest; for the day shall declare it, because it shall be revealed by fire; and the fire shall try every man's work of what sort it is. If any man's work abide which he hath built thereupon, he shall receive a reward. If any man's work shall be burned, he shall suffer loss; but he himself shall be saved, yet so as by fire.'—1 Cor. iii. 11-15.

The Angel-messenger declares that Dante cannot proceed without entering the Fire. His heart quails, but revives at the name of Beatrice.

PURGATORIO, CANTO XXVII. 5-36.

<blockquote>

ONDE 'l giorno sen giva,   5
   Quando l' angel di Dio lieto ci apparse.
   Fuor della fiamma stava in su la riva,
E cantava: *Beati mundo corde,*
   In voce assai più che la nostra viva.
Poscia: Più non si va, se pria non morde,   10
   Anime sante, il fuoco; entrate in esso,
   Ed al cantar di là non siate sorde.
Sì disse, come noi gli fummo presso;
   Per ch' io divenni tal, quando lo 'ntesi,
   Quale è colui che nella fossa è messo.   15
In su le man commesse mi protesi,
   Guardando 'l fuoco, e immaginando forte
   Umani corpi già veduti accesi.
Volsersi verso me le buone Scorte;
   E Virgilio mi disse: Figliuol mio,   20
   Qui puote esser tormento, ma non morte.
Ricordati, ricordati . . . E se io
   Sovr' esso Gerïon ti guidai salvo,
   Che farò or che son più presso a Dio?
Credi per certo che, se dentro all' alvo   25
   Di questa fiamma stessi ben mill' anni,
   Non ti potrebbe far d' un capel calvo.
E se tu credi forse ch' io t' inganni,
   Fatti vêr lei, e fatti far credenza
   Con le tue mani al lembo de' tuoi panni.   30
Pon giù omai, pon giù ogni temenza:
   Volgiti 'n qua, e vieni oltre sicuro.
   Ed io pur fermo, e contra coscïenza.
Quando mi vide star pur fermo e duro,
   Turbato un poco disse: Or vedi, figlio,   35
   Tra Beatrice e te è questo muro.

</blockquote>

'When thou walkest through the Fire thou shalt not be burned.'

(LI)

A TERRIBLE ordeal opens before the Pilgrim as the Evening hour draws on. The Evening hour made the flames appear more terrible, and the waning light of the day depresses the courage. But the Angel is a 'glad one,' and he chants the benediction that awaits the Pilgrim. 'Blessed are the pure in heart, for they shall see God.' He comes, as each divine Messenger has come before, when the Pilgrim has passed through a Circle, to point out the further path, and to endow with fresh blessing, so that a dead self should become a stepping-stone to higher life.

As the Seventh Circle is left, the glad Angel of Purity appears standing on the verge of the fiery furnace, and in penetrating voice, 'much more living than our own,' he sings the sacred words of hope and encouragement, but adds that no holy soul may go further unless he feels the pang of the fire. He bids the pilgrims enter it and to 'be not deaf to the song beyond.' Dante's heart and flesh utterly fail him as he hears these words of doom. His memory and imagination supply him with realizing conceptions of the suffering and destruction that await him.

On the verge of piercing pain of body or soul what assailing visions come forth to meet and encompass the onward-driven Pilgrim, who is too often compelled with added poignancy of grief to own himself an abject coward. Conscience and reason have to do their part, as well as the Messenger of grace, and the divine Hope of the heavenly vision beyond the trial.

The injunction to listen for melodies to be heard, even while in the furnace, is a blessed reminder to the Pilgrim of the songs that *are given* in the night-season, even when the Supreme Sun and the Stars are hidden in the darkness of anguish.

Dante is at last persuaded to enter the Fire. A voice on the other side sings, 'Come, ye blessed of my Father.'

——————————— (LII) ———————————

PURGATORIO, CANTO XXVII. 46-63, 87-90.

POI dentro al fuoco innanzi mi si mise,
 Pregando Stazio che venisse retro,
 Che pria per lunga strada ci divise.
Come fui dentro, in un bogliente vetro
 Gittato mi sarei per rinfrescarmi ;   50
 Tanto er' ivi l' incendio senza metro.
Lo dolce Padre mio, per confortarmi,
 Pur di Beatrice ragionando andava,
 Dicendo : Gli occhi suoi già veder parmi.
Guidavaci una voce che cantava   55
 Di là ; e noi attenti pure a lei
 Venimmo fuor, là ove si montava.
Venite, benedicti Patris mei,
 Sonò dentro ad un lume che lì era,
 Tal che mi vinse, e guardar nol potei.   60
Lo Sol sen va, soggiunse, e vien la sera ;
 Non v' arrestate, ma studiate 'l passo
 Mentre che l' occidente non s' annera.
  * * * * *
 Fasciati quinci e quindi dalla grotta,   87
Poco potea parer lì del di fuori ;
 Ma per quel poco vedev' io le stelle
 Di lor solere e più chiare e maggiori.   90

'*He is like a refiner's fire, and like fullers' soap.*'—
MAL. iii. 2.

(LII)

THE reluctance and terror of the Pilgrim are at last overcome by the magic name of Beatrice. Her own past image, with its inspiration of purity, and his present identification of her with the Celestial Wisdom awaiting him beyond, are necessary to his fainting spirit, ere he can summon resolution to follow the leading of Virgil into the purifying furnace.

> ' When I was in it, into molten glass
> I would have cast me to refresh myself,
> So without measure was the burning there.'

What a fierce conflict with a besetting sin these words indicate! Pain and torment he had been told there might be, but not the destruction of one hair of his head. His Guide, who goes before, encourages him by his pre-vision of Beatrice's eyes; and the sound of a voice beyond directed them to the further margin of the fire.

The voice singing 'Come, ye blessed of my Father,' proceeded from a Splendour too glorious to gaze upon. This glorious being warned them that the Sun was setting, and urged on their footsteps while there was yet light.

The solemnity of that night (the last in Purgatory), into which they passed from the searching, revealing flames, must have been intense.

Each made a bed of one of the stony steps to await the new day. Dante compares himself to a goat on the Mountains, and his two spirit friends to Shepherds who keep watch.

He could see but little of things without, the rocky ascent walling him in; but through that narrow opening the stars appeared larger and more lucent than their wont. His vision had been purified, and, as the silence and solitude encircled him, the new heavens and new earth within his own soul were unfolding to his spirit.

The early morning dream of the Lady gathering flowers, who calls herself Leah, and describes her sister Rachel.

PURGATORIO, CANTO XXVII. 92-114.

MI prese 'l sonno; il sonno che sovente,
    Anzi che 'l fatto sia, sa le novelle.
    Nell' ora, credo, che dall' oriente
    Prima raggiò nel monte Citerea,   95
    Che di fuoco d' amor par sempre ardente,
Giovane e bella in sogno mi parea
    Donna vedere andar per una landa,
    Cogliendo fiori; e cantando dicea :
Sappia qualunque il mio nome dimanda,   100
    Ch' io mi son Lia, e vo movendo intorno
    Le belle mani a farmi una ghirlanda.
Per piacermi allo specchio qui m' adorno;
    Ma mia suora Rachel mai non si smaga
    Dal suo miraglio, e siede tutto giorno.   105
Ell' è de' suoi begli occhi veder vaga,
    Com' io dell' adornarmi con le mani ;
    Lei lo vedere, e me l' ovrare appaga.
E già, per gli splendori antelucani,
    Che tanto ai peregrin surgon più grati,   110
    Quanto, tornando, albergan men lontani,
Le tenebre fuggian da tutti i lati,
    E 'l sonno mio con esse; ond' io leva'mi,
    Veggendo i gran Maestri già levati.

The twofold Life of Union with God in the activities of His works and the reception of His Light.

──────── (LIII) ────────

SLEEP seizes on the Pilgrim after his inner communings and his contemplation of the 'more lucent' stars, and again he dreams an early morning dream of special import, forecasting the coming day.

He had dreamed, in the dawn after the first night in Ante-Purgatory, of the fiery Eagle snatching him upwards into the consuming light. This dream had prefigured the long ascent towards the Beatific Vision, initiated on that new day by Lucia, the Lady of divine Grace and Light, who carried him, even while he dreamed, to the portals of the realm of Purification. On the second night, ere he entered the last three Circles for the purification of the senses, he dreamed of the Siren Enchantress, who lured men to their destruction through the dominion of the senses, wherein her power lay. He had also seen in that vision the Siren's great opponent Wisdom, who reveals the foulness of the 'strange woman' and her flatteries.

Now, on the verge of the Terrestrial Paradise, he dreams a prophetic dream of the twofold life of union of man with God; the active and the contemplative life, typified, as these had hitherto been, by Leah and Rachel.

Leah gathers her flowers and adorns herself with the works of her hands; Rachel gazes all day long into the mirror which reflects her own contemplation of God, and is absorbed with that vision.

The dream ushers in the wondrous day of revelation, when the full powers of the New Man are opening before him in all their activities for service, and in all their capacities for beholding the Truth.

As the Pilgrim awakens to behold the hues which precede the sunrise, his heart seems beating with joyful anticipation; he welcomes the day, even 'as it is welcomed by grateful Pilgrims, home returning and less remotely lodged—the darkness fleeing away on every side, and slumber with it.'

*Virgil hails Dante as King and Priest through
self-conquest in Eden restored.*

———————— (LIV) ————————

PURGATORIO, CANTO XXVII. 115-142.

Q UEL dolce pomo, che per tanti rami   115
    Cercando va la cura de' mortali,
    Oggi porrà in pace le tue fami.
Virgilio inverso me queste cotali
    Parole usò ; e mai non furo strenne,
    Che fosser di piacere a queste eguali.   120
Tanto voler sovra voler mi venne
    Dell' esser su, che ad ogni passo poi
    Al volo mi sentia crescer le penne.
Come la scala tutta sotto noi
    Fu corsa, e fummo in su 'l grado superno,   125
    In me ficcò Virgilio gli occhi suoi,
E disse : Il temporal fuoco e l' eterno
    Veduto hai, figlio ; e se' venuto in parte,
    Ov' io per me più oltre non discerno.
Tratto t' ho qui con ingegno e con arte ;   130
    Lo tuo piacere omai prendi per duce ;
    Fuor se' dell' erte vie, fuor se' dell' arte.
Vedi il Sol, che in la fronte ti riluce ;
    Vedi l' erbetta, i fiori e gli arboscelli,
    Che quella terra sol da sè produce.   135
Mentre che vegnon lieti gli occhi belli,
    Che lagrimando a te venir mi fenno,
    Seder ti puoi, e puoi andar tra elli.
Non aspettar mio dir più, nè mio cenno :
    Libero, dritto, sano è lo tuo arbitrio,   140
    E fallo fòra non fare a suo senno ;
Per ch' io te sopra te corono e mitrio.

'The heir of hopes too fair to turn out false.'

(LIV)

THE Pilgrim has become the New Man, the regenerated Adam in Christ, restored to Eden, with the rights of the heir to his Kingdom.

He may enjoy all its beauty and fruitfulness, and may now partake of that Apple 'that grows on the many branches of the blended Trees of Knowledge and of Life'—those fruits whose sweet odours have awakened his longings, and those of other hungering and thirsting mortals. His will is free from every bias of self and from all bewildering darkness; his own pleasure, his own true instincts, are to be henceforth his guides. No check from without, no monition of law, except that of his own perfected affections, is to lead him, and he will find his environment in complete harmony with the full-grown powers of his being.

Is this the Golden Age of the ancients realized or restored, or the fulfilment of the prophetic dreams of the Millennium reign on Earth?

Virgil seems to give voice to the realized aspirations of all the ages in this Coronation and Consecration Ode of the King and the Priest, and even to the earnest expectation of Creation itself. He beholds in the New Man 'the goal of Nature's restless, painful waiting'—the manifestation of a Son of God, a joint heir with Christ, who, having suffered with Him, is glorified also with Him. We should like to linger with him here, but we see he does not linger. He must explore his new Kingdom, and is to experience the urging of the new wings, whose growth he is conscious of, to carry him beyond this stage of its expression to the Fountainhead of all its joys.

> 'To roll, and sweep, and bend,
>   Suffice for Nature's part;
> But motion to an endless end
>   Is needful for the heart.'
>   G. MACDONALD.

'Where the Spirit of the Lord is, there is liberty.'

(LIV)

We saw the Pilgrim at the foot of the Mountain baptized with morning dew, and with tears. We have seen him disentangled from the distortions and maiming consequences of Pride, Envy, Anger, and Sloth; and have also seen the cleansing of the Temple of his body, by interventions of Grace, by emancipated Will, and finally by the Spirit's Baptism of Fire. He is now clothed with the Armour of God in righteousness and strength. He has not been thus equipped to dwell in the delights of a Garden, even though it be the Garden of God. He is to pause here, indeed, and to enter into his inheritance of the fulness of the Earth. It is a Station in the Divine Country for the rounding of his soul by rest and beauty; through the expansion of his powers in its stillness, he will learn the interpretation of his former life and see visions of the past, present, and future history of man; but he is bound for the City of God, and the claims of that great Commonwealth are urging him upwards.

A new Enterprise is to open before his enlarged vision; and the severely penetrating and inexorable eyes of his ideal Love will detect yet more that he needs, ere this Son of the Resurrection may ascend, as Christ ascended, to the right hand of Power.

'When thou art wholly given up to the obedience of the Light and the Spirit of God within thee, then wheresoever thou goest thou wilt have a Priest and an Altar along with thee. Thou shalt then will only in His will, love only in His love, be wise only in His Wisdom; then it is that everything thou doest is a song of praise.'—W. LAW.

'*It is sown in dishonour; it is raised in glory.*'

(LIV)

'—— life is not as idle ore,
 But iron dug from central gloom,
  And heated hot with burning fears,
  And dipt in baths of hissing tears,
 And batter'd with the shocks of doom
 To shape and use . . . .'
                      '*In Mem.*,' cxviii.

'As Conqueror and King he mounts the throne,
And wears the crown of human glory—whence
Throne over throne surmounting he shall reign
One with the Last and First Intelligence.'
                                    FITZGERALD.

The new morning in Eden regained by the new Adam.

(LV)

PURGATORIO, CANTO XXVIII. 1-36.

VAGO già di cercar dentro e dintorno
    La divina foresta spessa e viva,
      Ch' agli occhi temperava il nuovo giorno
Senza più aspettar lasciai la riva,
    Prendendo la campagna lento lento   5
      Su per lo suol che d' ogni parte oliva.
Un' aura dolce, senza mutamento
    Avere in sè, mi feria per la fronte,
      Non di più colpo che soave vento;
Per cui le fronde, tremolando pronte,   10
    Tutte quante piegavano alla parte,
      U' la prim' ombra gitta il santo monte :
Non però dal lor esser dritto sparte
    Tanto, che gli augelletti per le cime
      Lasciasser d' operare ogni lor arte :   15
Ma con piena letizia l' aure prime,
    Cantando, riceveano intra le foglie,
      Che tenevan bordone alle sue rime,
Tal, qual di ramo in ramo si raccoglie
    Per la pineta in sul lito di Chiassi,   20
      Quand' Eölo Scirocco fuor discioglie.
Già m' avean trasportato i lenti passi
    Dentro all' antica selva tanto, ch' io
      Non potea riveder dond' io m' entrassi :
Ed ecco l' andar più mi tolse un rio,   25
    Che 'nvêr sinistra con sue picciole onde
      Piegava l' erba che in sua ripa uscío.

'And he showed me a pure river of water of life, clear as crystal.'—REV. xxii. 1.

(LV)

Tutte l' acque, che son di qua più monde,
  Parrieno avere in sè mistura alcuna
  Verso di quella, che nulla nasconde,   30
Avvegna che si muova bruna bruna
  Sotto l' ombra perpetua, che mai
  Raggiar non lascia Sole ivi, nè Luna.
Co' piè ristetti e con gli occhi passai
  Di là dal fiumicello, per mirare   35
  La gran variazion de' freschi mai.

NO longer a Pilgrim needing a Guide, the new man leads the way in his own land, the two Poets following his footsteps.

Who should venture to mingle his poor words with the impressions of the unfolding morning hour of the new day, here so wonderfully opened to us.

The Song of Songs will not be discordant with the melody that has awakened our inward ear.

'Rise up, my love, my fair one, and come away,
  For lo, the Winter is past,
  The rain is over and gone;
  The flowers appear on the Earth;
  The time of the singing of birds is come,
  And the voice of the turtle is heard in our land;
  The fig-tree ripeneth her green figs,
  And the vines are in blossom;
  They give forth their fragrance.
  Arise, my love, my fair one, and come away.'

Cant. ii. 10-14.

Matilda gathering flowers and singing was seen beyond the clear stream; she drew near, and the words of her Song were heard by Dante.

PURGATORIO, CANTO XXVIII. 37-63.

E LÀ m' apparve (sì com' egli appare
    Subitamente cosa, che disvia
      Per maraviglia tutt' altro pensare)
Una Donna soletta, che si gía   40
    Cantando ed iscegliendo fior da fiore,
      Ond' era pinta tutta la sua via.
Deh bella Donna, ch' a' raggi d' amore
    Ti scaldi, s' io vo' credere a' sembianti,
      Che soglion esser testimon del core,   45
Vegnati voglia di trarreti avanti,
    Diss' io a lei, verso questa riviera,
      Tanto ch' io possa intender che tu canti.
Tu mi fai rimembrar dove e qual era
    Proserpina nel tempo che perdette   50
      La madre lei, ed ella primavera.
Come si volge con le piante strette
    A terra ed intra sè donna che balli,
      E piede innanzi piede appena mette;
Volsesi in su' vermigli ed in su' gialli   55
    Fioretti verso me, non altrimenti
      Che vergine che gli occhi onesti avvalli;
E fece i prieghi miei esser contenti
    Sì appressando sè, che 'l dolce suono
      Veniva a me co' suoi intendimenti.   60
Tosto che fu là dove l' erbe sono
    Bagnate già dall' onde del bel fiume,
      Di levar gli occhi suoi mi fece dono.

Matilda gathering flowers ' is made glad with the works of God's hands.'

———————————— (LVI) ————————————

WE are told later that the following was the song that Matilda was singing, whose sound with its meaning came across the clear streamlet to Dante's ear.

' It is a good thing to give thanks unto the Lord,
And to sing praises to Thy Name, O Most High :
To show forth Thy loving kindness in the morning,
And Thy faithfulness every night,
With an instrument of ten strings and with the Psaltery,
With a solemn sound upon the harp ;
For Thou, Lord, hast made me glad through Thy work ;
I will triumph in the works of Thy hands.'
Ps. xcii. 1-5.

Ruskin's words will teach us to see in Matilda the sublimated Leah of the more spiritual Dispensation.

' The Vision of Rachel and Leah has been always, and with unquestionable truth, received as a type of the Active and Contemplative life, and as an introduction to the two divisions of the Paradise which Dante is about to enter.

' Therefore the unwearied spirit of the Countess Matilda is understood to represent the Active life, which forms the felicity of Earth ; and the spirit of Beatrice the contemplative life, which forms the felicity of Heaven·

' This interpretation appears at first straightforward and certain ; but it has missed count of exactly the most important fact in the two passages we have to explain. Observe (xxvii. 100) : Leah gathers the flowers to decorate *herself*, and delights in her own labour. Rachel sits silent, contemplating herself, and delights *in her own image*. These are the types of the unglorified Active and Contemplative powers of man. But Beatrice and Matilda are the same powers glorified. And how are they glorified ? Leah took delight in her own labour ; but Matilda— " in operibus manuum Tuarum "—in God's labour. Rachel in the sight of her own face ; Beatrice in the sight of God's face.'—' Modern Painters,' vol. iii. 222.

Matilda instructs Dante concerning the living seeds and the Waters of Eden.

(LVII)

PURGATORIO, CANTO XXVIII. 118-144.

E SAPER dèi che la campagna santa
    Ove tu se', d' ogni semenza è piena ;
    E frutto ha in sè, che di là non si schianta. 120
L' acqua che vedi non surge di vena,
    Che ristori vapor che giel converta,
    Come fiume ch' acquista o perde lena ;
Ma esce di fontana salda e certa,
    Che tanto dal voler di Dio riprende,   125
    Quanto ella versa da duo parti aperta.
Da questa parte con virtù discende,
    Che toglie altrui memoria del peccato ;
    Dall' altra d' ogni ben fatto la rende.
Quinci Letè, così dall' altro lato   130
    Eünoè si chiama ; e non adopra,
    Se quinci e quindi pria non è gustato.
A tutt' altri sapori esto è di sopra.
    Ed avvegna ch' assai possa esser sazia
    La sete tua, perch' io più non ti scuopra,   135
Darotti un corollario ancor per grazia ;
    Nè credo che 'l mio dir ti sia men caro,
    Se oltre promission teco si spazia.
Quelli, che anticamente poetaro
    L' età dell' oro e suo stato felice,   140
    Forse in Parnaso esto loco sognaro.
Qui fu innocente l' umana radice ;
    Qui primavera sempre ed ogni frutto ;
    Nèttare è questo di che ciascun dice.

Joyous Infancy.

(LVII)

MATILDA unfolded to Dante the secrets of Eden, as it was in the infancy of Man, and as it became after his innocent laughter and sweet play 'were changed by his own default to weeping and to toil.' She tells him the Garden of Delights was then lifted up high towards Heaven, but that seeds from thence fall down to fructify the lower Earth, wherever they can find a worthy soil. She also intimates that memories or thoughts fall from thence, or have lingered or been engendered from thence, in the hearts of men; and have inspired the dreams of the Golden Age and haunted men's imagination with sensations of the abiding Spring and of the Nectar, which make the Poets sing.

It seems the Ideal Childhood known to Wordsworth and other poet-souls, with its trails of glory; and it is the spiritual Childhood opened to us by our Lord, that is entered at the new birth, and enjoyed in fresh tides from the inflowing of the Kingdom of Heaven, which must enter our hearts before we can enter Heaven.

The Water of Life flows through this region, purging away in Lethe every memory of Sin, and renewing in Eunöe the strength of Memory's hold on every good which it has received.

So Innocence, as well as Virtue, becomes again the heritage of the true Man.

The three stars and four stars as Seven Nymphs upon the right and left hand of the Triumphal Car.

——————————— (LVIII) ———————————

PURGATORIO, CANTO XXIX. 121-132.

TRE donne in giro dalla destra ruota
   Venian danzando: l' una tanto rossa,
   Ch' appena fòra dentro al fuoco nota ;
L.' altr' era, come se le carni e l' ossa
   Fossero state di smeraldo fatte ;   125
   La terza parea neve testè mossa.
Ed or parevan dalla bianca tratte,
   Or dalla rossa ; e dal canto di questa
   L' altre togliean l' andare e tarde e ratte.
Dalla sinistra quattro facean festa,   130
   In porpora vestite, dietro al modo
   D' una di lor, ch' avea tre occhi in testa.

The perfected Seven, or Heaven and Earth united.
(The Seen and Unseen in Union.)

(LVIII)

VISIONS are opened in this Canto of the seven Candlesticks, seven rainbow-tinted Banners, the twenty-four Elders of the Apocalypse, the four Living Creatures with eyes within and without, the Chariot of the Church, drawn by the Mystic Wonder (the Gryphon), Symbol of the double-natured Human-Divine Christ (the semblance of the Eagle and Lion in One), the Seven Damsels representing the four Cardinal Virtues and the three Christian Graces—all these are seen, with the triumphal Car of the Church in their midst. These Seven Damsels appeared to us as distant stars in the opening Purgatorio, where the first four, paling before the glory of the rising Three, disappeared. They are now restored in new development and relationship. The number seven has been associated for centuries with the union of Heaven and Earth.

At the left hand Chariot Wheel the four early acknowledged Virtues of Justice, Courage, Temperance, and Prudence, were represented by four Maidens clothed in regal purple. Prudence with her three eyes was their leader. 'Respice, Aspice, Prospice,' we are told by commentators, were her three capacities of Vision, implying Memory of the Past, Knowledge of the Present, and Foresight of the Future.

At the right hand wheel of the Chariot were the three blessed Maidens, the Christian Graces of Faith, Hope, and Charity. Faith is white and glistening as the newly fallen Snow, Hope as the Emerald in ever enduring depths of Green, and Charity as flaming Crimson. Note that the steps of the following two were directed always by the Song of either Love or Faith. Hope has no consistency without the leadership of One or the other.

The glorified Beatrice is revealed, clothed in the colours of the Christian graces in the midst of a cloud of flowers. Virgil has disappeared.

PURGATORIO, CANTO XXX. 28-54.

Così dentro una nuvola di fiori,
 Che dalle mani angeliche saliva,
 E ricadeva giù dentro e di fuori,   30
Sovra candido vel cinta d' oliva
 Donna m' apparve, sotto verde manto
 Vestita di color di fiamma viva.
E lo spirito mio, che già cotanto
 Tempo era stato, ch' alla sua presenza   35
 Non era di stupor tremando affranto,
Sanza dagli occhi aver più conoscenza,
 Per occulta virtù, che da lei mosse,
 D' antico amor sentì la gran potenza.
Tosto che nella vista mi percosse   40
 L' alta virtù, che già m' avea trafitto,
 Prima ch' io fuor di puerizia fosse,
Volsimi alla sinistra col respitto,
 Col quale il fantolin corre alla mamma,
 Quando ha paura, o quando egli è afflitto,   45
Per dicere a Virgilio: Men che dramma
 Di sangue m' è rimasa, che non tremi;
 Conosco i segni dell' antica fiamma.
Ma Virgilio n' avea lasciati scemi
 Di sè, Virgilio dolcissimo padre,   50
Virgilio, a cui per mia salute die'mi:
 Nè quantunque perdeo l' antica madre
 Valse alle guance nette di rugiada,
Che lagrimando non tornassero adre.

The Bride from Lebanon or Celestial Wisdom becomes visible as the beloved Beatrice.

──────────── (LIX) ────────────

AFTER solemn thunder and glorious preludings of Music and processions of Angels and Saints and amid clouds of flowers, the manifestation to Dante of Celestial Wisdom and of his own Ideal of Womanhood, his own from his early childhood, bursts upon his Vision. She is clothed in the three colours of the Christian Graces already seen, with green mantle, veiled in pure white so that her face is concealed, crowned like Minerva, yet with the more sacred Olive-leaves, and vested in colour of living flame. Her beloved presence was felt through the occult Virtue dwelling therein, though her countenance was unseen. Dante's awe and agitation were so great, that he turned away to the Guide and Consolation of his pilgrimage, as a Child would turn to his Mother for support, but the faithful Virgil had disappeared.

We could hardly resist weeping with Dante unless we learnt to let go the literal Virgil ('Virgilio! Virgilio! dolcissimo Padre!') and to see him here as the living Soul of limited human reason now gathered up into, and flooded with, the Light of the fuller glory of Celestial Wisdom which henceforth shines into his Scholar's heart and mind. By the decrease of John the Baptist in the increase of the Bridegroom, he, who had been less than the least in the Kingdom of Heaven, entered that Kingdom; and in our Lord's rapture over the fields, white unto the Harvest, He foresaw the joying together of those that had sowed (as John the Baptist and Virgil) with those who reaped.

*Beatrice calls Dante by name, and declares her own name
to him, yet severely rebukes him.*

(LX)

PURGATORIO, CANTO XXX. 55-81.

DANTE, perchè Virgilio se ne vada,   55
   Non pianger anco, non piangere ancora ;
   Chè pianger ti convien per altra spada.
Quasi ammiraglio, che in poppa ed in prora
   Viene a veder la gente che ministra
   Per gli altri legni, ed a ben far l' incuora ;   60
In su la sponda del carro sinistra,
   Quando mi volsi al suon del nome mio,
   Che di necessità qui si registra,
Vidi la Donna, che pria m' apparío
   Velata sotto l' angelica festa,   65
   Drizzar gli occhi vér me di qua dal rio.
Tutto che 'l vel che le scendea di testa,
   Cerchiato dalla fronda di Minerva,
   Non la lasciasse parer manifesta ;
Regalmente nell' atto ancor proterva   70
   Continuò, come colui che dice,
   E 'l più caldo parlar dietro riserva :
Guardami ben : ben son, ben son Beatrice.
   Come degnasti d' accedere al monte?
   Non sapei tu che qui l' uomo è felice ?   75
Gli occhi mi cadder giù nel chiaro fonte ;
   Ma veggendomi in esso, io trassi all' erba :
   Tanta vergogna mi gravò la fronte
Così la madre al figlio par superba,
   Com' ella parve a me ; perchè d' amaro   80
   Sente 'l sapor della pietade acerba.

> '*Love is not Love without Truth;*
> *Truth is not Truth without Love.*'

(LX)

THE transfigured Lady now calls Dante by name—by his baptismal name. It is the only time throughout the Poem that any one of the multitudes who address him utters that name; here he says he must necessarily record it. From her lips it must have pierced him with a wondrous appeal; and soon afterwards she declares herself to him, though still veiled, as Beatrice: 'Look at me well; I am indeed, indeed I am Beatrice.'

These words of personal recognition and revelation perhaps rendered this first speech of reunion more endurable than it could otherwise have been. We can trace no tone of tenderness in her words; they have revolted many from the Poet who could put them into the lips of his ideal Woman.

'Queenlike in look and gesture and severe,' she stood before him, and seemed to hold in reserve yet deeper condemnation.

Dante teaches us, in his 'Vita Nuova,' what his ideal of woman was, as she was seen in earthly relationship with others and with himself. He says that, when she is with other ladies, she does not only make herself pleasing to them, but each one receives honour from her, and that so much strength or virtue is in her beauty that it causes no envy to others. Rossetti's translation is given further on of his first Sonnet, portraying his perfect conception of his Lady's gentleness and humility.

No reproaches such as those we have been studying in Canto XXX. could have escaped the lips portrayed in that Sonnet while she lived in Dante's sight at Florence. She did, indeed, once refuse him her salutation, which seems to indicate a moral conviction stronger than her loving desire

Wisdom passeth and goeth through all things by reason of her pureness.

to please; but the wide difference between Beatrice on earth and Beatrice glorified should make us seek for Dante's meaning.

Here, it seems, we see Beatrice as one with Dante's own highest spiritual life; and her voice, *as his very own*, condemns that past condition of his lower nature which remained beneath the Mount of Aspiration, as though all joys were below.

As his purged inward eye again beholds the glorified ideal of his life, he is constrained to lower his eyelids, and there, in the clear stream at her feet, to behold the image of what he had actually been, in intense contrast to the personalized Purity, Faith, Hope, and Love now revealed. It is a renewed vision of the white polished marble step at the stern portal of Purgatory, and of the crystal stream that separated him from Matilda. Light, as we can bear it, must ever more and more make manifest the darkness that flees before it.

Dante feels its controlling dominion and the bitter savour of its severe compassion; even as a boy shrinks from a Mother's lofty rebuke, he shrank before the stern requirements of Wisdom.

Dante has much to teach us concerning noble Love, which is very different from the lessons taught us in this generation. We need to learn '*with all Saints*' in each generation in order to comprehend that which is deeper, higher, and broader than any individual comprehension, 'the love of Christ which passeth knowledge.'

Beatrice at Florence.

(LX)

'My lady looks so gentle and so pure
When yielding salutation by the way,
That the tongue trembles and has naught to say,
And the eyes which fain would see may not endure.
And still, amid the praise, she hears secure;
She walks with humbleness for her array,
Seeming a creature sent from Heaven to stay
On Earth, and show a miracle made sure;
She is so pleasant in the eyes of men
That through the sight the inmost heart doth gain
A sweetness which needs proof to know it by;
And from between her lips there seems to move
A soothing essence that is full of love,
Saying for ever to the spirit, "Sigh!"'

Dante feels the compassion of the heavenly choirs, but Beatrice still insists on his having fallen short of his glorious destiny.

PURGATORIO, CANTO XXX. 91-120.

COSÌ fui senza lagrime e sospiri
    Anzi 'l cantar di que' che notan sempre
    Dietro alle note degli eterni giri :
Ma poichè intesi nelle dolci tempre
    Lor compatire a me, più che se detto   95
    Avesser : Donna, perchè sì lo stempre?
Lo gel, che m' era intorno al cuor ristretto,
    Spirito ed acqua fessi, e con angoscia
    Per la bocca e per gli occhi uscì del petto.
Ella, pur ferma in su la detta coscia   100
    Del carro stando, alle sustanzie pie
    Volse le sue parole così poscia :
Voi vigilate nell' eterno die,
    Sì che notte nè sonno a voi non fura
    Passo, che faccia il secol per sue vie ;   105
Onde la mia risposta è con più cura,
    Che m' intenda colui che di là piagne,
    Perchè sia colpa e duol d' una misura.
Non pur per ovra delle ruote magne,
    Che drizzan ciascun seme ad alcun fine,   110
    Secondo che le stelle son compagne ;
Ma per larghezza di grazie divine
    (Che sì alti vapori hanno a lor piova,
    Che nostre viste là non van vicine),
Questi fu tal nella sua vita nuova   115
    Virtualmente, ch' ogni abito destro
    Fatto averebbe in lui mirabil pruova.
Ma tanto più maligno e più silvestro
    Si fa 'l terren col mal seme, e non colto,
    Quant' egli ha più di buon vigor terrestro.   120

'*As many as I love, I rebuke and chasten; be zealous
therefore and repent.*'—REV. iii. 19.

---------- (LXI) ----------

WHEN Beatrice's voice was silent, and Dante's shame was further increased by the image he read of himself in the clear fount, the Choir of Angels, to comfort him, suddenly sang the words from Psalm xxxi. : 'In Thee, O Lord, have I put my trust, let me never be ashamed.' When he heard in their sweet melodies, 'that always follow the notes of the spheres,' compassion expressed for himself, his frozen heart was melted, and sighs and tears broke forth.

Let us think for a moment of that choir. No note has its source in the Singers themselves; they are always listening to the larger melodies awakened by the breath that moves throughout the mighty Universe, its Keynote of Love being heard by them; they re-echo it in perfect harmony and adaptation to every awakened ear.

Beatrice speaks again, turning to the Angels, who are ever faithfully watching in the light of Day, and recounts to them all the influences which had contributed to endow Dante with the promise and potency of good. Not only, she says, 'those great wheels that destine every seed unto some end' were in his favour. The abundant bounties of celestial graces, with rains that descended from lofty summits beyond the reach of the eye, had been poured out upon him, so that the good seed might have borne fruit a hundred-fold :

> '*But all the more perverse, and wild, and rude,
> Becomes the soil, with ill seed, left untilled,
> As 'tis with more of natural strength endued.*'

She recounts all her own endeavours to lead and sustain him in the right way. After her ascension from flesh to spirit, when beauty and virtue had increased in her, she failed not to call upon him in dreams and otherwise; but these availed not, for he turned his steps into fallacious paths, so that nothing remained for his salvation but to show him the people of perdition.

Beatrice further declares it would infringe the decree of God, should he drink of the Waters of Lethe ere the penitence due to such dereliction had burst forth in tears. The self-convicted Dante stands as a culprit before the judgment of Love; and she does not hasten to close the wounds she has opened. She turns from the Angels, and brings the keen point of her scathing words straight to his own heart.

Love speaks at sundry times in divers manners. There are tender caresses and joyful surprises for one season, and they are precious, for nothing else could have been apprehended by our dulness as Love; and there is the passionate, personal appreciation, that seems blind to our defects and lifts us on to a pedestal of its own, making us 'forget our self-despisings,' and this is precious, for nothing else would have imparted power to our benumbed and discouraged affections; and there are the severe requirements of a Love that is not blind, but has 'eyes of flame,' that will search and try the beloved and hold up the mirror to his heart, so lifting him on to the stepping-stone of his dead self that he may rise to higher things. Few in the flesh, perhaps none, are worthy to give or to receive such supreme tokens of love as these last; they belong to the realm of the spirit, where the Celestial Wisdom and Love are worshipped as One. Dante conceives Beatrice to be one in worship with himself, as well as one with himself in personal love; the reproofs he puts into her lips are therefore his own; in such love 'the distinction of Me and Thee is swept away, and there pulses in two individuals one warm life·

The Dominion of Love.

(LXI)

In the 'Vita Nuova' Dante speaks of 'the intolerable Beatitude of Love.' The Lord of Love visits him in a dream, and appears weeping over him. Dante asks his Lord of all nobility, why he weeps? He is answered in these words, 'I am as the Centre of a Circle to which all parts of the Circumference bear an equal proportion; but with thee it is not thus.' After this Vision many and diverse questionings arose in his mind to be weighed or combated; two of these present themselves thus: Good is the dominion of Love, for He draws His faithful disciple from all petty things. The second was this: Not good is the dominion of Love, for the more faithful the disciple, so much the more must he pass through difficult and dolorous pathways.

Dante is forced to reconsider his life in the light of Wisdom and Truth, and to confess its error ere he may bathe in Lethe.

———————————(LXII)———————————

PURGATORIO, CANTO XXXI. 1-30.

O TU, che se' di là dal fiume sacro
    (Volgendo 'l suo parlare a me per punta,
    Che pur per taglio m' era parut' acro),
Ricominciò seguendo senza cunta:
    Di', di', se questo è vero; a tanta accusa   5
    Tua confession conviene esser congiunta.
Era la mia virtù tanto confusa,
    Che la voce si mosse, e pria si spense
    Che dagli organi suoi fosse dischiusa.
Poco sofferse; poi disse: Che pense?   10
    Rispondi a me; chè le memorie triste
    In te non sono ancor dall' acqua offense.
Confusione e paura insieme miste
    Mi pinsero un tal sì fuor della bocca,
    Al quale intender fur mestier le viste.   15
Come balestro frange, quando scocca
    Da troppa tesa la sua corda e l' arco,
    E con men foga l' asta il segno tocca;
Sì scoppia' io sott' esso grave carco,
    Fuori sgorgando lagrime e sospiri,   20
    E la voce allentò per lo suo varco.
Ond' ella a me: Per entro i miei desiri,
    Che ti menavano ad amar lo bene,
    Di là dal qual non è a che s' aspiri,
Quai fosse attraversate, o quai catene   25
    Trovasti, perchè del passare innanzi
    Dovessiti così spogliar la spene?
E quali agevolezze, o quali avanzi
    Nella fronte degli altri si mostraro,
    Perchè dovessi lor passeggiare anzi?   30

'I have somewhat against thee because thou hast left thy first Love.'—Rev. ii. 4.

(LXII)

THE whole of this Canto should be studied, for it offers much food for meditation.

The New Man who has been baptized by Water and Fire, who has climbed the steep ascent of the Holy Hill, and has been purged from the seven root-sins that had clung to him—he who has been crowned and mitred King and Priest, beholds again the transfigured Ideal of his soul in the, as ever, personally beloved Beatrice; and he stands before her abashed, ashamed, convicted, till he falls before her as one dead. We have to remind ourselves that he is in the Eden of restored man, for this is more like

> 'That sad, obscure, sequestered state
> Where God unmakes, but to remake, the soul
> He else made first in vain.'

Many have asked with Scartazzini, what are the sins which are reproved and censured in Dante, when he had passed through the second Kingdom where the human spirit is purged? See Vernon, vol. ii., 286.

The answer there given is, that these sins must be sought, in the symbolical, rather than in the personal, relationship between the two, and that the infidelity towards herself, with which Beatrice reproaches him, indicates his infidelity towards those who ought to guide man in accordance with the doctrines of revelation; that he had, in fact, followed the teachings of a philosophical School at variance with that of orthodox Theology. This may be a true explanation; but the passionate grief of his heart's overflow described here seems to manifest a more personal poignancy of remorse. His sins against his Ideal of Righteousness have been repented of, and cleansed, and, he knew, forgiven; we

(LXII)

believe that this cleansing and forgiveness has rendered him capable of a still deeper repentance, for we feel that it is here, for the first time, that he is conscious that his sin has been against Love.

The personal gifts of Providence are recounted, which, he sees with the eyes of Beatrice, he has left untilled; and her faithful and continued endeavours to lift him above the things of sense are seen to have been unfailing, both before and after her death, as they were never understood hitherto. Love has stood at his door and knocked; he knows it now, and it wounds him to the quick, as no general sense of transgression against a righteous law could wound. Peter went out and wept bitterly when the eyes of the beloved Master rested upon him, and revealed his denial to him. Dante knew that he had been false to the inward loyalty that such a love demanded. Only in the knowledge of a faithful, personal love can anything like deep contrition of heart be experienced. Before tasting of Evil's oblivion through the baptism of Lethe, he must become fully aware of that evil; he must own that the thing he had most loved was indeed his greatest foe. Only by seeing this in its true colour could he die to it and rise again with Her to the new Celestial life. 'How can two walk together except they be agreed?' This renewed Man has to rise to the purely spiritual man, to behold the Vision of the 'Holy, Holy, Holy' in the Holy of Holies—not to dwell in innocent childlike delights with his blessed Lady in the Garden of Eden, but to be endowed with power from the right hand on high to be a Ruler over many Cities.

> *'Except a corn of wheat fall into the ground and die,
> it abideth alone.'*

―――――――――――― (LXII) ――――――

After this overpowering taste of death, Matilda, as the Active Ministress of Eden, immerses him in, and draws him through, the cleansing Waters of Lethe. Then each Virtue covers him with her arm, and he is led by them to the 'Three beyond' who 'more profoundly look,' and these are to lead him again to Beatrice and to teach his eyes to behold in hers the vision of Christ, symbolized in the double-natured Gryphon. This 'Wonder,' in Itself unchanging, was reflected in her eyes as now Man, now God. In this vision of the Incarnation he finds a satisfying and yet stimulating food which is indescribable; a foretaste of the ultimate Vision, the Source and Goal of all life. His words here are few; his deepest Sanctuary is always veiled, as the wings of the Seraphim veil their faces.

The Canto closes with the gracious intercession of the blessed Three to Beatrice to do *them* the grace of unveiling her Second beauty to her devoted Servant and Lover.

> ' 'Tis somewhat late!
> And all thou dost enumerate
> Of power and beauty in the World,
> The righteousness of love was curled
> Inextricably round about.
> Love lay within it and without
> To clasp thee, but in vain! Thy Soul
> Still shrank from Him who made the whole,
> Still set deliberate aside
> His love! Now take love! well betide
> The tardy Conscience!'
>   R. BROWNING.

PURGATORIO, CANTO XXXIII. 106-129.

Sì come s'affigge,
   Chi va dinanzi a schiera per iscorta,
   Se trova novitade in sue vestigge,
Le sette donne al fin d'un' ombra smorta,
   Qual sotto foglie verdi e rami nigri   110
   Sovra suoi freddi rivi l' Alpe porta.
Dinanzi ad esse Eüfratès e Tigri
   Veder mi parve uscir d' una fontana,
   E quasi amici dipartirsi pigri.
O luce, o gloria della gente umana,   115
   Che acqua è questa, che qui si dispiega
   Da un principio, e sè da sè lontana?
Per cotal prego detto mi fu : Prega
   Matelda, che 'l ti dica. E qui rispose,
   Come fa chi da colpa si dislega,   120
La bella Donna : Queste ed altre cose
   Dette gli son per me ; e son sicura
   Che l' acqua di Letèo non gliel nascose.
E Beatrice : Forse maggior cura,
   Che spesse volte la memoria priva,   125
   Fatto ha la mente sua negli occhi oscura.
Ma vedi Eünoè, che là deriva :
   Menalo ad esso, e come tu se' usa,
   La tramortita sua virtù ravviva.

> '*The Best in me that sees the worst in me,*
> *And groans to see it.*'

------(LXIII)------

THE intercessions of the Three gracious Ladies—Faith, Hope, and Charity—prevailed on Beatrice to unveil her 'second beauty' to Dante's longing eyes.

His full self-conviction, and his confession that the fallacious 'present things' of the world had seduced him from his heart-allegiance to his highest and best love, and his subsequent baptism in the waters of Lethe, cleansing him from the memories of sin, seem to have been the preparation for the culminating vision that belongs to the apex of the Purgatorial Realm. The clash of the flesh and the spirit have been recognised all the uphill Way. The dream of the enchanting Siren, and of the overcoming Lady of Wisdom, embodied this conflict half-way up the Mountain.

The enchantments and illusions of things seen have now vanished, but the Visible is not to vanish, or to be resisted by the perfected King and Priest; for here a deeper vision is unfolded to him, which is to reconcile all things in Heaven and in Earth. The four Virtues of Earth and their three Heavenly Inspirers go before him; he is led by them to the profound and extended vision of the Incarnation. In mysterious language, in few words, he tells us that, fixing his eyes on the eyes of Beatrice, he beholds in those 'Emeralds' (eyes of enduring Hope as well as Wisdom) the Prodigy, or double-natured Being, now GOD, now Man, both inextricably One.

This perception of the point of contact, if we may so express it, of the unifying of the redeemed and redeeming flesh of Christ with the underlying substance of the creating and anointing Spirit, is the revelation of Eden restored.

This is the Sacramental region where the outward and visible Sign is regarded as the Word of GOD; the region

Dante is now bathed by Matilda in the life-renewing Waters of Eunoë.

———————— (LXIII) ————————

(*Continued from last page.*)

PURGATORIO, CANTO XXXIII. 130-145.

<pre>
Com' anima gentil, che non fa scusa,   130
  Ma fa sua voglia della voglia altrui,
  Tosto com' è per segno fuor dischiusa ;
Così, poi che da essa preso fui,
  La bella Donna mossesi, ed a Stazio
  Donnescamente disse : Vien con lui.   135
S' io avessi, lettor, più lungo spazio
  Da scrivere, io pur cantere' in parte
  Lo dolce ber, che mai non m' avria sazio :
Ma perchè piene son tutte le carte
  Ordite a questa Cantica seconda,   140
  Non mi lascia più gir lo fren dell' arte.
Io ritornai dalla santissim' onda
  Rifatto sì, come piante novelle
  Rinnovellate di novella fronda,
Puro e disposto a salire alle stelle.   145
</pre>

The Sacramental Witness of the Union of Heaven and Earth.

(LXIII)

where the indwelling Divine Spirit and the outward embodiment are seen to be in such intimate life-currents of unity, that the endeavour to wrench asunder the GOD-interwoven twain might seem to threaten the destruction of two worlds.

This Central revelation is the Key that opens avenues to many other visions appertaining to the same realm of miracle. Beatrice displays to the Disciple pictures of the Church and the Empire, present and future. She showed him also the Mystic Tree again, renewed in foliage after spoliation, and in lovely blossoming as with Apple blossoms, such as, he says, 'made the Angels long for its fruit and its perpetual marriage-feasts in Heaven' (xxxii. 75). The distinct interpretation of this Tree is hard to find. It seems to combine allusions to the Tree of Knowledge, the Tree of Life, the Cross, the Church, and the Tree of the restored Humanity in Christ.

Beatrice instructs him to make known what he has seen in fearless speech, and not to speak as in a dream.

These visions are far too intricate and need too much of historic interpretation to be meddled with here.

Venturing to seek, as we have done, the simpler and more personal spiritual nutriment of Pilgrims on the Way, to be found in this great Poem, and leaving so much aside, we yet must not fail to note the intense interest of the Representative Pilgrim in all the events of the actual matter-of-fact life around him. Unlike our own Bunyan's Way of the Pilgrim, this Way is almost inextricably interwoven with the actions and hopes and fears and indignations and protests of the Citizen, the Patriot, and the Churchman. As we might expect (if the Sign of the Prodigy, the Union of the redeemed Outward and Inward, has been truly interpreted) there could be no leaving behind thoughts or actions concerning such subjects ; they were to the Seer the 'visible speech of God' stamped within and without on the scroll of Christ-illumined Life. We find them indeed surrounding him in the highest heaven, in the very Courts of the Inner Sanctuary of the Beatific Vision. Perhaps no Mystic was ever so sensitive to external and practical things as Dante ; perhaps none has so much felt the unity in himself of the two worlds, as we are accustomed to call them, of the Visible and of the Spiritual.

Dante meets with no other traveller in this region of prophetic Vision ; though Statius follows him and is bathed by Matilda with him in Eunoë, they seem to have had no communion in words. Matilda, the active dispenser of the bounties of Paradise, is more like one of the Nymphs or Graces than any actual personality. She is the ministress of Beatrice's behests with regard to Dante ; her will is merged in that of Beatrice. The Angels and Graces and Processions of Saints and Elders seen by him are like those in the Apocalypse, changing phantasies, displayed for the teaching of the Seer alone, and for those who may learn of him.

Such an exceptional region has been entered by saints and mystics of all generations, and if the Key of this region be accepted, this picture may be a prophecy, a promise for all the race, when the due season of its purged and extended faculties permits the consummation of the Wedding of Earth and Heaven.

Our portion for to-day, the last lines of the Cantos of the Second Kingdom, leave the New Man reunited with the Love and Ideal of his personal life, not as yet in the perfect

The Sacramental Witness of the Union of Heaven and Earth.

——————————— (LXIII) ———————————

union of equality, but as a perfectly prepared disciple with the perfect Teacher:

> 'And what delights can equal those
> That stir the spirit's inner deeps,
> When one that loves, but knows not, reaps
> A truth from one that loves and knows.'

At her request the ready and gentle Matilda, 'who makes her own will of another's,' revives the fainting life of Dante by the Waters of Eunoë. This baptism is not unto any death, like that of Lethe; it is all unto Life. Lethe had destroyed in him the memory of sin in his past life; now Memory, re-dipt, is to restore to him every good thing that has been imprinted there. 'Behold, I make all things new.' Let us imagine the wealth of such a new world within as this. The familiar old benedictions, unstained by our sins, negligences and ignorances, in full potency; Childhood's gardens of delight and wonder re-opened; the loving looks and ways of Home alive, without the limiting irksomeness of its restraints; the unfolding stores of vital knowledge rescued from our dulness; the blessed intercommunion of rekindled ardour in friendships; each thought and word of love and of kindred mind that has 'exalted us above ourselves'; the strains of Poetry and of Music that have swayed our Souls; the flashes through Nature's grandeur or simplicity that have revealed their intimate Source; the breathings of Prayer or Adoration that have passed through or over us—these all in ordered ranks, unified by the hidden divine Love that lived in all. We may count up such things and thousands more, even now as we can recollect them, even under the chequered shades of our sorrows and our

The Sacramental Witness of the Union of Heaven and Earth.

sins, unobliterated by Lethe. We may drink of the two streams of the water of life in some measure each evening of our lives, practising to forget and to remember, learning more of the renewed life that stirred in the renewed man as he

> 'Returned from the most holy water
> Regenerate, in the manner of new trees
> That are renewed with a new foliage,
> Pure and disposed to mount unto the stars.'

PARADISO.

THE ASCENSION THROUGH THE HEAVENS TO THE PARADISO.

'Eye hath not seen, nor ear heard, neither have entered into the heart of man, the things which God hath prepared for them that love Him.

'But God hath revealed them unto us by His Spirit: for the Spirit searcheth all things, yea, the deep things of God. . . . Now we have received, not the spirit of the world, but the Spirit which is of God; that we might know the things that are freely given to us of God.'—1 Cor. ii. 9-12.

'I knew a man in Christ about fourteen years ago (whether in the body, I cannot tell; or whether out of the body, I cannot tell; God knoweth), such an one caught up to the third Heaven. And I knew such a man (whether in the body or out of the body, I cannot tell; God knoweth), how that he was caught up into Paradise and heard unspeakable words, which it is not lawful (or possible) for a man to utter.'—2 Cor. xii. 2-4.

'Grant, we beseech Thee, Almighty God, that like as we do believe Thy only-begotten Son, our Lord Jesus Christ, to have ascended into the Heavens, so we may also in heart and mind thither ascend and with Him continually dwell, who liveth and reigneth with Thee and the Holy Ghost, one God, world without end. Amen.'—Collect for Ascension Day.

IT is with this prayer alone, and in this spirit, that we venture to press into these opened Heavens.

We have, in the Inferno, studied the picture of the human heart in both ignorant and wilful antagonism to its Divine Centre and to right reason.

The Ascension through the Heavens to the Paradiso.

(2)

In the Purgatorio we have seen the human heart in its true filial relationship to the Divine Centre, yet trammelled with the consequences of the false conceptions that had dominated it.

How shall we follow the Pilgrim along this almost unbeaten path to the fully-developed spiritual consciousness, generated in complete union with God and with His Universe?

Experience, which has helped us in the former portions of the Poem, is in great measure lacking to us here, and the wings of our imagination fail us. We are warned by Dante himself (Canto II. 1-15) that we had better not try to follow his Bark across waters that have never been navigated, unless we have already, with a few, aspired to feed on Angels' Bread. By 'these few' the elements of well-being and of bliss here opened to us have, indeed, been tasted, and such divinely-nourished souls have said, and may say, as the spirits of Light here described say, ' His Will is our Peace.' 'Our joy is in receiving from Him and giving to others; our intellect finds its nourishment in His Truth; our heart is at rest in His Love.'

St. Paul tells the Ephesians that they have been 'raised up together with Christ, and made to sit with Him in Heavenly places'; and we have been taught to expect the revealings of the 'deep things of God by His Spirit.'

These things, 'freely given to us of God,' have been known, and may be increasingly known, even by those who are yet under the limitations of Sense and Time; but till these limitations are removed, and till the members of Christ's mystical Body are in full fellowship, the vision, as presented here, must continue an Ideal, towards which we may, indeed, continually approach, but which cannot be entirely realized.

In the Paradiso we naturally find less of external description and of varied symbolism than in the two first portions of the Poem.

Its lofty themes are: the Providence of God; the nature of Will in Man; the Order and Form of the Universe; the ideal justice of God as the cause of every manifestation of justice on Earth; the Incarnation; the Atonement; the Nature of Faith, Hope, and Charity; the Creation of Angels and Man; the Church militant and triumphant; and the final goal, the Vision of the Trinity, and Humanity One with God. These subjects are treated, probably, much as theologians have treated them before and since the time of Dante; but they are represented as received not on the authority of external teaching alone, but in inner communion with the Celestial Wisdom and with the spirits of just men made perfect; they are warmed with the heart's blood of the Seer, and inwoven with his living experience. He blends them with biographies of Saints, with the history of the age, and especially with that of the Church in his own day.

With such histories the heart of the renewed man is felt to be intimately connected, and the heavenly hierarchy is portrayed as vibrating in fullest sympathy.

The Heavens not only rejoice in the triumphs of the Church Militant, but blush with shame at her defeats.

The outward presentation of deep and spiritual conceptions in artistic framework, appealing to our sense apprehensions, must necessarily have its paradoxes. Here, however, this framework is, as has been said, less definite and outlined than in the preceding portions. The ascent through the nine Heavens is no longer a painful climb, as in Purgatory, but the spirit is borne aloft without effort, almost without sense of motion, as a necessary consequence of ardent desire and of the gaze into the eyes of Beatrice—Beatrice, the soul of Dante's soul and its divinely nurturing Mother. She is almost identified with Divine philosophy and with perfecting grace. 'Her two eyes,' Dante tells us in 'Convito,' II., and in the 'Vita Nuova,' 'are demonstrations which look into the soul; and her smiles are persuasions which enamour it, and emancipate it from all fettering conditions.'

Like St. Paul, he knows not how his body could be lifted beyond its own limits; but 'God knew who lifted him with His Light.' And he invents a word to express what, he says, language cannot express, the transition from the earthly to the heavenly—to 'transhumanize' (Canto I. 70).

We shall follow him through the nine Spheres of the encircling and encanopying Heavens, each one revolving with swifter and swifter motion as it approaches the Empyrean, or Tenth Heaven of motionless Rest and Peace. The swift and ardent desire of the soul is seen here as *spiritual motion*, 'that ne'er rests until she doth enjoy the thing beloved.'—Purgatorio, XVIII. 33. This Heaven is the Central point towards which all are pressing inwards with this ardent desire; yet this Central point is, at the same time, the Circumference that encloses our restlessness with its rest. Beneath its outstreaming light the Mystic White Rose of the glorified Church triumphant is brought into its ideal perfection. The Ninth, or first moved Heaven of swiftest motion, is the circle where 'they most know and most love.' This transmits its virtues to the Eighth, and in this way each receives from the Heaven above itself and gives to the one below, though with diminished vitality.

Divine giving and Divine receiving make the rhythm of the Spheres, and are the joy of the whole, manifesting the interaction and reciprocity of the Father and the Son.

The two great powers of the spiritual life, Love and Knowledge (dreamt of by the Pilgrim on the threshold of the Eden-Paradise as Rachel and Leah, the active and contemplative faculties of the soul), are seen in perfected equilibrium in God, Who is called, in this relationship, 'The Prime Equality.' The hunger of each soul is fed by partaking of this twofold perfection.

The Divine volition of St. John xvii. is seen to be fulfilled, 'I in them and Thou in Me, that they may be one, even as We are One.' Thousands, in the form of the Celestial Eagle, are imagined speaking of themselves as 'I and Me,' for all are of one spirit and one language. Though personality is never lost (for who could emphasize it more than Dante?), it is continually represented as subordinated to a social end. The blessed form themselves into figures or words for the enlightenment of others; the disciple of one Saint recounts the blessedness, not of his own Master, but of the Founder of another Order; and each fulfils in increased joy some special act of love. The Divine Elective Light mingles with the consenting light of each, and directs each to the action in which he rejoices, though he knows not wherefore he especially is elected to this office.— XXI. 85-95.

The Light is broken into thousands of mirroring spirits, that reflect it with joyful and varied capacity, but with equal consent, and It remains One and Unbroken as ever.

Different degrees of glory are evidenced by the Saints manifesting themselves in one or other of the nine graduated Heavens, yet each abides, indeed, in the very heart of Para-

The Ascension through the Heavens to the Paradiso.

(6)

dise. The Saint who has attained least is *there* as truly as the Seraphim who is 'most absorbed in God.'

Each and 'all make beautiful the primal circle, and have sweet life in different degrees by feeling more or less the Eternal Breath.'

Light, Music, and joyous rhythmic Motion are the only outward and visible signs of the Harmony and Joy that prevail. The forms of the redeemed spirits are not defined, except as concealed in their own light, till at last, in the mystic White Rose, the Seer is able to discern their unveiled countenances, or is, perhaps, granted a fore-gleam of their future glory in the white-robed garments of the restored body. For this restitution of the whole man they are represented as awaiting the Morning of the Resurrection.

The Beatific Vision, the consummation of the whole Poem, for which each step of the Way has been preparing the Pilgrim, must be reverently studied by itself after our gradual approach to its excelling Glory.

(7)

WISDOM OF SOLOMON VII. 22-27.

'WISDOM, which is the worker of all things, taught me: for in her is an understanding spirit, holy, one only, manifold, subtil, lively, clear, undefiled, plain, not subject to hurt, loving the thing that is good, quick, which cannot be letted, ready to do good, kind to man, steadfast, sure, free from care, having all power, overseeing all things, and going through all understanding, pure, and most subtil, spirits. For Wisdom is more moving than any motion: she passeth and goeth through all things by reason of her pureness. For she is the breath of the power of God, and a pure influence flowing from the glory of the Almighty: therefore can no defiled thing fall into her. For she is the brightness of the everlasting light, the unspotted mirror of the power of God, and the image of His goodness. And being but one, she can do all things: and remaining in herself, she maketh all things new: and in all ages entering into holy souls, she maketh them friends of God, and prophets.'

Dante has been, he says, in the highest Light of Heaven, and has seen that which, in his descent, he cannot repeat.

─── (I) ───

PARADISO, CANTO I. 1-12.

LA gloria di Colui, che tutto muove,
    Per l' universo penetra, e risplende
    In una parte più, e meno altrove.
Nel ciel, che più della sua luce prende,
    Fu' io, e vidi cose, che ridire   5
    Nè sa, nè può qual di lassù discende;
Perchè appressando sè al suo disire,
    Nostro intelletto si profonda tanto,
    Che la memoria retro non può ire.
Veramente quant' io del regno santo   10
    Nella mia mente potei far tesoro,
    Sarà ora materia del mio canto.

'Let Thy Light and Thy Truth lead me.'

— (I) —

'THE Glory of Him who moves and penetrates the Universe' are the first words we hear at the entrance of this third Realm of Spirits; they are addressed to us from the midst of the after-glow of its consummate Vision. The last quivering beam of transcendent Light seems to have just passed away, and the Seer, filled to overflowing with the effulgence he has beheld, knows that, in his descent from that glorious Mount of Transfiguration, his memory will not hold that which had flooded the depths of his mind. He invokes harmonious music to breathe forth from his soul, and with power Divine to make manifest the shadow, even, of the blessed realm that does remain treasured within.

We may recall here the concluding lines of each portion of the Poem, for these mark significantly steps in spiritual progress. We learn at the same time to behold the stars, as Dante plainly did, as Sacramental witnesses to the Order of God's Universe.

On issuing from the uttermost darkness of the Inferno he re-beholds them in the distant sky, and welcomes the sight of them as a restoration to a lost consciousness.

In the last line of the Purgatorio, cleansed with baptisms of Water and Fire, he recognises in himself the new life which disposes him to mount *unto the stars.* He would fain be amongst their undeviating courses and ministries, and in the secret of their abiding order.

Lastly, at the end of the Paradiso, he perceives that his own will and desires are moved by the 'same Love that moves the Sun and the other Stars,' and he is aware that his heart now beats in instinctive union with the Central Heart of the Universe.

Dante sees Beatrice's intense gaze at the Sun, and learns to direct his eyes to the same Source.

(II)

PARADISO, CANTO I. 37-57.

SURGE a' mortali per diverse foci
   La lucerna del mondo : ma da quella,
   Che quattro cerchi giunge con tre croci,
Con miglior corso e con migliore stella   40
   Esce congiunta, e la mondana cera
   Più a suo modo tempera e suggella.
Fatto avea di là mane, e di qua sera
   Tal foce ; e quasi tutto era là bianco
   Quello emisperio, e l' altra parte nera ;   45
Quando Beatrice in sul sinistro fiance
   Vidi rivolta, e riguardar nel Sole :
   Aquila sì non gli s' affisse unquanco.
E sì come secondo raggio suole
   Uscir del primo, e risalire in suso,   50
   Pur come peregrin che tornar vuole ;
Così dell' atto suo, per gli occhi infuso
   Nell' immagine mia, lo mio si fece ;
   E fissi gli occhi al Sole oltre a nostr' uso.
Molto è licito là, che qui non lece   55
   Alle nostre virtù, mercè del loco
   Fatto per proprio dell' umana spece.

The Pilgrim of the sky with larger, other eyes transcends his former powers of vision.

(II)

THE Sun arose, we are told, at the most propitious moment for Dante's mysterious ascent, when he and Beatrice stood to welcome the advent of the World's Lamp. This was when the Sun was in Aries and the three Circles —the Equator, Ecliptic, and the Equinoctial Colure—meet, forming three crosses with the horizon. These are supposed to awaken associations with the Creation, Incarnation, and the Crucifixion, each mystery having been manifested in the season of Spring.

Statius and Matilda have vanished, leaving Dante and his Celestial Guide alone for their ascent of Heart and Mind. She intently fixes her eyes on the Sun, more intently than the upsoaring Eagle, who mounts thitherward on strongest wing; and he, whom she guides and inspires, learns from her gaze the first law of the purely Spiritual Kingdom—to seek the uncreated Light, the Source of all illumination.

He finds he may transcend the natural laws of Earth, for he starts from the plane of the restored Eden, to which environment the primal man had been adjusted, with whose powers the regenerate man is supposed to be reinstated.

Can we, indeed, measure or define the limits of man's powers in the Spirit, since we know that we are born of the Infinite One, and that our Lord has not only said, 'With God all things are possible,' but 'All things are possible to him that believeth'?

Note lines 48-54, and the beautiful simile of the second ray that issues from the first, and reascends 'like to a Pilgrim who would fain return.' Dante likens himself to this second ray, which he deems as kindled through beholding Beatrice's gaze on the Sun.

Dante learns to assimilate the new element by fixing his eyes on Beatrice's eyes.

───── (III) ─────

PARADISO, CANTO I. 58-84.

IO nol soffersi molto nè sì poco,
   Ch' io nol vedessi sfavillar d' intorno,
   Qual ferro che bollente esce dal fuoco.   60
E di subito parve giorno a giorno
   Essere aggiunto, come Quei che puote
   Avesse 'l ciel d' un altro Sole adorno.
Beatrice tutta nell' eterne ruote
   Fissa con gli occhi stava, ed io in lei   65
   Le luci fissi, di lassù remote ;
Nel suo aspetto tal dentro mi fei,
   Qual si fe Glauco nel gustar dell' erba,
   Che 'l fe consorto in mar degli altri Dei.
Trasumanar significar per verba   70
   Non si poria ; però l' esempio basti
   A cui l' esperïenza grazia serba.
S' io era sol di me quel che creasti
   Novellamente, Amor che 'l ciel governi,
   Tu 'l sai, che col tuo lume mi levasti.   75
Quando la ruota, che tu sempiterni
   Desiderato, a sè mi fece atteso
   Con l' armonia che temperi e discerni,
Parvemi tanto allor del cielo acceso
   Dalla fiamma del Sol, che pioggia o fiume   80
   Lago non fece mai tanto disteso.
La novità del suono, e 'l grande lume,
   Di lor cagion m' accesero un disio
   Mai non sentito di cotanto acume.

'Then by a Sun-beame I will climb to Thee.'

───────────── (III) ─────────────

THE light of the Sun is doubled as they ascend, and the Aspirant's eyes have not yet learnt to continue the steadfast gaze he had for a short time maintained. He finds he must withdraw them and fix them upon Beatrice. Even the regenerate man, led by the Spirit, cannot concentrate his vision on the Supreme Source of Light alone. 'The Light of the Knowledge of the glory of God is revealed in the face of Jesus Christ'—revealed, yet veiled also, in the flesh of the Son of Man.

Dante must be nourished by the food of the new element he has entered. Ere he could bear the splendour of the Light, and be lifted by it beyond himself, he must 'transhumanize' or pass over from human to Divine consciousness. Some measure of these transcendent things must be experienced, for language cannot convey them to us.

A new sound broke upon the Pilgrim's ear, as the double flaming of the Sun's light broke upon his vision. He was in the midst of the music of the spheres. Their motion uttered, and was caused by, their desire for God. These sounds, in orderly harmony, spoke the Peace of Heaven.

He longs to know the cause of the sound, and of the light, and is told by Beatrice that he is no longer, as he had falsely imagined, on Earth, but has unconsciously passed into the first Heaven.

Through pure desire, and through Divine Grace, not through effort, the transition has been made.

*Dante cannot understand the contradiction of physical
laws in the spiritual world.*

(IV)

PARADISO, CANTO I. 97-123.

GIÀ contento requïevi
    Di grand' ammirazion ; ma ora ammiro
    Com' io trascenda questi corpi lievi.
Ond' ella, appresso d' uno pio sospiro,   100
    Gli occhi drizzò vèr me con quel sembiante
    Che madre fa sopra figliuol deliro ;
E cominciò : Le cose tutte quante
    Hann' ordine tra loro ; e questo è forma,
    Che l' universo a Dio fa somigliante.   105
Qui veggion l' alte creature l' orma
    Dell' eterno valore, il quale è fine,
    Al quale è fatta la toccata norma.
Nell' ordine ch' io dico sono accline
    Tutte nature per diverse sorti   110
    Più al principio loro, e men vicine :
Onde si muovono, a diversi porti
    Per lo gran mar dell' essere ; e ciascuna
    Con istinto a lei dato che la porti.
Questi ne porta il fuoco invèr la Luna :   115
    Questi ne' cuor mortali è permotore :
    Questi la terra in sè stringe ed aduna.
Nè pur le creature, che son fuore
    D' intelligenzia, quest' arco saetta,
    Ma quella c' hanno intelletto ed amore.   120
La provvidenza, che cotanto assetta,
    Del suo lume fa 'l ciel sempre quïeto,
    Nel qual si volge quel c' ha maggior fretta.

'Not with Outward Maker's force' but 'like inward Father.'

―――――――――― (IV) ――――

D ANTE is puzzled by his strange ascent in contradiction to the law of gravitation. In the realm of spirit we cannot reason from physical laws; his questionings are like those of Nicodemus: 'How can a man be born again? Can he enter a second time into his mother's womb and be born?'

The paradoxes of the worlds of sense and of Spirit must, indeed, continually puzzle us here. The answer of Beatrice and the imagery of lines 100-102 suggest to us that we are all immature, and not only so, but mostly sick with fever and delirium, and that it is with a sigh and with tender motherly compassion that the Celestial Wisdom looks upon us and listens to our babblings.

Beatrice teaches the disciple something of the Providence and Order of the Universe, whose pattern is in God; and he learns that all things, by a law within, are tending towards the great Centre of Being. So, truly, another law of gravity is disclosed, which must as necessarily draw his spirit upwards as the rivulet must necessarily, in the physical world, gravitate from a high mountain to the lowlands.

If the Spirit of the living God be in us, we must needs draw Homewards to Him. The marvel would be 'to be *seated down below*' while that living fire, ever tending upwards to its home, is within.

Order is the technical expression for dependence of the lower beings on the Highest, and for the revelation of the Power of the Highest in the lower (103-105).

The new law of gravitation revealed to Dante.

―――――――――― (IV) ――――――――

(Continued from last page.)

PARADISO, CANTO I. 136-142.

*   *   *   *   *

Non déi più ammirar, se bene stimo,
  Lo tuo salir se non come d' un rivo,
  Che d' alto monte scende giuso ad imo.
Maraviglia sarebbe in te, se, privo
  D' impedimento, giù ti fossi assiso,   140
  Com' a terra quïeto il fuoco vivo.
Quinci rivolse invèr lo cielo il viso.

'―― *that which drew from out the boundless deep
Turns again Home.*'

(IV)

In the 'Convito' (IV. 8) Dante quotes St. Thomas Aquinas as saying, 'To know the order of one thing to another is the proper Act of reason.' 'To perceive dependencies in Nature is to perceive unity, and therefore to perceive the Form that makes the Universe resemble God. . . . The lowest rests on the highest, and not the highest on the lowest. Things are substantial just in proportion to their degree of participation in the Divine self-activity.—W. T. HARRIS.

In our selection for to-day it is as though we caught the distant sound of the music of the spheres. Hope, with its lyre of many broken strings, vibrates again to the assurance that every creature, from the highest, 'with intellect and love,' to the lowest, 'with instinct given,' is endowed with its innate Pilot, who conducts each, 'freighted with experience,' by diverse passages to the one true Haven of Rest.

'Who dost so strongly and so sweetly move,
While all things have their will, yet none but Thine.'
GEO. HERBERT.

The swift motion of desire carries Dante into the first Heavens, the Eternal Pearl of the Moon.

———— (V) ——

PARADISO, CANTO II. 19-45.

<blockquote>

LA concreata e perpetua sete
   Del deiforme regno cen portava   20
   Veloci quasi come 'l ciel vedete.
Beatrice in suso, ed io in lei guardava:
   E forse in tanto, in quanto un quadrel posa
   E vola e dalla noce si dischiava,
Giunto mi vidi, ove mirabil cosa   25
   Mi tolse 'l viso a sè. E però quella,
   Cui non potea mia cura essere ascosa,
Volta vêr me sì lieta, come bella:
   Drizza la mente in Dio grata, mi disse,
   Che n' ha congiunti con la prima stella.   30
Pareva a me che nube ne coprisse
   Lucida, spessa, solida e pulita,
   Quasi adamante che lo Sol ferisse.
Per entro sè l' eterna margherita
   Ne ricevette, com' acqua recepe   35
   Raggio di luce, permanendo unita.
S' io era corpo (e qui non si concepe
   Com' una dimensione altra patìo,
   Ch' esser convien se corpo in corpo repe),
Accender ne dovria più il disio   40
   Di veder quella essenzia, in che si vede
   Come nostra natura e Dio s' unìo.
Lì si vedrà ciò che tenem per fede,
   Non dimostrato, ma fia per sè noto,
   A guisa del ver primo, che l' uom crede.   45

</blockquote>

' —— *that which drew from out the boundless deep*
Turns again Home.'

(IV)

In the 'Convito' (IV. 8) Dante quotes St. Thomas Aquinas as saying, 'To know the order of one thing to another is the proper Act of reason.' 'To perceive dependencies in Nature is to perceive unity, and therefore to perceive the Form that makes the Universe resemble God. . . . The lowest rests on the highest, and not the highest on the lowest. Things are substantial just in proportion to their degree of participation in the Divine self-activity.—W. T. HARRIS.

In our selection for to-day it is as though we caught the distant sound of the music of the spheres. Hope, with its lyre of many broken strings, vibrates again to the assurance that every creature, from the highest, 'with intellect and love,' to the lowest, 'with instinct given,' is endowed with its innate Pilot, who conducts each, 'freighted with experience,' by diverse passages to the one true Haven of Rest.

'Who dost so strongly and so sweetly move,
While all things have their will, yet none but Thine.'
GEO. HERBERT.

The swift motion of desire carries Dante into the first Heavens, the Eternal Pearl of the Moon.

——————(V)——

PARADISO, CANTO II. 19-45.

LA concreata e perpetua sete
    Del deiforme regno cen portava   20
    Veloci quasi come 'l ciel vedete.
Beatrice in suso, ed io in lei guardava:
    E forse in tanto, in quanto un quadrel posa
    E vola e dalla noce si dischiava,
Giunto mi vidi, ove mirabil cosa   25
    Mi tolse 'l viso a sè. E però quella,
    Cui non potea mia cura essere ascosa,
Volta vêr me sì lieta, come bella:
    Drizza la mente in Dio grata, mi disse,
    Che n' ha congiunti con la prima stella.   30
Pareva a me che nube ne coprisse
    Lucida, spessa, solida e pulita,
    Quasi adamante che lo Sol ferisse.
Per entro sè l' eterna margherita
    Ne ricevette, com' acqua recepe   35
    Raggio di luce, permanendo unita.
S' io era corpo (e qui non si concepe
    Com' una dimensione altra patío,
    Ch' esser convien se corpo in corpo repe),
Accender ne dovria più il disio   40
    Di veder quella essenzia, in che si vede
    Come nostra natura e Dio s' unío.
Lì si vedrà ciò che tenem per fede,
    Non dimostrato, ma fia per sè noto,
    A guisa del ver primo, che l' uom crede.   45

God communicates Himself to the longing soul, for His nature and ours are blended.

(V)

THE Picture of the great Sea of Being tarries in Dante's mind's eye, and he imagines 'his own Ship that singing sails along' upon the bosom of the Ocean of unseen Spirit life, piloted by Divine Wisdom, Harmony, and Art. With something like a smile of scornful pity, he addresses others in 'some pretty little boats' that may be following in his wake, and bids them beware of being lost on such an untried voyage, unless, indeed, they had been fitted for it by the Bread of Angels—the 'daily Manna' without which (as the Lord's Prayer is paraphrased, Purgatorio, XI. 12),

'In this rough wilderness,
Backward goes he who toils most to advance.'

But fed thus, he says, and with their own thirst for the Deiform realm, others may follow him and be borne onwards as he and Beatrice were, as swiftly as the Heavens themselves.

Our own thirst for the spiritual, inspired by heavenly grace can alone carry us on to Divine knowledge.

The Heaven of the Moon, that nearest to the Earth, is the first symbol perceived by Dante of one of many Mansions, or resting-places, in the Father's House. The Cone of the Earth's shadow touches it, and this (as Dante supposes) extends also over the two succeeding heavens of Mercury and Venus. This shadow intimates that the spirits who manifest themselves in these three spheres are in lower degrees of the glory that differentiates one star from another.

Dante describes his entrance into this star as being like that of a ray of light into water, without any displacement of matter, and is led to feel after the intimate union of the Divine and the Human.

PARADISO, CANTO III. 37-57.

O BEN creato spirito, che a' rai
    Di vita eterna la dolcezza senti,
    Che, non gustata, non s' intende mai,
Grazïoso mi fia, se mi contenti   40
    Del nome tuo e della vostra sorte.
    Ond' ella pronta e con occhi ridenti:
La nostra carità non serra porte
    A giusta voglia, se non come quella
    Che vuol simile a sè tutta sua corte.   45
Io fui nel mondo vergine sorella;
    E se la mente tua ben mi riguarda,
    Non mi ti celerà l' esser più bella;
Ma riconoscerai che io son Piccarda,
    Che, posta qui con questi altri beati,   50
    Beata son nella spera più tarda.
Li nostri affetti, che solo infiammati
    Son del piacer dello Spirito santo,
    Letizian dal suo ordine formati.
E questa sorte, che par giù cotanto,   55
    Però n' è data, perchè fur negletti
    Li nostri voti, e vôti in alcun canto.

'Unstable as Water, thou shalt not excel.'
Yet—'Out of weakness made strong.'

(VI)

IN this first heaven of imperfect wills, spirits were seen by Dante as though reflected in water, or as outlines of faces, no more salient than a pearl on a white forehead. He fancied them but mirrored semblances, till Beatrice encouraged him to speak to one who seemed anxious to address him.

Perhaps weakness of character is intended to be expressed by such faint and shadowy images.

Dante places infirmity of purpose and weak refusal of responsibility as signs of the first downward steps in hell, and makes them characteristic also of the lowest grade in Paradise. It is Piccarda Donati, the sister of Corso and Forese, and (it is believed) Dante's own sister-in-law, with whom he converses. She was a Nun, and against her will was forced to leave her Convent and marry.

It is affirmed later that 'Will is never quenched unless it will'; and, even where physical violence prevails, Will must triumph in death rather than yield. Dante begins to question her with reverent curiosity concerning the sweetness of Eternal life, 'which being untasted ne'er is comprehended.' She answers with laughing eyes, and says he does not at once recognise her, because she is more fair. He had in purgatory met Forese and inquired of him concerning her; he spoke of his sister as not knowing whether she was more beautiful or good, and as having already obtained her crown. She declares herself to be blest in the slowest and lowest sphere of the Heavens, for she rejoices in the Holy Spirit and in the Order ordained by Him.

Dante learns from Piccarda that the supreme joy of Heaven is perfect union with the Divine Will.

(VII)

PARADISO, CANTO III. 64-90.

MA dimmi: Voi che siete qui felici,
   Desiderate voi più alto loco,   65
     Per più vedere, o per più farvi amici?
Con quell' altr' ombre pria sorrise un poco;
   Da indi mi rispose tanto lieta,
     Ch' arder parea d' amor nel primo fuoco:
Frate, la nostra volontà quïeta   70
   Virtù di carità, che fa volerne
     Sol quel ch' avemo, e d' altro non ci asseta.
Se disiassimo esser più superne,
   Foran discordi gli nostri disiri
     Dal voler di Colui che qui ne cerne;   75
Che vedrai non capere in questi giri,
   S' essere in caritate è qui necesse,
     E se la sua natura ben rimiri;
Anzi è formale ad esto beato esse
   Tenersi dentro alla divina voglia,   80
     Perch' una fansi nostre voglie stesse.
Sì che, come noi siam di soglia in soglia
   Per questo regno, a tutto il regno piace,
     Com' allo re, che in suo voler ne invoglia.
In la sua volontade è nostra pace: 85
   Ella è quel mare, al qual tutto si muove
     Ciò ch' ella cria, o che natura face.
Chiaro mi fu allor com' ogni dove
   In cielo è paradiso, e sì la grazia
     Del sommo ben d' un modo non vi piove.   90

Humility is the Throne of Love and Peace.

(VII)

THERE is great sweetness in these questions and answers on the lowest step of the heavenly throne.

Dante, with his soaring nature and intense earnestness to know and to extend fellowship in the joy of Communion, inquires of Piccarda, whether she and other spirits in this slowest, lowest sphere are not 'desirous of a higher place, and to make more friends.' [Or, perhaps, to make more friends with God. See line 66; also XXV. 90.]

Her look round on her companions, sure of full assent from them while giving her own smiling answer, and her glow in the grace and fire of love, seem to pulsate with Heaven's own atmosphere. The One Will, the fount of Peace filling and attracting every lower Will, is the Goal of the onward movement of every form of life on the Ocean of Being, which we read of in Beatrice's revealing utterance (Canto I. 112):

> 'And His Will is our peace; this is the Sea
> To which is moving onward whatsoever
> It doth create, and all that nature makes.'

Though Piccarda had failed in the strength of purpose she would have attained by allying herself completely with the Divine Will on Earth, here she is presented to us as a blossom floating on the bosom of that Ocean of rest, swayed by its undulations alone, in absolute peace of Union with itself. Her words convince Dante that every part and grade within that Will's dominion of Peace is Paradise, even though God rain His Graces in different measures upon different spheres.

Dante is taught that all in Paradise are alike near to God, but are manifested according to sense-apprehension in different grades of merit.

———————————— (VIII) ————————

PARADISO, CANTO IV. 28-48.

DE' Serafin colui che più s' india,
    Moisè, Samuello, e quel Giovanni,
    Qual prender vuogli, io dico, non Maria,   30
Non hanno in altro cielo i loro scanni,
    Che quegli spirti che mo t' appariro,
    Nè hanno all' esser lor più o men anni :
Ma tutti fanno bello il primo giro ;
    E differentemente han dolce vita,   35
    Per sentir più e men l' eterno spiro.
Qui si mostraro, non perchè sortita
    Sia questa spera lor, ma per far segno
    Della celestïal, c' ha men salita.
Così parlar conviensi al vostro ingegno ;   40
    Perocchè solo da sensato apprende
    Ciò, che fa poscia d' intelletto degno.
Per questo la Scrittura condiscende
    A vostra facultate, e piedi e mano
    Attribuisce a Dio, ed altro intende :   45
E santa Chiesa con aspetto umano
    Gabbriele e Michel vi rappresenta,
    E l' altro, che Tobbia rifece sano.

(VIII)

FURTHER questions arise in Dante's mind as he turns again to Beatrice; questions concerning Free-will and Force with regard to broken vows; questions also about the Platonic doctrine of the Soul's return to the Stars. We cannot follow these. His Celestial Guide reads his inner questioning without his utterance. She assures him that the Seraphim who is most *immersed* in God (remark the expression, line 28, 'che più s'india'), and the most exalted Saint, with these who appear in lower spheres, have all one standing in the abode of God, though they manifest themselves according to their merits to make sign to his limited apprehension, even as Scripture language is fitted to men's sense-apprehensions.

She says 'all make beautiful the primal sphere,' as though the more or less of the Eternal Breath that filled each contributed in some way to the beautiful motion and scintillation of the 'sweet life.' No thought of exclusion or remoteness could be the portion of any one palpitating with this Life of Love's unity and variety.

Dante expresses his joyful gratitude to Beatrice for her life-giving words of Truth.

(IX)

PARADISO, CANTO IV. 115-132.

COTAL fu l' ondeggiar del santo rio,   115
  Ch' uscì del fonte ond' ogni ver deriva,
  Tal pose in pace uno ed altro disio.
O amanza del primo Amante, o diva,
  Diss' io appresso, il cui parlar m' innonda
  E scalda sì, che più e più m' avviva ;   120
Non è l' affezion mia tanto profonda,
  Che basti a render voi grazia per grazia ;
  Ma Quei, che vede e puote, a ciò risponda.
Io veggio ben che giammai non si sazia
  Nostro intelletto, se 'l ver non lo illustra,   125
  Di fuor dal qual nessun vero si spazia.
Posasi in esso come fera in lustra,
  Tosto che giunto l' ha : e giunger puollo ;
  Se non, ciascun disio sarebbe frustra.
Nasce per quello, a guisa di rampollo,   130
  Appiè del vero il dubbio ; ed è natura,
  Ch' al sommo pinge noi di collo in collo.

'When He, the Spirit of Truth, is come, He will guide you into all Truth.

(IX)

IN this address to Beatrice, Dante leads us beyond any limit of the personality that clings to her name by speaking of her words as—

' The flowing of the holy river
That issued from the font whence springs all truth ;'

and of herself as being 'the Beloved of the first Lover.' Wisdom, speaking of the Creator, says, 'Then I was by Him as one brought up with Him, and I was daily His delight, rejoicing always before Him.'—Prov. viii. 30.

The holy River's reviving power convinced Dante that the mind could never be satisfied without Truth. He sees it is fitted for its resting-place as a *creature fits its lair*. Man desires Truth, which proves (he believes) that man can attain it (128).

'Man is in quest of truth, is in perplexity about it ; he was created in it and for it, for none can seek for anything but that which is lost, *is wanted*—nor could one form the least idea of it, but because it has belonged to him and ought to be his.'—WM. LAW.

Lines 130-132 are especially to be noted, as showing us the Seer's conception of Doubt in its healthy condition. He regards it as an offshoot from the living tree of Truth, springing up at its root, and stimulating to further inquiry and to further attainment of vital knowledge. Contrast with this the Doubt, represented by Medusa's stony gaze, which quenched all vitality (Inferno, IX. 51).

'The Inquiry of Truth, which is the love-making or wooing of it ; the Knowledge of Truth, which is the presence of it ; and the Belief of Truth, which is the enjoying of it ; is the sovereign good of human nature.'—BACON'S 'Essays.'

Beatrice tells Dante her flaming love arises from her perfect vision of the Eternal Light.

(X)

PARADISO, CANTO V. 1-12.

S' IO ti fiammeggio nel caldo d' amore
   Di là dal modo che in terra si vede,
   Sì che degli occhi tuoi vinco 'l valore,
Non ti maravigliar, chè ciò procede
   Da perfetto veder, che, come apprende,   5
   Così nel bene appreso muove il piede.
Io veggio ben sì come già risplende
   Nello intelletto tuo l' eterna luce,
   Che vista sola sempre amore accende:
E s' altra cosa vostro amor seduce,   10
   Non è se non di quella alcun vestigio
   Mal conosciuto, che quivi traluce.

'We needs must love the highest when we see it.'

(X)

THE fuller vision of the Truth must ever kindle the heart into a more ardent embrace of the Truth. This thought is continually presented to us, as we ascend the pathway that lies before us for heart and mind. Dante teaches that the mind, or the capacity for perception, must go before the capacity for loving and set that on fire.

Wisdom's eyes are aflame with love, through her gaze into the Light or Truth. We are not taught to weigh the Heart and the Mind in the balances one against the other, but rather that 'they are halves of one dissevered world'—the one hemisphere of intelligence awakening first, as it were, through the shining of the Light into darkness, and then causing the affections to awaken and to rejoice with the mind in their object.

> 'I too have sought to KNOW as thou to LOVE—
> Excluding love as thou refusedst knowledge.
>   *   *   *   *   *
> Are we not halves of one dissevered world?
>   l'art? never!
> Till thou the lover, know; and I, the knower
> Love—until both are saved.'
>   PARACELSUS.

Swiftly, as an arrow finds its mark, they reach Mercury, where those are seen who for Fame did great deeds.

———————————— (XI) ————————————

PARADISO, CANTO V. 85-105.

<pre>
COSÌ Beatrice a me com' io lo scrivo :   85
   Poi si rivolse tutta disïante
   A quella parte ove 'l mondo è più vivo.
Lo suo tacere e 'l tramutar sembiante
   Poser silenzio al mio cupido ingegno,
   Che già nuove quistioni avea davanti,   90
E sì come saetta, che nel segno
   Percuote pria che sia la corda queta,
   Così corremmo nel secondo regno.
Quivi la Donna mia vid' io sì lieta,
   Come nel lume di quel ciel si mise,   95
   Che più lucente se ne fe il pianeta.
E se la stella si cambiò e rise,
   Qual mi fec' io, che pur di mia natura
   Trasmutabile son per tutte guise !
Come in peschiera ch' è tranquilla e pura   100
   Traggono i pesci a ciò che vien di fuori,
   Per modo che lo stimin lor pastura ;
Sì vid' io ben più di mille splendori
   Trarsi vêr noi ; ed in ciascun s' udia :
   Ecco chi crescerà li nostri amori.   105
</pre>

'Life upsprings aspiring to be Immortality.'

(XI)

AFTER further discourse on broken vows and imperfection of Will, Beatrice turns again towards 'that part where the world is most alive,' most alive with Light: both were silent as they beheld and received it. 'Voir, c'est avoir,' it has been said. Seeing with eyes of the Spirit is truly to hold and to have, and so they found themselves swiftly borne into the Heaven of Mercury.

The spirits of those who have done great deeds manifest themselves here; but their great deeds were not done from wholly pure motives, rather for Fame than for the noble cause itself.

'Fame is the reflection not of the deed itself, shining in us, as inspired by the deepest conviction, but the reflection of the deed shining in the recognition of our fellow-men.'—W. T. HARRIS.

'Nay, rather for the sake of me, their King,
And the deed's sake, my knighthood do the deed,
Than to be noised of.'—TENNYSON.

The star was changed and became more luminous as they entered it, and still more, Dante says, he, 'so mutable,' was changed by this further ascent. Beatrice was welcomed by more than a thousand 'splendours,' as the spirits are called.

The simile of the gold-fish in the pure and tranquil pool, drawing to that part where something reaches them from without, deeming it as food, intimately pictures that welcome. They say, 'Lo, this is one who shall increase our Love!' as the newcomer reaches their Circle. We long for such expansiveness and such ardour in our own social life, as well as for the vital power that would so welcome Wisdom's Divine nutrition within.

The little Star is adorned with good and active spirits whose desires had deviated from the highest goal.

— (XII) —

PARADISO, CANTO VI. 112-126.

QUESTA piccola stella si correda
   De' buoni spirti, che son stati attivi,
   Perchè onore e fama gli succeda:
E quando li desiri poggian quivi   115
   Sì disvïando, pur convien che i raggi
   Del vero amore in su poggin men vivi.
Ma nel commensurar de' nostri gaggi
   Col merto, è parte di nostra letizia,
   Perchè non li vedem minor nè maggi.   120
Quinci addolcisce la viva giustizia
   In noi l' affetto sì, che non si puote
   Torcer giammai ad alcuna nequizia.
Diverse voci fanno dolci note:
   Così diversi scanni in nostra vita   125
   Rendon dolce armonia tra queste ruote.

'*Law seen as a Divine Element, immanent in human nature.*'

(XII)

JUSTINIAN, the Lawgiver and the Emperor, speaks in this Canto as the representative of the orderly rule established on earth for the right conduct of men. He recounts the history and triumph of the Sacred Symbol of the Roman Eagle. Later, in the sixth Heaven of Jupiter, we shall see the Celestial Eagle, the ideal and sublimated Justice, by virtue of which alone this lower manifestation of Law and Justice had existed.

Justinian explains the deviation from the highest motive that has characterized the active spirits that belong to this sphere of Mercury.

They have nobly worked, in order that fame and honour might come after them, but not with that single-eyed love that mounts directly upwards. They were, however, so disinterested, so kindled, by living Justice, that their happiness is increased by reason of the measure of their joy being so truly adjusted to their deserts. Again, as in the first Heaven, the varieties of diverse voices and spheres are dwelt upon as contributing to the harmony of the whole.

Beatrice assures Dante that God's mode of redemption could only be understood by love; and restoration could only be through Divine Humility.

───────── (XIII) ─────────

PARADISO, CANTO VII. 55-60, 97-120.

TU dici : Ben discerno ciò ch' i' odo ;   55
  Ma perchè Dio volesse, m' è occulto,
  A nostra redenzion pur questo modo.
Questo decreto, frate, sta sepulto
  Agli occhi di ciascuno, il cui ingegno
  Nella fiamma d' amor non è adulto.   60

  *   *   *   *   *

Non potea l' uomo ne' termini suoi
  Mai satisfar, per non potere ir giuso
  Con umiltade, obbediendo poi,
Quanto disubbidiendo intese ir suso.   100
  E questa è la ragion, perchè l' uom fue
  Da poter satisfar per sè dischiuso.
Dunque a Dio convenia con le vie sue
  Riparar l' uomo a sua intera vita :
  Dico con l' una, ovver con ambedue.   105
Ma perchè l' opra tanto è più gradita
  Dell' operante, quanto più appresenta
  Della bontà del cuore ond' è uscita ;
La divina bontà, che 'l mondo imprenta,
  Di proceder per tutte le sue vie   110
  A rilevarvi suso fu contenta.
Nè tra l' ultima notte e 'l primo die
  Sì alto e sì magnifico processo,
  O per l' una o per l' altro fue, o fie.
Chè più largo fu Dio a dar sè stesso   115
  In far l' uom sufficiente a rilevarsi,
  Che s egli avesse sol da sè dimesso.
E tutti gli altri modi erano scarsi
  Alla giustizia, se 'l Figliuol di Dio
  Non fosse umiliato ad incarnarsi.   120

'So deeply had human pride sunk us, that nothing but Divine Humility could raise us.'

---(XIII)---

THE Crucifixion under the Roman rule is spoken of earlier in this Canto, and leads to Dante's questionings concerning the mysteries of Adam's Fall, the Incarnation and the Atonement. These should be studied with the context, and not divided here into fragments. Dean Plumptre tells us that Dante's theory of the Atonement is not identical with that of the early Church, or that of Anselm, or that of Aquinas, or that of a Vicarious Satisfaction, which has been predominant in Protestant theology. Among the great mediæval theologians, Hugh of St. Victor seems the one in whose footsteps he treads most closely.

Whatever may be our Christian creed, the two portions that have been selected cannot but aid our thoughts concerning these great themes.

Dante's question has been one that has arisen in many minds. Could not God have pardoned man without the Incarnation and the Passion? In our first six lines for to-day he is told that this mystery of the Atonement must remain buried before the eyes of one whose very nature has not been matured in the flame of Love. In the second part, he seems taught that mankind, in proud and independent aspiration (or presumption?) had so lost the possibility of the lowliness necessary for the reception of God's Truth, that nothing but the sinking of the Divine Son within humanity could restore man's nature and render possible Humility's descent with Himself. So God would descend into the very depths of man's littleness, with its debased flesh conditions, that He might renew His creature's whole life with the gift of Himself, and raise man to the Divine Goodness. In such a way, God's love would be brought infinitely more within touch than by a free pardon without it.

The ways of Providence are spoken of by Charles Martel as astral influences.

— (XIV) —

PARADISO, CANTO VIII. 97-111.

LO Ben che tutto 'l regno che tu scandi
    Volge e contenta, fa esser virtute
    Sua provedenza in questi corpi grandi;
E non pur le nature provvedute   100
    Son nella mente, ch' è da sè perfetta,
    Ma esse insieme con la lor salute.
Per che quantunque quest' arco saetta,
    Disposto cade a provveduto fine,
    Sì come cocca in suo segno diretta.   105
Se ciò non fosse, il ciel, che tu cammine,
    Producerebbe sì li suoi effetti,
    Che non sarebber arti, ma ruine :
E ciò esser non può, se gl' intelletti,
    Che muovon queste stelle, non son manchi,   110
    E manco 'l primo, che non gli ha perfetti.

'If man constantly aspires, is he not elevated?'

(XIV)

IN the earlier lines of this Canto we read of the ascent of the Aspirant to the third Heaven of Venus, and are again told that he was only aware of the ascent through beholding more radiancy and beauty in the Countenance of his Celestial Guide.

The spirits in this sphere of Venus are seen as lamps, and their motion is described as circulating more or less swiftly in proportion to their inward vision; a beautiful revelation of the unity here, between the active and contemplative life! One of those spirits, Charles Martel, son of Charles II. of Naples, had been known to Dante; he tells Dante that he is concealed from him by the gladness that is rayed round about him, and 'hides him even as a creature is swathed in its own silk.' As the poor souls were seen in the dark world, swathing themselves in the flames of their passions, so it is intimated here that the clothing of good works, which these spirits had spun like silk-worms in their earth-life, was shining with their own transfiguring joy. We are reminded here of Milton's Sonnet:

> 'Thy works, and alms, and all thy good endeavour
> Stay'd not behind, nor in the grave were trod;
> But, as Faith pointed with her golden rod,
> Follow'd thee up to joy and bliss for ever.
> Love led them on, and Faith, who knew them best,
> Thy handmaid, clad them o'er with purple beams
> And azure wings, that up they flew so drest,
> And spake the truth of thee on glorious themes
> Before the Judge, who thenceforth bid thee rest
> And drink thy fill of pure immortal streams.'

Seed unadapted to its soil develops ill, and men are warped from Nature's calling by perverse interference.

———————————— (XIV) ————————————

(*Continued from last page.*)

PARADISO, CANTO VIII. 139-148.

Sempre natura, se Fortuna truova
    Discorde a sè, come ogni altra semente   140
    Fuor di sua regïon, fa mala pruova.
E se 'l mondo laggiù ponesse mente
    Al fondamento che natura pone,
    Seguendo lui, avria buona la gente.
Ma voi torcete alla religïone   145
    Tal, che fu nato a cingersi la spada,
    E fate re di tal ch' è da sermone ;
Onde la traccia vostra è fuor di strada.

Heaven-born instincts are not to be resisted.

——————— (XIV) ———————

Dante is awakened into fuller joy by seeing his friend's joy. By Charles Martel's history of himself and of his successor the question is aroused in Dante's mind, given in the first line of our extract :

'How from sweet seed can bitter issue forth ?'

Truly a deep and universal question ! Our Lord Himself asks the same in His parable, but can hardly be said to answer it, 'From whence, then, hath it tares ?' (though He speaks, indeed, of an Enemy and of the sleep of man as the immediate cause). Here some interesting thoughts on the Providence of God are given, always in Dante's mind connected with the Stars, as channels of His influences and of His orderly will ; 'they receive from above and give to those below.' Charles Martel speaks of Providence as a power or law, implanted within all those vast bodies, which keeps them from falling into ruins. He also speaks of their influences preventing the effects of natural heredity amongst men by endowing them with varied qualities and varied circumstances, and tells him men are destined for diverse offices in the Commonwealth of a City ; but that Fortune's Wheel or the perverseness or carelessness of parents or governors wrests a man's natural bias aside, and makes the born soldier a monk, or the born preacher a king, and that this is one cause of much divergence from the true course.

Dante recognises a Spirit or 'Gladness' like a fine ruby bright in sunshine, Folco of Marseilles, whom he eagerly questions.

(XV)

PARADISO, CANTO IX. 67-81.

L' ALTRA letizia, che m' era già nota,
   Preclara cosa mi si fece in vista,
   Qual fin balascio in che lo Sol percuota.
Per letiziar lassù fulgor s' acquista,   70
   Sì come riso qui : ma giù s' abbuia
   L' ombra di fuor, come la mente è trista.
Dio vede tutto ; e tuo veder s' inluia,
   Diss' io, beato spirto ; sì che nulla
   Voglia di sè a te puote esser fuia.   75
Dunque la voce tua, che 'l ciel trastulla
   Sempre col canto di que' fochi pii,
   Che di sei ale fannosi cuculla,
Perchè non satisface a' miei desii ?
   Già non attendere' io tua dimanda,   80
   S' io m' intuassi, come tu t' immii.

'But when Love turns to ill, or doth pursue
Good with more eager care, or less, than right,
The thing made to its Maker works untrue.'

(XV)

THE third Heaven, like the two preceding and lower Heavens, is a heaven of imperfect wills; the imperfections of those in this sphere have been especially fostered by the influences of Love that fell short of the Divine Charity, and were allied with selfishness and disorderly action.

'The planet Venus gives notice of the rising Sun as Lucifer, and it follows the setting Sun as Hesperus; its course is back and forth along the heavenly pathway, and not always progressive.'—W. T. HARRIS.

One who speaks with Dante here says, that over it ends the shadowy Cone cast by our world; so, allegorically, it is still in the shadow of imperfect earthly affections, and excluded from the higher degrees of glory.

Yet the joys of those manifesting themselves here are undimmed by memories of their sins, though they are aware that the 'splendour of the Star had overcome their virtue.'

'We must remember that Lethe has taken away all memory of evil, and it is known to have been only what, when repented of, it actually was—a stepping-stone to higher things.'—DEAN PLUMPTRE.

Their joy flashes forth like jewels, even as smiles make radiant the countenance on earth, and as grief in the dark world darkens the sad mind's outward expression.

Dante's eager desire to know the history of one of these 'joys,' or 'glad ones,' is expressed in to-day's portion. He speaks of them as bringing joy to Heaven by their songs that ever flow from the Seraphim above, an intimation of the blessed circulation of joyous harmony throughout the many Mansions of the Father's House. The intimacy of

Dante is told that Rahab is at rest in this Heaven.

———————————— (XV) ————————————

(*Continued from last page.*)

PARADISO, CANTO IX. 115-125.

Or sappi che là entro si tranquilla 115
   Raab ; ed a nostr' ordine congiunta,
   Di lei nel sommo grado si sigilla.
Da questo cielo, in cui l' ombra s' appunta
   Che 'l vostro mondo face, pria ch' altr' alma
   Del trionfo di Cristo fu assunta, 120
Ben si convenne lei lasciar per palma,
   In alcun cielo, dell' alta vittoria,
   Ch' ei s' acquistò con l' una e l' altra palma ;
Perch' ella favorò la prima gloria
   Di Giosuè in su la terra santa. 125

the interpenetrating of spirit with spirit is expressively uttered by the verbs coined by Dante (line 81), 'S' io m' intuassi, come tu t' immii '—If I could in-thee myself as thou in-me-est thyself.

Amongst those who have been impressed by the influences of this Star, Dante is told that Rahab is resting, like a Sunbeam in the pure water. 'Before all other souls was she taken up,' set free from amongst the imprisoned ones when Christ descended into Hades.

> 'Full meet it was to leave her in some Heaven,
> Even as a palm of the high victory
> Which He acquired with one palm and the other.'

She is spoken of as having 'set her seal on the order of the Star in its *supremest grade*.' We must remember that she was looked upon as the representative of the Faith that foresaw the triumph of Joshua in opening the Land of Canaan to the Israelites, symbolizing the greater One who was to open the Kingdom of Heaven to all believers. The writer of the Hebrews cites her amongst the victorious by faith, and St. James amongst those whose faith was quickened by works. She was the ancestress of David, and therefore of David's greater Son, and is a representative of one circle of the lost ones whom He came to seek and to save. We cannot but wonder why the Magdalen's name should not be mentioned here.

Dante finds himself within the Sun, but is not conscious of his ascension except as a man is conscious, ere it come, of a first thought.

───────────── (XVI) ─────────────

PARADISO, CANTO X. 28-40.

LO ministro maggior della natura,
    Che del valor del cielo il mondo imprenta
    E col suo lume il tempo ne misura,   30
Con quella parte che su si rammenta
    Congiunto, si girava per le spire,
    In che più tosto ognora s' appresenta:
Ed io era con lui; ma del salire
    Non m' accors' io, se non com' uom s' accorge,   35
    Anzi 'l primo pensier, del suo venire.
Oh, Beatrice, quella che si scorge
    Di bene in meglio sì subitamente,
    Che l' atto suo per tempo non si porge,
Quant' esser convenia da sè lucente!   40

'The breath of God within, to Him returning.'

(XVI)

A FOURTH ascension, by means of the "radiance of grace kindling true Love, which afterwards grows by loving,' brings the Aspirant into the fourth family of Heaven. This is a wonderful description of Prayer, or Heavenly Communion. 'The love kindled from above,' that must increase by exercise (St. Thomas Aquinas, who speaks here, tells Dante), 'becomes so resplendent within, that it conducts thee upward by that stair,* where without reascending none descends.' Once having gained those heights, none can again contentedly remain below.

This is the Heaven of the Sun, the greatest Minister of Nature, who with his strength impresses the world and measures for us Time.

This sphere stands between the triplet of lower Heavens of imperfect wills and the triplet of higher Heavens of perfected Wills. It is the antithesis to the descent into the abyss of Malebolge with Geryon, which marked the transition from the weak compliance with evil impulses to that of deliberate and wilful choice of evil for self-ends. Here we are amongst the mighty who have set their faces steadfastly to the Light, and are now in the full illumination of the Spirit of God.

The great Theologians are 'the splendours,' or Suns, that belong to this Sun region of Light and Heat.

---

* The same golden stairway that will reappear later.

Dante beholds that which is incommunicable in the Source of Light, for it transcends genius and art and experience.

———————————— (XVI) ————————————

(*Continued from last page.*)

PARADISO, CANTO X. 41-48.

E quel ch' er' entro al Sol, dov' io entra' mi,
 Non per color, ma per lume, parvente,
Perch' io l' ingegno e l' arte e l' uso chiami,
 Sì nol direi, che mai s' immaginasse :
 Ma creder puossi, e di veder si brami. 45
E se le fantasie nostre son basse
 A tanta altezza, non è maraviglia ;
 Chè sovra 'l Sol non fu occhio ch' andasse.

(XVI)

In the three opening lines of this tenth Canto the doctrine of the Trinity is mystically expressed. The Holy Spirit—the Spirit of Love—is breathed forth from Father to Son and from Son to Father, and is manifested in the Order of the Universe, especially in the flaming source of Light. Dante thinks we must needs contemplate this Light with joy, and find the art of that Work-Master, 'who doth love it so within Himself, His eyes ne'er part from it.'

The Poet beseeches his readers to remain seated at the Table he spreads for them, to pursue in thought what they have foretasted, and to feed themselves (line 22); he is continually pressing upon us the truth that we cannot receive these heavenly jewels at second hand, that they cannot be transported from the realm he has visited, that each must go thither himself, if he would behold them. It is, however, a step towards seeing them to believe that another has seen beyond our own limited horizon, and we may at least long that our eyes may penetrate further. 'Come and see,' said Philip to Nathaniel.

'The greatest of the Ministers of Nature' is pointed out to us in our portion for to-day as the Visible or Sacramental form of deepest mystical significancy given to man in Nature—the wondrous sign of the invisible and spiritual grace within its rays and properties; perhaps if we knew more of these, we might through them discern more of the unseen spiritual Reality that causes them.

'For the invisible things of Him . . . are clearly seen, being understood by the things that are made.'—Rom. i. 20.

Dante, brought into the fourth Family of the Father, rejoices in thanksgiving, and becomes absorbed in God. The Sun spirits circle round him.

(XVII)

PARADISO, CANTO X. 49-66, 139-148.

TAL' era quivi la quarta famiglia
   Dell' alto Padre, che sempre la sazia,   50
   Mostrando come spira, e come figlia.
E Beatrice cominciò : Ringrazia,
   Ringrazia il Sol degli angeli, ch' a questo
   Sensibil t' ha levato per sua grazia.
Cuor di mortal non fu mai sì digesto   55
   A divozione ed a rendersi a Dio
   Con tutto 'l suo gradir cotanto presto,
Com' a quelle parole mi fec' io;
   E sì tutto 'l mio amore in lui si mise,
   Che Beatrice ecclissò nell' oblio.   60
Non le dispiacque, ma sì se ne rise,
   Che lo splendor degli occhi suoi ridenti
   Mia mente unita in più cose divise.
Io vidi più fulgor vivi e vincenti
   Far di noi centro, e di sè far corona,   65
   Più dolci in voce, che in vista lucenti.

*   *   *   *   *

Indi, come orologio, che ne chiami
   Nell' ora che la sposa di Dio surge   140
   A mattinar lo sposo perchè l' ami,
Che l' una parte l' altra tira ed urge,
   Tin tin sonando con sì dolce nota,
   Che 'l ben disposto spirto d' amor turge;
Così vid' io la gloriosa ruota   145
   Muoversi, e render voce a voce in tempra
   Ed in dolcezza, ch' esser non può nota
Se non colà dove il gioir s' insempra.

> *'God in us, from our hearts veil after veil*
> *Keeps lifting, till we see with His own sight*
> *And altogether run in unity's delight.'*

(XVII)

A GLORIOUS Vision of the Light of God, of His satisfying Portion, of the regenerating Power breathed forth in His Holy Spirit, seems to be experienced by Dante. The Celestial Guide bids the receiver of so much grace give thanks, and he tells us that never was heart of mortal so disposed

'To worship and to give itself to God.'

He was so absorbed in love to Him that for a time even Beatrice was forgotten, 'and this displeased her not'; but his human consciousness, which had been for a moment one with God (63), 'was restored to its perception of the plurality of Creation by her smile.'—PLUMPTRE.

The Lady of grace had still to continue her work of 'making the Aspirant strong for Heaven.' The spirits, whom he sees after his act of adoration and love to the 'Sun of Angels,' were vivid and triumphant as they circled three times around those whom they welcomed; they were even 'more sweet in voice than luminous in aspect.' These were great Theologians, whose voices had taught and charmed the Church. The names of seven were given by Thomas Aquinas, who was himself one of this seven-stringed lute of sweet voices. The fifth amongst these, strangely enough, was Solomon—perhaps placed with them on account of his 'Song of Songs.'

Dante is reminded of musical chimes, that call the Bride of God to matins, by the echoing of voice in answer to voice of these encircling, flaming spirits; doubtless he intends to convey the harmony of the truths they uttered and confirmed through the testimony that each gave to the teaching of the other.

PARADISO, CANTO XI. 28-42.

LA provvidenza, che governa 'l mondo,
 Con quel consiglio, nel quale ogni aspetto
 Creato è vinto, pria che vada al fondo,   30
Però ch' andasse vêr lo suo Diletto
 La sposa di Colui ch' ad alte grida
 Disposò lei col sangue benedetto,
In sè sicura ed anche a lui più fida,
 Duo principi ordinò in suo favore,   35
 Che quinci e quindi le fosser per guida.
L' un fu tutto serafico in ardore,
 L' altro per sapïenza in terra fue
 Di cherubica luce uno splendore.
Dell' un dirò, perocchè d' ambodue   40
 Si dice l' un pregiando, qual ch' uom prende,
 Perchè ad un fine fûr l' opere sue.

*'Why live
Except for love—how love, unless they know?'*

(XVIII)

IN this Canto, and the next, we are given the histories of St. Francis of Assisi and of St. Dominic, who belong to this sphere.

The first is recounted by St. Thomas Aquinas, who was a disciple of St. Dominic; while that of St. Dominic is told by St. Bonaventura, who belonged to the Order of St. Francis. Dante points out the degeneracy of these orders in later days, and evidently desires to remind them of the unity of their Founders and early disciples, as well as of the absence of all rivalry and jealousy in true spiritual life. We are told, in the portion before us, that the Providence, which cannot be fathomed by mortal sense, ordained these two spiritual Princes for His Bride the Church, that she might go towards her own Beloved between them more safely and more faithfully. One, St. Francis, was seraphic in his ardour of love; the other, St. Dominic, 'a splendour of Cherubic light and knowledge.' These two have already been represented to us in the Earthly Paradise as supporting the Biga of the Church, one at each wheel, as the Love Power and the Knowledge, or Wisdom, Power. St. Francis, portrayed by Art, bears the signs of the love-wounds of Christ; St. Dominic, the reflected Star of Christ-light. The necessity for the interaction of Heart and Mind is again brought before us.

The spirits of the Sun-realm are all spoken of as Suns, and in these two Children of the Sun we are reminded of the Heat and Light that emanate from the heavenly body.

We cannot forbear wishing that the heart of St. Dominic had been more penetrated with the love-rays which had been kindled by the Christian Creed, of which, as we are told, he was the holy Athlete. He is spoken of in relation

St. Dominic.

(XVIII)

to the Church as (XII. 55-57) 'Benignant to its own and to its enemies cruel.' Those who persecute, 'thinking they are doing God service,' need the illumination of Light as much as the warmth of Love. Our Lord tells us that they do these things because they have not known the Father nor the Son. The Divine-human relationship has not enlightened their thoughts about 'doing God service' (John xvi. 2, 3).

The following lines from the history of St. Dominic are fine in their portrayal of him as the Champion of the Church. He would ask nothing for himself but permission to do battle against the erring world (Canto XII. 97):

> ' With will and doctrine then himself he threw
>   In Apostolic office to proceed,
>   Like torrent which its streams from high source drew;
> And so upon the heretics' false breed
>   He fiercely swept, most vehemently there,
>   Where rebel will did most his course impede.'
>
> DEAN PLUMPTRE'S translation.

> ' Poi con dottrina e con volere insieme
>   Con l' ufficio apostolico si mosse,
>   Quasi torrente che l 'alte vene preme;
> E negli sterpi eretici percosse
>   L' impeto suo, più veramente quivi,
>   Dove le resistenze eran più grosse.'

Three lines from the history of St. Francis must be quoted. After speaking of his mystical marriage with Poverty, St. Thomas Aquinas, who recounts the story, says (Canto XI. 76-78):

> 'Their concord, and their looks of joy profuse,
>   The love, the wonder, and the aspect sweet,
>   Made men in holy meditation muse.'

> 'La lor concordia, e i lor lieti sembianti,
>   Amore e maraviglia, e 'l dolce sguardo,
>   Faceano esser cagion de' pensier santi.'

St. Francis of Assisi.

(XVIII)

Poverty was made of joyous aspect by St. Francis, as well as St. Francis by Poverty, so that many became enamoured of her.

The daily Prayer of the blessed St. Francis was: 'My God and my All, who art Thou, sweetest Lord, my God? And who am I, a poor worm, Thy Servant? Holiest Lord, I would love Thee! Sweetest Lord, I would love Thee! Lord, my God, I give to Thee all my heart and body, and vehemently desire, if I might know how, to do more for Thy love.'

He would often say, 'My brethren, let us now begin to serve God,' and in the waning years of his life would add, 'Up to this time, we have done nothing.'

THE SONG OF THE CREATURES.

Praised by His Creatures all,
   Praised be the Lord my God;
By Messer Sun, my brother, above all,
Who by his rays lights us and lights the day—
Radiant is She with his great splendour stored,
   Thy glory, Lord, confessing.

By Sister Moon and Stars my Lord is praised,
Where clear and fair they in the heavens are raised.

By Brother Wind, my Lord, Thy praise is said,
By air and clouds, and the blue sky o'erhead,
By which Thy creatures all are kept and fed.

By one most useful, humble, precious, chaste,
By Sister Water, O my Lord, Thou art praised.

   And praised is my Lord
By Brother Fire—he who lights up the night,
Jocund, robust is he, and strong and bright.
Praised art Thou, my Lord, by Mother Earth—
Thou Who sustainest her, and governest,
And to her flowers, fruit, herbs, dost colour give and birth.

S. FRANCIS OF ASSISI.

Dante is instructed to behold God's ideal signet shining more or less through each created thing.

(XIX)

PARADISO, CANTO XIII. 52-81.

CIÒ che non muore, e ciò che può morire,
　Non è se non splendor di quella idea,
　Che partorisce, amando, il nostro Sire:
Chè quella viva luce, che sì mea　　　　　　　55
　Dal suo lucente, che non si disuna
　Da lui, nè dall' amor che in lor s' intrea,
Per sua bontate il suo raggiare aduna,
　Quasi specchiato, in nove sussistenze,
　Eternalmente rimanendosi una.　　　　　　60
Quindi discende all' ultime potenze
　Giù d' atto in atto, tanto divenendo,
　Che più non fa che brevi contingenze:
E queste contingenze essere intendo
　Le cose generate, che produce,　　　　　　65
　Con seme e senza seme, il ciel movendo.
La cera di costoro, e chi la duce,
　Non sta d' un modo; e però sotto 'l segno
　Ideale poi più e men traluce:
Ond' egli avvien ch' un medesimo legno,　　70
　Secondo spezie, meglio e peggio frutta;
　E voi nascete con diverso ingegno.
Se fosse appunto la cera dedutta,
　E fosse il cielo in sua virtù suprema,
　La luce del suggel parrebbe tutta:　　　　75
Ma la natura la dà sempre scema,
　Similemente operando all' artista,
　C' ha l' abito dell' arte e man che trema.
Però se 'l caldo amor la chiara vista
　Della prima virtù dispone e segna,　　　　80
　Tutta la perfezion quivi s' acquista.

'Thy will but holds me to my life's fruition.'

(XIX)

THIS is the third passage on almost the same theme that we find in the Paradiso. There is so much to awaken our thoughts in each that all are given.

The first—Canto I. 103—brings before us especially the idea of the Form and Order of the Universe, 'that makes it resemble God,' and each created thing, with its instinct or tendency leading it by various ways homewards to God.

The second—Canto VIII.—with a repetition of the same thought, dwells rather more on the perfection of the Mind that foresees and preserves each form unto its fruition, and who has fore-ordained diversity of personality for divers offices in Earthly polities, also providing against the uniformity that heredity would otherwise produce.

This third passage seems to emphasize, in its opening beautiful lines, that each animate and inanimate object is manifested by the splendour of the Divine Idea that resides within it. In the later lines the inadequacy of the soil or wax that must receive the Idea is dwelt upon. It is affirmed, in the lines that follow our quotation, that the primal Earth and Adam in Paradise had received, in rightly prepared soil, the 'signet seal' of God. The first and the second Adam alone of the human family had the resulting perfection of 'prepared wax' with the 'true brilliance' of the Idea. It is implied, therefore, throughout this passage that it was Adam's transgression that caused the failure in his descendants and in his environment of Nature to correspond at all adequately to the effulgence of the Idea that caused the existences we behold. The origin of Evil is left untouched.

'The Life was the Light of men.'

(XIX)

Turning again to the first lines of to-day's portion, we are taught—if this be the true interpretation of the difficult passage—that the Love of the Father is ever flowing forth in the Word or Idea, who as the Son is ever manifesting His thoughts through the effulgence of the Spirit. That intrined rays of Light, from which the Living Source of Light Himself is never separated, pass into nine Spheres or Subsistencies as into a Mirror, the Unity of the Light ever remaining unbroken in Itself.

These nine Subsistencies are the nine Hierarchies of the Heavens. Each Circle is swift in motion and in power to receive and transmit the Vision of God, as each is in proximity to the Tenth Encircling Heaven of Stillness and Rest, whence the Effulgence of Light emanates.

Each Hierarchy receives the unbroken ray, and transmits it to the next beneath without imperfection or distortion, as it appears, but with diminishing splendour, till the remotest Heaven that encompasses this Earth is reached. Here, as it has been said, 'the wax' of Nature, through its own inherited powerlessness, is but inadequately fitted to receive and manifest the impress of the Divine ray that informs it. Our poor wax may be likened 'to an Artist's trembling hand,' that can but ill produce the idea of his brain.

The products of the Idea are called, in Scholastic language, its 'contingencies.'

Such utterances as these, we know, are but the strivings of human lips to make known a man's own concepts of the unutterable workings and ways of God in His Universe. In the minds of some they may awaken quickening suggestions of the manifoldness and fulness within and around the Child of God and Inheritor of the Kingdom of Heaven.

The out-flowing Life perfecting Itself in expression.

(XIX)

The inspired words of St. Paul tell us that we are all *Children of the Light* (1 Thess. v. 5), and the words we have been studying might seem an expansion of the same thought.

To behold every living thing, and every human being, as existing by virtue of its intrined ray of Light, consciously or unconsciously endeavouring to respond to its impress, can hardly fail to enrich our outlook. We may be helped by such imaginative suggestions to behold each flower more gloriously arrayed than Solomon, and each child of man with Christ 'in him the Hope of Glory,' even though he may be at the moment obscuring that glory.—See Col. i. 15-19, 26, 27 ; John i. 1-14.

> 'One Almighty is, from whom
> All things proceed, and up to Him return,
> If not depraved from good : created all
> Such to perfection, one first matter all,
> Endued with various forms, various degrees
> Of substance, and, in things that live, of life ;
> But more refined, more spiritous, and pure,
> As nearer to Him placed, or nearer tending
> Each in their several active spheres assigned,
> Till body up to spirit work, in bounds
> Proportioned to each kind. So from the root
> Springs lighter the green stalk ; from thence the leaves
> More aëry ; last the bright consummate flower
> Spirits odorous breathes.'
>
> 'Paradise Lost,' v. 469.

St. Thomas Aquinas warns Dante against hasty judgments.

———————————— (XX) ————————————

PARADISO, CANTO XIII. 112-123, 130-142.

E QUESTO ti fia sempre piombo a' piedi,
   Per farti muover lento, com' uom lasso,
   Ed al sì ed al no, che tu non vedi:
Chè quegli è tra gli stolti bene abbasso,   115
   Che senza distinzione afferma o niega,
   Così nell' un come nell' altro passo;
Perch' egli incontra che più volte piega
   L' opinïon corrente in falsa parte,
   E poi l' affetto l' intelletto lega.   120
Vie più che indarno da riva si parte,
   Perchè non torna tal qual ei si muove,
   Chi pesca per lo vero, e non ha l' arte:
    *   *   *   *   *
Non sien le genti ancor troppo sicure   130
   A giudicar, sì come quei che stima
   Le biade in campo pria che sien mature:
Ch' io ho veduto tutto 'l verno prima
   Il prun mostrarsi rigido e feroce,
   Poscia portar la rosa in su la cima;   135
E legno vidi già dritto e veloce
   Correr lo mar per tutto suo cammino,
   Perire alfine all' entrar della foce.
Non creda monna Berta e ser Martino,
   Per vedere un furare, altro offerére,   140
   Vedergli dentro al consiglio divino;
Chè quel può surgere, e quel può cadere.

> *'Everything holds a slender guiding clue*
> *Back to the Mighty One-ness.'*

(XX)

ST. THOMAS AQUINAS, who is supposed to have been conversing with Dante in the last two Cantos, winds up with a warning against hasty judgments on subjects imperfectly understood. In lines 130-142 he speaks of ignorant and hasty judgments of our fellow-creatures.

We were led (No. xviii.) to consider the life of each as in progress towards the realization of its Divinely-impressed innate ideal; the concluding lines of this Canto might well have sprung from such a thought, and have suggested the question, Can we pronounce on an incomplete and growing life? As an answer to this question, how captivating to both reason and imagination is the Poet's simile in lines 133-135!

With Dame Bertha and Master Martin we might well have judged through the long winter 'a rigid and fierce Thorn' as only fit for burning; later we find it crowned with the outbreathing of the consummate Summer's Soul— the Briar-Rose! What Prophet could have predicted such a miracle of lavish grace and beauty as the 'brilliant signet' impressed within that harsh and prickly plant of the dry ground!

We may easily pronounce on the failure of an action or an enterprise when it is concluded, as on the perishing of the ship at the Harbour's mouth; but we venture to ask, Does any mortal eye see the conclusion of a Life?

'Absolute terms are not applicable to man who is ever *on the way*, progressively manifesting the power of the Ideal that dwells in him, and whose very life is conflict and acquirement' through mistake and failure. — PROFESSOR HENRY JONES on Browning.

'From centre unto rim, from rim to centre.'

(XXI)

PARADISO, CANTO XIV. 1-12.

DAL centro al cerchio, e sì dal cerchio al centro
    Muovesi l' acqua in un ritondo vaso,
    Secondo ch' è percossa fuori o dentro.
Nella mia mente fe subito caso
    Questo ch' io dico, sì come si tacque   5
    La gloriosa vita di Tommaso,
Per la similitudine che nacque
    Del suo parlare e di quel di Beatrice,
    A cui sì cominciar, dopo lui, piacque :
A costui fa mestieri (e nol vi dice,   10
    Nè colla voce, nè pensando ancora)
    D' un altro vero andare alla radice.

'Where thine meets mine is my life's true condition.'

(XXI)

THE opening lines of this Canto convey to us a very vivid impression of spiritual Communion.

As a circular vessel of water vibrates from the Circumference to the Centre, and then again from the Centre to the Circumference, so the mind of the receiver of spiritual emotion had stirred beneath the breath of St. Thomas Aquinas while he had spoken; it came 'from rim to centre,' and the answer awakened within himself from 'centre to rim,' as the speaker ceased. It is yet more suggestive to find that the answering thought (which takes the form of another question) was not one which Dante himself formulated in speech or mind (lines 10, 11), though it came from the Centre; it is uttered for him by the Soul of his Soul, Beatrice.

The ensuing lines (omitted in order to shorten the portion for to-day) contain a question, whether such blossoming Light as Dante has witnessed can remain the same eternally; and if it does, after the glad flames shall be revestured in flesh at the Resurrection, how shall physical sight sustain such glories? What a natural misgiving of satiety is apparent in these questions! The new joy that seemed to quicken the song of those encircling him reassured Dante and made him exclaim (lines 25-27):

> 'Whoso lamenteth him that here we die
> That we may live above, has never there
> Seen the refreshment of the Eternal rain!'

Light and its glorious effulgence have been hitherto much dwelt upon; now we are called to imagine the quickening joy of refreshing showers.

*The melody of the spirits under the refreshing showers.
The 'modest voice' of Solomon?*

(*Continued from last page.*)

PARADISO, CANTO XIV. 25-27, 34-51.

Qual si lamenta perchè qui si muoia 25
   Per viver colassù, non vide quive
   Lo refrigerio dell' eterna ploia.
*   *   *   *   *
Ed io udii nella luce più dia
   Del minor cerchio una voce modesta, 35
   Forse qual fu dell' angelo a Maria,
Risponder: Quanto fia lunga la festa
   Di Paradiso, tanto il nostro amore
   Si raggerà d' intorno cotal vesta.
La sua chiarezza seguita l' ardore, 40
   L' ardor la visïone; e quella è tanta,
   Quanta ha di grazia sovra suo valore.
Come la carne glorïosa e santa
   Fia rivestita, la nostra persona
   Più grata fia, per esser tutta quanta: 45
Per che s' accrescerà ciò che ne dona
   Di gratuito lume il sommo Bene,
   Lume ch' a lui veder ne condiziona:
Onde la visïon crescer conviene,
   Crescer l' ardor, che di quella s' accende, 50
   Crescer lo raggio, che da esso viene.

*'Can God provide
For the large heart of man what shall not pall?'*

──────── (XXI) ────────

No dead-level of one over-powering and 'sober certainty of bliss' can Life Eternal unfold, but waves of unexpected union with the manifold many-coloured expressions of that Life—descents of Divine Grace as refreshing dew and rain, ever producing ascents of renewed adoration and love. It is, indeed, our mortal dulness that finds satiety anywhere; it is our death in the very midst of life. The more abundant life of the Spirit uncurtains new joys and brings refreshment and sweetness, even with the tears that are to be wiped away.

'A modest voice, perhaps like that of Gabriel to Mary,' answered from the Lustre most Divine of all those around them; not that of St. Thomas Aquinas, but, strange to say, the wise King's—perhaps because his voice had been attuned to a sweetness that Dante so much loved in the Song of Songs.

The fifteen lines that follow (37 to 51) and beyond (to line 60) are placed in Solomon's lips; they will well repay our study. He says that all the glory of the Saints is derived from their vision of God, and is proportioned to the ardour of their vision; and that, when re-clothed with body, all powers will be more complete, and well able to sustain all the graces received.

Dante then perceives that the glorious Sun-spirits are desiring their re-vesturing—not for themselves chiefly, 'but for the Mothers, the Fathers, and the rest who had been dear, before they became eternal flames.'

'The new life which is accorded to man by means of his regeneration in the power of faith and prayer is not mere spirit, but corporeal and substantial. "The body of the resurrection," even if it is invisible to mortal eyes, is far more durable and indestructible than any imaginable physical form.'—J. BOEHME.

PARADISO, CANTO XIV. 94-108.

CHÈ con tanto lucore e tanto robbi
    M' apparvero splendor dentro a duo raggi, 95
    Ch' io dissi : O Eliòs, che sì gli addobbi !
Come, distinta da minori e maggi
    Lumi, biancheggia tra' poli del mondo
    *Galassia sì, che fa dubbiar ben saggi ;
Sì costellati facean nel profondo   100
    Marte quei raggi il venerabil segno,
    Che fan giunture di quadranti in tondo.
Qui vince la memoria mia lo ingegno :
    Chè in quella croce lampeggiava Cristo
    Sì, ch' io non so trovare esemplo degno.   105
Ma chi prende sua croce e segue Cristo,
    Ancor mi scuserà di quel ch' io lasso,
    Vedendo in quell' albor balenar Cristo.

---

* The Milky Way, or
    'Galaxy, that maketh wise men doubt.'

*'Desperate tides of the whole great world's anguish
Forced through the channels of a single heart.'*

(XXII)

ANOTHER Ascension translates this 'Pilgrim of the Sky' into the fifth Heaven of Mars; he knew he was more uplifted

> 'By the enkindled smiling of the Star,
> That seemed to me more ruddy than its wont.'

The new grace called forth an ardent thanksgiving from his heart, and in a moment he was assured it was accepted by the 'red splendours that appeared.'

We know that colour was ever to him the vesture of Love. The glorious Army of Martyrs are found here, and the Crusaders who died fighting for the Faith.

These heroes of the Cross have accomplished great deeds, like those in Mercury; but they are unlike those in the purity of the motive that inspired them. Not through love of fame, but through the self-sacrificing spirit born of the constraining love of Christ, had they overcome.

These are placed nearer the Empyrean than even the Sun-spirits, for, as this has been interpreted by Buti, 'a greater and more burning ardour of love is in those who fight and conquer the world, the flesh, and the devil, than in those who exercise themselves with the Scriptures.'

In this Heaven 'the Cross shines forth in mystic glow,' and here in vision, as in a flash of lightning Christ gleamed forth in the whiteness of dawn upon the Cross. The reverence that will not further describe—that can find no similitude for His appearance—is like Dante's, who ever travels along his way with bowed head. He tells us that one who himself takes up his Cross and follows Christ will forgive his reticence, for he will have the vision and know it to be unutterable; and he only who lives in Christ's Spirit can behold the Vision.

Dante hears the melody of the spirits united in the venerable Sign.

(XXII)

(*Continued from last page.*)

PARADISO, CANTO XIV. 118-129.

E come giga ed arpa, in tempra tesa
   Di molte corde, fan dolce tintinno
   A tal, da cui la nota non è intesa;   120
Così da' lumi che lì m' apparinno
   S' accogliea per la croce una melode,
   Che mi rapiva senza intender l' inno.
Ben m' accors' io ch' ell' era d' alte lode,
   Perocchè a me venia : *Risurgi, e vinci,*   125
   Com' a colui che non intende ed ode.
Ed io m' innamorava tanto quinci,
   Che infino a lì non fu alcuna cosa
   Che mi legasse con sì dolci vinci.

The mysterious melody of the Cross, loved, though not understood, by the Pilgrim.

(XXII)

It is noteworthy that here, and in other places where the Sacred Name is mentioned, it is three times repeated (if at the end of a line), for Dante will not make another word rhyme with it.

The spirits of this sphere are seen passing up and down and across the great Sign like motes in a Sunbeam or like flames behind Alabaster. They passed, 'some swift, some slow,' and from them arose the lute-like sounds of a Hymn that was rendered indistinct, as it might seem, by softening distance and mysterious import—the music of the Cross; its words were not distinguished by the listener's uncomprehending ears; yet he says he well perceived that it was of lofty praise, and that it was addressed to Him who had conquered, and who was called upon to go forth conquering yet! 'Risurgi e vinci' were the words that he was able to distinguish.

The undefined vision, the music of tenderness and yet of triumph, the indistinguishable words, and the soul more captivated than by aught else, reveal to us again, as in Canto VII. 58, the condition of heart and mind Dante deems necessary for the contemplation of the mystery of the Cross—'maturity in the fire of Love.' He speaks of the fifth Heaven of Mars in his 'Convito' as the central sphere between the Empyrean and Earth, and has doubtless therefore placed the manifestation of the central truth of the Incarnation of Love even unto death, at this point, in the crimson glow. He, at the same time, marks self-sacrifice as the keynote of Heaven's life; as he made its antithesis, self-interest and its progressive isolation, the centre of the stagnation and death that pervades Hell.

Dante cannot at first understand the profound speech of Cacciaguida.

(XXIII)

PARADISO, CANTO XV. 37-54.

INDI, ad udire ed a veder giocondo,
    Giunse lo spirto al suo principio cose
    Ch' io non intesi ; sì parlò profondo.
Nè per elezïon mi si nascose,   40
    Ma per necessità ; chè 'l suo concetto
    Al segno de' mortai si soprappose.
E quando l' arco dell' ardente affetto
    Fu sì sfogato, che 'l parlar discese
    Invèr lo segno del nostro intelletto,   45
La prima cosa, che per me s' intese,
    Benedetto sie Tu, fu, trino ed uno,
    Che nel mio seme se' tanto cortese.
E seguitò : Grato e lontan digiuno,
    Tratto leggendo nel magno volume,   50
    U' non si muta mai bianco nè bruno,
Soluto hai, figlio, dentro a questo lume
    In ch' io ti parlo, mercè di colei
    Ch' all' alto volo ti vestì le piume.

Cacciaguida's ardour had to be calmed before he could adapt himself to Dante's incapacity.

―――――――――――(XXIII)――― ―― ― ―

THERE was silence amongst the blessed spirits when the melody of the Cross subsided. Silence, to give him who longed to know opportunity of asking. One of the lights (even as a falling star) was seen to pass from the right extremity of the transverse line of the Cross, down its Central bar to its foot, and seemed a flame behind Alabaster. The eyes of Beatrice were beaming such a smile that Dante thought his own, in beholding them, had sounded the depths of the grace vouchsafed to him, and that he must have seen the culminating point of his own Paradise. The love that knew what the joy of this meeting would be both to Dante and to his ancestor Cacciaguida (for he was the descending Light) was overflowing in Beatrice.

As the spirit drew down to Dante's level, he was aware that pleasant words were spoken and that a vision of happiness was before him, but he understood not; not because the spirit was unwilling to manifest himself plainly, 'but by necessity' (line 41) by reason of Dante's incapacity to grasp either language or vision—surely the constant impediment to our reception of messages from above. It was by reason, also, of the spirit's high mental conception and of the ardour of his love in projecting this conception, as it were, far beyond our mortal mark. At length Dante began to distinguish words, after the spirit's burning sympathy had slackened through its first overflow; and these words were of thanksgiving to God for loving kindness to his descendant. Cacciaguida, who spoke, made Dante understand that he had been awaiting his approach, and that he had foreseen it in the mighty Volume of the unchanging decrees of God's Providence. This Volume he read in the light of God's Countenance, whether its contents were light or dark.

Cacciaguida's ardour had to be calmed before he could adapt himself to Dante's incapacity.

(XXIII)

(Continued from last page.)

PARADISO, CANTO XV. 55-69.

Tu credi che a me tuo pensier mei 55
    Da quel ch' è primo, così come raia
    Dall' un, se si conosce, il cinque e 'l sei.
E però, ch' io mi sia, e perch' io paia
    Più gaudioso a te, non mi dimandi,
    Che alcun altro in questa turba gaia. 60
Tu credi 'l vero; chè i minori e i grandi
    Di questa vita miran nello speglio,
    In che, prima che pensi, il pensier pandi.
Ma perchè 'l sacro amore, in che io veglio
    Con perpetua vista, e che m' asseta 65
    Di dolce disiar, s' adempia meglio,
La voce tua sicura, balda e lieta
    Suoni la volontà, suoni 'l desio,
    A che la mia risposta è già decreta.

'God's breath in Prayer returning to his birth.'

(XXIII)

Cacciaguida continues, that he is aware that Dante does not ask him his name because he knows that all in the heavenly land who behold the Source of Life and Light can read therein the thoughts, even unborn, of another. But, he says, in order *to satisfy the sacred love:*

> 'Now let thy voice secure and frank and glad
> Proclaim the wishes, the desire proclaim,
> To which my answer is decreed already.'

Here the great paradox of Prayer is touched; God knows thy thoughts and desires though unformulated even to thyself; yet shalt thou utter thy will and desires in a voice bold and glad and certain; 'for so shall the Sacred Love which decrees the answer be satisfied.' We see the mystery of Prayer here presented, as was presented the mystery of the Atonement; it is opened alone to those whose 'eyes were matured in the flame of Love.'

'The heart has its reasons as well as the head.' The Heart of God and the heart of man have to be satisfied by communion. 'My Son, give Me thy heart' is the Father's cry. The Father loves to be asked for good things by His children, as well as to give them; the Children love to ask and to receive from Him, knowing that this reciprocity is the very food of Love, nay more, it is Love; for there need to be two conscious hemispheres, of giving and receiving, in perfected Love.

'The 'glad certainty' reminds us of the words, 'All things are yours, and ye are Christ's, and Christ is God's.' Christ inspired His disciples with the same confidence when He said, 'Whatsoever things ye ask, believe that ye receive them, and ye shall have them.'

The Power in the Word.

(XXIII)

To the logical understanding the paradox of Prayer must perhaps remain a paradox and foolishness, and the question remain a question—'If God is wise and good, will He not do what is best for us without our asking Him to do so?' May a hint come to us of some Divine necessity for Prayer, by our consideration of the Name of Him (the Word) who is the Utterer of God to man and of man to God?

The Creative Act, as expressed to us in Genesis, is linked with God's utterance 'Let there be Light.' May it be that man's utterance, or formulated desire through the Word, has to unlock, as with Milton's golden key, the treasures of Eternity, our own though unappropriated?

We learn the power of prayer—'the power of our own sonship is not power to over-ride God's law, but to co-operate with it; it depends on our intelligent co-operation with the Divine method. . . . "Nature, as Lord Bacon said, can only be controlled by being obeyed." In accurate theology God has been generally regarded as inherent in nature as well as transcending it; as working out a Divine purpose *in* the whole ordered system . . . the laws of nature are limits in His working, only so far as they express something of that law of perfect reason against which, says St. Augustine, God can no more work than He can work against Himself.'— GORE'S Bampton Lectures, V.

'God's breath in Prayer returning to his birth.'

(XXIII)

To the Supreme Being.

The prayers I make will then be sweet indeed
If Thou the Spirit give by which I pray;
My unassisted heart is barren clay,
That of its native self can nothing feed;
Of good and pious works Thou art the seed,
That quickens only where Thou say'st it may;
Unless Thou show to us Thine own true Way
No man can find it. Father, Thou must lead.
Do Thou, then, breathe those thoughts into my mind
By which such virtue may in me be bred,
That in Thy holy footsteps I may tread;
The fetters of my tongue do Thou unbind,
That I may have the power to sing of Thee
And sound Thy praises everlastingly.
Michael Angelo.

*Dante affirms that heat and radiance are
equal in the Sun.*

──────────── (XXIV) ────────────

PARADISO, CANTO XV. 70-83.

I' MI volsi a Beatrice; e quella udío 70
 Pria ch' io parlassi, ed arrisemi un cenno,
 Che fece crescer l' ale al voler mio:
Poi cominciai così: L' affetto e il senno,
 Come la prima Egualità v' apparse,
 D' un peso per ciascun di voi si fenno; 75
Perocchè al Sol, che v' allumò ed arse
 Col caldo e con la luce, èn sì iguali,
 Che tutte simiglianze sono scarse.
Ma voglia ed argomento ne' mortali,
 Per la cagion ch' a voi è manifesta, 80
 Diversamente son pennuti in ali.
Ond' io, che son mortal, mi sento in questa
 Disagguaglianza.

The equality of Love and Knowledge among the Blessed received through their vision of God.

(XXIV)

THE invitation to speak out gladly and boldly his desire is at once responded to by the well-instructed soul. The words that he uses have been chosen for one of our subjects of meditation, partly on account of the remarkable name by which he speaks of God, 'the primal Equality.' The lines that follow show his meaning to be that in God Love and Knowledge are equal, even as (Dante believes) Light and Heat are equal in the Sun.

The varying degrees of Love and Knowledge in the Church Militant have often been referred to in the Poem; the necessity for both has been repeatedly affirmed, and here the reading all in God's Countenance, where Truth and Love are equal, seems, to the more and more ascending soul, the primal bliss of Heaven. Dante reminds Cacciaguida that, being mortal himself, he is opprest with the inequality of capacity in the two wings that bear him aloft; his knowledge is not equal to his desire or love; even with the Celestial Wisdom at his side, he cannot, as the souls of the emancipated Saints, read all in the Divine Countenance. He therefore begs to learn from the spirit who speaks to him his name and the reason of his paternal welcome. In answer to these questions a long history is given, not only with regard to Dante's ancestors, of whom Cacciaguida was one, but concerning the condition of Florence in earlier and simpler days; and protest is made against the luxury and degeneracy of the current time.

Cacciaguida foretells to Dante his separation from all pleasant things.

PARADISO, CANTO XVII. 19-45.

MENTRE ch' i' era a Virgilio congiunto
    Su per lo monte che l' anime cura,   20
    E discendendo nel mondo defunto,
Dette mi fûr di mia vita futura
    Parole gravi; avvegna ch' io mi senta
    Ben tetragono ai colpi di ventura.
Per che la voglia mia sarà contenta   25
    D' intender qual fortuna mi s' appressa;
    Chè saetta previsa vien più lenta.
Così diss' io a quella luce stessa,
    Che pria m' avea parlato: e, come volle
    Beatrice, fu la mia voglia confessa.   30
Non per ambage, in che la gente folle
    Già s' invescava, pria che fosse anciso
    L' agnel di Dio che le peccata tolle;
Ma per chiare parole, e con preciso
    Latin rispose quell' amor paterno,   35
    Chiuso e parvente nel suo proprio riso:
*La contingenza, che fuor del quaderno
    Della vostra materia non si stende,
    Tutta è dipinta nel cospetto eterno.
Necessità però quindi non prende,   40
    Se non come dal viso in che si specchia
    Nave che per corrente giù discende.
Da indi, sì come viene ad orecchia
    Dolce armonia da organo, mi viene
    A vista 'l tempo che ti s' apparecchia.   45

* 'Contingency, that which from our standpoint may or may not come to pass, is ever-present in the eternal Now of the mind of God.'— DEAN PLUMPTRE.

*'Its discords, quenched by meeting harmonies,
Die in the large and charitable air.'*

(XXV)

DANTE inquires concerning his own future, which had been partly foretold to him on the Mountain of Purgatory, and he says he feels himself 'foursquare against the blows of chance'; for what is the meaning of chance or Fortune to one who is beyond the realm of the wheel that goes up and down? Cacciaguida answers 'not as those ancient oracles who spoke in vague phrases before the manifestation of the great At-one-ment of Heaven and Earth, but with clear and unambiguous words.' It seems intimated that the paternal love was by this Divine manifestation set free to express itself.

He again declares that all is depicted in the Eternal aspect, for in that which is transitory the Truth can never be read. In this Love-enlightened Knowledge, Dante's forefather read the sad history of his offspring's separation from everything he cared for, his banishment from Florence, and the bitterness of a stranger's food and of dwelling in a strange land. Yet all these impressions of woe reach Cacciaguida as he gazes into the Divine Light, 'even as the sweet harmony of an Organ reaches the ear'; their discords are resolved into harmonies, and the sequence and unity of the whole is seen to be good.

In the spiritual region it is clearly discerned that all the changes and chances of this troublesome world (though each is not good in itself), 'work *together* for good' to those who receive them in the love of God.

(XXVI)

PARADISO, CANTO XVII. 103-132.

Io cominciai, come colui che brama,
    Dubitando, consiglio da persona,
    Che vede e vuol dirittamente, ed ama :   105
Ben veggio, padre mio, sì come sprona
    Lo tempo inverso me, per colpo darmi
    Tal, ch' è più grave a chi più s' abbandona ;
Per che di provedenza è buon ch' io m' armi,
    Sì che, se 'l luogo m' è tolto più caro,   110
    Io non perdessi gli altri per miei carmi.
Giù per lo mondo senza fine amaro,
    E per lo monte, dal cui bel cacume
    Gli occhi della mia Donna mi levaro,
E poscia per lo ciel di lume in lume,   115
    Ho io appreso quel, che, s' io 'l ridico,
    A molti fia savor di forte agrume.
E s' io al vero son timido amico,
    Temo di perder vita tra coloro
    Che questo tempo chiameranno antico.   120
La luce, in che ridea lo mio tesoro
    Ch' io trovai lì, si fe prima corrusca,
    Quale a raggio di Sole specchio d' oro ;
Indi rispose : Coscïenza fusca
    O della propria, o dell' altrui vergogna,   125
    Pur sentirà la tua parola brusca.
Ma nondimen, rimossa ogni menzogna,
    Tutta tua visïon fa' manifesta ;
    E lascia pur grattar dov' è la rogna.
Chè, se la voce tua sarà molesta   130
    Nel primo gusto, vital nutrimento
    Lascerà poi, quando sarà digesta.

'That utterance may be given me, that I may open my mouth boldly.'—EPH. vi. 19.

(XXVI)

THE opening words, that introduce Dante's further rejoinder to Cacciaguida, picture for us in strong simple outline the ideal Counsellor :

'Persona
Che vede, e vuol dirittamente, ed ama.'
(*One who sees, and uprightly wills, and loves.*)

Desiring counsel from such an one as this, Dante speaks the wrestling doubts that arise within his heart. In his passage through the three spiritual worlds, he says, he has learned truth which to tell again would be to many a savour of pungent herbs; yet, on the other hand, to prove only a timid friend to Truth would cost him his own enduring life. At once the light flashed forth from him, 'who saw, and uprightly willed, and loved'; it flashed back to the questioner as sunlight in a golden mirror. Dante is told that he must lay aside utterly all falsehood and make his vision manifest.

Some, whose consciences were o'ercast, would wince under the 'parola brusca,' but vital nutriment should remain behind, when the harsh and molesting words should be digested.

The power of the Word, both towards Heaven and in the world, seems meant to be the instruction for the spiritual man throughout this paternal discourse. He is instructed to be bold, glad, and confident towards Heaven ; bold and sincere also in declaring God-given truth to man; he must declare it without disguise, even should it be distasteful and bitter. It is hinted, that all excuse for veiling the truth in vague and foolish words is done away since the Lamb of God was slain, who taketh away the sins of the World.

*Dante ascends to the White Star of Jupiter,
the Home of just Rulers.*

(XXVII)

PARADISO, CANTO XVIII. 58-79.

E COME, per sentir più dilettanza
    Bene operando, l' uom di giorno in giorno
    S' accorge che la sua virtute avanza ;   60
Sì m' accors' io che il mio girare intorno
    Col cielo insieme avea cresciuto l' arco,
    Veggendo quel miracolo più adorno.
E quale è il trasmutare, in picciol varco
    Di tempo, in bianca donna, quando l' volto   65
    Suo si discarchi di vergogna il carco ;
Tal fu negli occhi miei quando fui vôlto,
    Per lo candor della temprata stella
    Sesta, che dentro a sè m' avea ricolto.
Io vidi in quella gioviäl facella   70
    Lo sfavillar dell' amor che lì era,
    Segnare agli occhi miei nostra favella.
E come augelli surti di riviera,
    Quasi congratulando a lor pasture,
    Fanno di sè or tonda or lunga schiera ;   75
Sì dentro a' lumi sante creature
    Volitando cantavano, e faciensi
    Or D, or I, or L, in sue figure.
Prima cantando a sua nota moviensi.

The Celestial Eagle as Ideal Justice.

(XXVII)

THE personal communication between Dante and his Ancestor being ended, the latter uttered the names of many of the great spirits in that fifth sphere of the Heavens. Even as each name was uttered, the 'splendour' of each spirit was revealed, moving athwart or revolving in the great Cross. Again the power of the Word calls forth the manifestation of light and personality. Looking to Beatrice to learn what his next action should be, Dante beholds her again surpassing herself in radiancy and beauty, and in this way he became aware of their having made a further ascent. They had left the glowing Mars, and had reached the white and temperate Sphere of Jupiter, the Sixth Heaven; the habitation of Ideal Justice, personified in the righteous rulers of the World. As we saw in Mars the sublimated, self-sacrificing Love, that in Venus had fallen short through admixture of selfish passion, we see in Jupiter the finer and more ideal Justice, which was represented in imperfect fashion under the Standard of the Roman Eagle in Mercury. Here is the soaring Celestial Eagle, where dwell the spirits of enlightened Righteous Rulers.

From this Sphere spring the cause and inspiration of all lower manifestations of Justice.

The Birds of Light form themselves as Vowels and Consonants into words.

(XXVII)

(*Continued from last page.*)

PARADISO, CANTO XVIII. 88-93.

* * * * *

Mostrârsi dunque cinque volte sette
　Vocali e consonanti ; ed io notai
　Le parti sì, come mi parver dette.　　　　90
Diligite justitiam, primai
　Fur verbo e nome di tutto 'l dipinto :
　Qui judicatis terram, fur sezzai.

The Pilgrim instructed in the love of pure Justice.

(XXVII)

The Bird of God, in which all the spirits are here unified, seems, like St. John's Eagle, to be the symbol of the Spirit of God inspiring the Rule of Justice. The holy beings who show themselves in the figure of this Eagle (as the Martyrs and Crusaders in Mars showed themselves within the form of the Cross), when they disperse themselves for special objects, are seen in companies like flights of birds. These, 'moving to their own song,' form themselves into figures and letters to welcome with love and instruction the soul newly arrived amongst them. The first sentence flashed into him by these birds of light was 'Love Justice, you who govern the world.'

' As we rise from Heaven to Heaven in the Paradiso, we reach a more adequate state of devotion of the individual to the welfare of the social whole. Each one unites with his fellows to produce an aggregate social result. As in Mars they are arranged within the form of a colossal Cross, so in Jupiter they spell out Ethical principles, or present a great Eagle.'—'Spiritual Sense of Dante,' by W. T. HARRIS.

'True Justice . . . lies for the most part beyond the limits of any acknowledged law. The idea of Justice involves the idea of rights; but at bottom rights are equivalent to that which really *is*; and the recognition of these rights, therefore, the justice required of our hands or our thoughts, is the recognition of that which the person or the thing in its inmost nature really is; and as sympathy alone can really discover that which really is in matter of feeling or thought, true justice is in its essence a finer knowledge through Love.'—PATER'S Essays.

*The just spirits show themselves in the Celestial Eagle,
and thousands speak as 'I and my' in this unity.*

(XXVIII)

PARADISO, CANTO XIX. 1-27.

PAREA dinanzi a me coll' ali aperte
    La bella image, che nel dolce frui
    Liete faceva l' anime conserte.
Parea ciascuna rubinetto, in cui
    Raggio di Sole ardesse sì acceso,   5
    Che ne' miei occhi rifrangesse lui.
E quel che mi convien ritrar testeso,
    Non portò voce mai, nè scrisse inchiostro,
    Nè fu per fantasia giammai compreso ;
Ch' io vidi, ed anche udii parlar lo rostro,   10
    E sonar nella voce ed Io e Mio
    Quand' era nel concetto e Noi e Nostro.
E cominciò : Per esser giusto e pio
    Son io qui esaltato a quella gloria,
    Che non si lascia vincere a desio.   15
Ed in terra lasciai la mia memoria
    Sì fatta, che le genti lì malvage
    Commendan lei, ma non seguon la storia.
Così un sol calor di molte brage
    Si fa sentir, come di molti amori   20
    Usciva solo un suon di quella image.
Ond' io appresso : O perpetui fiori
    Dell' eterna letizia, che pur uno
    Sentir mi fate tutti i vostri odori,
Solvetemi, spirando, il gran digiuno,   25
    Che lungamente m' ha tenuto in fame,
    Non trovando lì in terra cibo alcuno.

One perfume, one beauty, one love-language.

(XXVIII)

THE perfect unity of 'just men made perfect' is here symbolized by thousands speaking together, in one voice uttering 'I and my,' though they should have said literally 'We and Our.' In the purgatorio (Canto XV.) we were taught the beauty of the word 'Ours' rather than 'Mine,' with regard to possessions shared; here unanimity is expressed by many speaking as One. 'That they may be One even as we are One' is fulfilled in this Vision of Union. All separate self-assertion, all desire to be distinguished, must vanish, before this bliss of Heaven can be welcomed as bliss. Personality is submerged, though not extinguished, in the conception of the whole; each, in union with the whole, represents the whole. Later, names and characteristics are dwelt upon; but here we are shown the sacrifice of each to the social community, in joy and song and word. The illustrations given of the love and beauty of these interwoven, intermingled spirits are very forcible. As many embers give out one feeling of warmth, so the many loves as from one large heart gave out one love-language; and again, manifold odours from the various flowers of eternal joy were perceived as one perfume.

Dante appeals to the Sempiternal Justice for an answer to his burning question, and is reminded of man's short sight.

(XXIX)

PARADISO, CANTO XIX. 70-81.

UN uom nasce alla riva 70
    Dell' Indo; e quivi non è chi ragioni
    Di Cristo, nè chi legga, nè chi scriva;
E tutti suoi voleri ed atti buoni
    Sono, quanto ragione umana vede,
    Sanza peccato in vita od in sermoni; 75
Muore non battezzato e senza fede:
    Ov' è questa giustizia che 'l condanna?
    Ov' è la colpa sua, sed ei non crede?
Or tu chi se', che vuoi sedere a scranna,
    Per giudicar da lungi mille miglia 80
    Con la veduta corta d' una spanna?

'*Son of man, can these bones live?*'—EZEK. xxxvii.

―――――――― (XXIX) ――――――――

IN this central home of Love and 'Living Justice' the soul that has long ached with hunger to know, under the burden of one great question, eagerly seeks to be satisfied. The question (with others akin to it) has burdened many a heaven-taught heart growing in the knowledge and love of God and man; it has been answered differently through the ages by saints of God, or left untouched as a mystery not to be fathomed by the mind of man. 'Where is the justice that condemneth him who dies without baptism and without faith, who has yet lived a sinless life? Where is his fault (if it has been caused by circumstances for which he is not responsible) if he do not believe?' (lines 77, 78). The answer given here may silence, if it does not satisfy:

> 'Now who art thou, that on the bench would sit
> In judgment at a thousand miles away,
> With the short vision of a single span?'

The Voice, or rather concurrent voices, continued, implying, or seeming to imply, that Scripture answers the doubt.* The Voice then affirms that it is the primal Will, never disjoined from the Good Supreme, that, in raying forth, occasions every idea of justice amongst finite beings, and must therefore be the only standard of Justice. After a pause, it is declared in distinct language that 'Unto that Kingdom never had one ascended who had not faith in Christ.' Yet the absolute exclusion from that Kingdom seems modified, by the terms of more or less near to Christ, in the lines that follow:

> 'But look thou, many crying are Christ, Christ!
> Who at the judgment shall be far less near
> To Him, than some shall be who knew not Christ.'
> Lines 106-108.

―――――――――――――――――――――
* Those who would see how much of Scripture has been cited in support of opposite views on this subject, with an attempt to harmonize the two sides, are referred to 'The Restitution of All Things,' by the Rev. A. Jukes (Longmans).

The murmuring river and the Lark's song.

(XXX)

PARADISO, CANTO XX. 19-30, 73-78.

UDIR mi parve un mormorar di fiume,
 Che scenda chiaro giù di pietra in pietra, 20
 Mostrando l' ubertà del suo cacume.
E come suono al collo della cetra
 Prende sua forma, e sì come al pertugio
 Della sampogna vento che penètra;
Così, rimosso d' aspettare indugio, 25
 Quel mormorar dell' aquila salissi
 Su per lo collo, come fusse bugio.
Fecesi voce quivi, e quindi uscissi
 Per lo suo becco in forma di parole,
 Quali aspettava 'l cuore, ov' io le scrissi. 30
  * * * * *
Qual lodoletta, che in aere si spazia
 Prima cantando, e poi tace contenta
 Dell' ultima dolcezza che la sazia; 75
Tal mi sembiò l' imago della imprenta
 Dell' eterno piacere, al cui disio
 Ciascuna cosa, quale ell' è, diventa.

How hear we every man in our own tongue wherein we were born?

(XXX)

THE One voice of united Voices is again brought to the ear; it is heard as the murmuring of a clear river, awakened into varied sound by its descent from rock to rock. Though the many-voiced Voice speaks as 'I and My' through the organ of utterance of one celestial bird, it comes not upon the ear as a monotone, but as one of blended harmonies; the many personalities which enrich its notes are throbbing through it, not merged in one, but in conscious combination. The fulness of that outflowing Spirit, and His continual supply of the Water of Life, is imaged to us by the 'affluence' of the Fountain Head on the Mountain-top, that, descending from rock to rock, is scattered into countless drops of the crystal stream.

From the united speakers came such a language 'as the heart of the listener awaited' (line 30). It is the heart of the exile that awaits and longs for this harmonious language amid the confused and alien Babel tongues of the strange land in which he sojourns. The cessation of this language is compared (75-78) to the Lark's silent rapture, satisfied with the last sweetness of his song; and such (the Poet seems to suggest) is the joy of the Creator in imprinting His ideal in each creature, and in bringing each into that perfectness which makes it the thing it is.

In the omitted portion of this Canto five righteous Rulers are named as belonging to this Sphere of the sixth Heaven. Amongst these Hezekiah is cited (49-54), and we learn that in his spiritual condition he becomes aware that his penitent prayer did not change the righteous purpose of GOD, but delayed its Time-manifestation.

*Dante is taught that warm love and living hope prevailed
in the salvation of two righteous heathen.*

―――――――――――― (XXXI) ――――――――

PARADISO, CANTO XX. 94-99, 127-132.

R*EGNUM cœlorum* violenza pate
   Da caldo amore, e da viva speranza,   95
   Che vince la divina volontate ;
Non a guisa che l' uomo all' uom sovranza,
   Ma vince lei, perchè vuol esser vinta ;
   E vinta vince con sua beninanza.
   *   *   *   *   *
Quelle tre donne gli fûr per battesmo,   127
   Che tu vedesti dalla destra ruota,
   Dinanzi al battezzar più d' un millesmo.
O predestinazion, quanto rimota   130
   È la radice tua da quegli aspetti,
   Che la prima cagion non veggion tota !

> *'True prayer is not a mere wishing or desiring, but an action within the Power of the Omnipotent God.'*

——————————— (XXXI) ———————————

THE mystery of Prayer is again touched upon as an apparent, but not a real, conflict of the human and divine volition. It is shown us here as rather the fervour of Divine love and living hope, awakening in man the conquering force that belongs to the Kingdom of Heaven, and wins the Kingdom of Heaven.

The burden of the question concerning the Salvation of the righteous heathen still oppresses Dante's yearning heart. Among the five righteous Rulers named in this Canto, he finds two that belonged to the heathen world—Trajan and Riphæus. He learns that they had passed from their mortal bodies not as Gentiles, as was supposed, but as Christians 'in the steadfast faith of feet that were to suffer, and had suffered,' Trajan having lived after those wounded feet had trodden the way home to God, and Riphæus a thousand years before. There was a tradition that the intercession of St. Gregory had resuscitated Trajan, and that he lived on earth a short time as a Christian, and was made worthy to attain the blessed life. It is said of Riphæus that through grace he set all his love on righteousness, and that from grace so deep 'a fountain wells that never hath the eye of any creature reached its primal wave.' No rite of baptism had then been ordained, but the Three eternal Maidens themselves were his baptism.

Dante learns that the ignorance of man cannot sound the depths of God's grace. With Him all things are possible, and in the two exceptional instances of Riphæus and Trajan miracles were worked to save them from perdition. He adds, 'nor can the mystery of Predestination be sounded by any who see not the First Cause entire'—'tota,' or as a Whole.

Dante ascends to the Home of the contemplative spirits, and beholds the golden Stairway that mounts beyond.

──────── (XXXII) ────────

PARADISO, CANTO XXI. 28-51.

DI color d' oro, in che raggio traluce,
    Vid' io uno scaleo eretto in suso
    Tanto, che nol seguiva la mia luce.   30
Vidi anche per li gradi scender giuso
    Tanti splendor, ch' io pensai ch' ogni lume
    Che par nel ciel, quindi fosse diffuso.
E come per lo natural costume
    Le pole insieme, al cominciar del giorno,   35
    Si muovono a scaldar le fredde piume;
Poi altre vanno via senza ritorno,
    Altre rivolgon sè, onde son mosse,
    Ed altre roteando fan soggiorno;
Tal modo parve a me che quivi fosse   40
    In quello sfavillar che insieme venne,
    Sì come in certo grado si percosse.
E quel che presso più ci si ritenne
    Si fe sì chiaro, ch' io dicea pensando:
    Io veggio ben l' amor che tu m' accenne.   45
Ma Quella, ond' io aspetto il come e 'l quando
    Del dire e del tacer, si sta: ond' io,
    Contra 'l disio, fo ben s' io non dimando.
Per ch' ella, che vedeva il tacer mio
    Nel veder di Colui che tutto vede,   50
    Mi disse: Solvi il tuo caldo disio.

'*Henceforth* [*N.V.*] *ye shall see Heaven opened, and the Angels of God ascending and descending upon the Son of Man.*'—JOHN i. 51.

――――――――――― (XXXII) ―――――――――――

THE harmonious voice in Jupiter had ceased, and the eyes of Dante's aspiring spirit were again concentrated on those of his Celestial Guide. Hitherto the attainment of each new Sphere had been known to him by his perception of fuller splendour in the radiant smile of Beatrice, but in the Seventh Heaven of Saturn (the Heaven of the contemplative) she smiled not. 'If I were to smile,' she says, 'thy mortal power would in such glory be consumed, even as a leaf by the lightning.' Perhaps for such a reason as this the eyes of the Apostles 'were holden,' when their risen Lord appeared to them and they knew Him not.

Beatrice bids Dante fix his mind in the direction of his eyes (for she had told him they were now in the seventh splendour of Saturn), and read in that mirror the figure that should appear to him.

Obedience to her commands was as great a joy as the contemplation of her countenance, and he perceived at once the shining golden Stairway that led too far upwards for his eyes to reach its goal. Innumerable flashes of splendour descended these wonderful steps, as though all Heaven were pouring down them; some advancing, some retreating, some wheeling about them like flights of rooks around their home-trees. One of these sparkling spirits as he drew near became so clear to Dante's eyes that he said within himself, 'Well I perceive the love thou showest me.' But these ethereal splendours seem to have presented no outline of form recognisable to the outward eye. The form of each is apparently concealed by its vesture of dazzling light; this has been remarked since the three Heavens have been left below over which the Earth's shadow extends.

St. Peter Damiano explains why music is silent and Beatrice smiles not, in the Seventh Heaven.

———————— (XXXIII) ————————

PARADISO, CANTO XXI. 52-72.

E D io incominciai: La mia mercede
  Non mi fa degno della tua risposta,
  Ma per colei, che il chieder mi concede,
Vita beata, che ti stai nascosta   55
  Dentro alla tua letizia, fammi nota
  La cagion che sì presso mi t' accosta;
E di' perchè si tace in questa ruota
  La dolce sinfonia di Paradiso,
  Che giù per l' altre suona sì devota.   60
Tu hai l' udir mortal, sì come 'l viso,
  Rispose a me; però qui non si canta
  Per quel che Beatrice non ha riso.
Giù per li gradi della scala santa
  Discesi tanto, sol per farti festa   65
  Col dire, e con la luce che m' ammanta.
Nè più amor mi fece esser più presta;
  Chè più e tanto amor quinci su ferve,
  Sì come il fiammeggiar ti manifesta.
Ma l' alta carità, che ci fa serve   70
  Pronte al consiglio che il mondo governa,
  Sorteggia qui, sì come tu osserve.

'Who maketh His Angels spirits, and His ministers a flame of fire.'

(XXXIII)

THE unknown Splendour, pausing on the Golden Stairway, desiring lovingly to speak with Dante, was addressed by him with great reverence and courtesy in these very perfect lines. He asks why the sweet music which he has heard in each preceding Sphere should here be silent? Peter Damiano answers him and reminds him that his senses of sight and hearing are mortal, and that for the same reason that Beatrice smiled not, the Symphonies of the Seventh Heaven must needs be silent; the ravishing sounds and sight would destroy the frail vessel that received them. The perfection of the Seventh Heaven is here expressed—the Home, as it were, of Beatrice and of Contemplatives, who are ever ascending its Golden Stairway. Dante longed to inquire what the relationship of this Spirit was with himself, yet waited till he was authorized to do so by Beatrice. Divine Wisdom, who reads all in Him who sees *all things* (not only the Pilgrim's individual needs and desires), bids him now let loose and make these desires known. He is told that the readiness of Love shown by this Spirit arose from no more ardour in himself than burnt in those above, but that the office had been allotted to him by the High Charity that controls the world, and makes His ministers these flames of love. He apparently perceives no unveiled countenance amongst these Flames; the submergence of external identity seems to convey to us the ideal state of the unity of Love and Service in which all were conjoined. 'Not I but Christ' was the language of every heart; Christ was to be supremely 'admired in all His Saints.'

Dante is taught that the reason of election to any office is cut off from every created mind.

(XXXIV)

PARADISO, CANTO XXI. 73-102.

IO veggio ben, diss' io, sacra lucerna,
   Come libero amore in questa corte
   Basta a seguir la provvidenza eterna.   75
Ma quest' è quel ch' a cerner mi par forte,
   Perchè predestinata fosti sola
   A questo uficio tra le tue consorte.
Non venni prima all' ultima parola,
   Che del suo mezzo fece il lume centro,   80
   Girando sè come veloce mola.
Poi rispose l' amor che v' era dentro:
   Luce divina sovra me s' appunta,
   Penetrando per questa, in ch' io m' inventro;
La cui vertù col mio veder congiunta   85
   Mi leva sovra me tanto, ch' io veggio
   La somma essenzia, della quale è munta.
Quinci vien l' allegrezza, ond' io fiammeggio;
   Perchè alla vista mia, quant' ella è chiara,
   La chiarità della fiamma pareggio.   90
Ma quell' alma nel ciel che più si schiara,
   Quel serafin che in Dio più l' occhio ha fisso,
   Alla dimanda tua non satisfára;
Perocchè sì s' inoltra nell' abisso
   Dell' eterno statuto quel che chiedi,   95
   Che da ogni creata vista è scisso.
Ed al mondo mortal, quando tu riedi,
   Questo rapporta, sì che non presuma
   A tanto segno più muover li piedi.
La mente, che qui luce, in terra fuma;   100
   Onde riguarda come può laggiùe
   Quel che non puote, perchè 'l ciel l' assuma.

'*Oh, the depths of the riches, both of the Wisdom and knowledge of God! how unsearchable are His judgments, and His ways past finding out!*'

(XXXIV)

THE questioning spirit would fain know why Peter Damiano was sent down the Golden Stairway to welcome him rather than any other who loved as much '*or more*' (68).

The swift, whirling motion of the flame gave sign of the joy of the spirit in the Will that attuned all in these happy spheres into harmony with Himself; and then the Love within the flame expressed, as far as the Seer could grasp it, the secret of the consciousness of One who acts in the Light and Love of the Spirit, conjoined with the full acquiescence and energy of his own spirit. He is aware, he says, that a Divine Light pierces the light in which he is ever living and moving, and that a power of vision beyond his own, yet combining with his own, lifts him so far above himself that he can behold the beatific vision of the Supreme Essence. This Vision, he adds, causes the joy with which he flames; and in the measure of his own clearness of vision his flame becomes more or less clear. But he declares that no created being can penetrate that abyss from which the cause of election springs; and Dante is charged to carry back this message to the mortal world: that none with the denser mind of earth should attempt to fathom this mystery, for to heavenly beings, in fullest light, it is unfathomable.

'In Sophocles the Divine righteousness asserts itself not in the award of happiness or misery to the individual, but in the providential Wisdom which assigns to each individual his place and function in a universal moral order.'—'Some Aspects of Greek Genius,' PROFESSOR BUTCHER.

St. Benedict describes the Missionary's work at Monte Cassino.

(XXXV)

PARADISO, CANTO XXII. 28-57.

E LA maggiore e la più luculenta
   Di quelle margherite innanzi fèssi,
   Per far di sè la mia voglia contenta.   30
Poi dentro a lei udi': Se tu vedessi,
   Com' io, la carità che tra noi arde,
   Li tuoi concetti sarebbero espressi.
Ma perchè tu, aspettando, non tarde
   All' alto fine, io ti farò risposta   35
   Pure al pensier, di che sì ti riguarde.
Quel monte, a cui Cassino è nella costa,
   Fu frequentato già in su la cima
   Dalla gente ingannata e mal disposta.
Ed io son quel che su vi portai prima   40
   Lo nome di Colui che in terra addusse
   La verità, che tanto ci sublima.
E tanta grazia sovra me rilusse,
   Ch' io ritrassi le ville circostanti
   Dall' empio culto che 'l mondo sedusse.   45
Questi altri fuochi tutti contemplanti
   Uomini furo, accesi di quel caldo
   Che fa nascere i fiori e i frutti santi.
Qui è Maccario, qui è Romualdo;
   Qui son li frati miei, che dentro a' chiostri   50
   Fermaro i piedi, e tennero 'l cuor saldo.
Ed io a lui: L' affetto che dimostri
   Meco parlando, e la buona sembianza
   Ch' io veggio e noto in tutti gli ardor vostri,
Così m' ha dilatata mia fidanza,   55
   Come 'l Sol fa la rosa, quando aperta
   Tanto divien quant' ell' ha di possanza.

'Man, then, must open himself, almost as a Rose which can no longer remain closed.'

------- (XXXV) -------

EVEN in this Sphere of holy Contemplatives a loud cry arose, overpowering Dante with terror, and reminding us of the close interweaving of events and lives on Earth with those who dwell within the veil. The Saints in light, here or beyond, are supposed to thrill with Divine indignation at Sin, as well as with joy at the conversion of sinners.

Dante turns for refuge to Beatrice, 'as a pale and breathless boy to his Mother.' The character of Motherhood is the one that appears dominant in Beatrice's relationship with Dante in her 'Second beauty.' St. Benedict tells Dante that, if he could only see the living and glowing Love as he himself sees it, the desires that fill his heart would be called out into expression.

He recounts his own life at Monte Cassino, the first who carried to those deluded and ill-disposed people

> 'The name of Him who brought upon the earth
> The truth that so much sublimateth us' (42).

He describes his fellow-labourers as 'enkindled by that heat which maketh holy flowers and fruits spring up'—a fine motto for the Missionary, who by this vivid illustration is reminded that he himself should be as a burning glass to concentrate the rays of the Sun of Righteousness and Love upon the plants of the Lord, in order that they may burst into flower and fruits. Dante answers that the blessed warmth he feels there has so much fostered his own confidence, that it is like the Rose opened with all her powers by the Sunshine, so that the flower becomes in actualized fact what she truly is in potentiality.

What a glorious moral atmosphere to inbreathe and to breathe out is this, wherein each is emboldened to become his truest, noblest self, and each is prompted to draw forth others towards their own special perfection !

St. Benedict instructs Dante that his requests are to be fully answered in God, beyond Time and Space.

———————————— (XXXVI) ————————

PARADISO, CANTO XXII. 58-74.

PERÒ ti prego; e tu, padre, m' accerta,
   S' io posso prender tanta grazia, ch' io
   Ti veggia con immagine scoverta.   60
Ond' egli : Frate, il tuo alto disio
   S' adempierà in su l' ultima spera,
   Ove si adempion tutti gli altri e 'l mio.
Ivi è perfetta, matura ed intera
   Ciascuna disïanza ; in quella sola   65
   È ogni parte là, dove sempr' era :
Perchè non è in luogo, e non s' impola,
   E nostra scala infino ad essa varca,
   Onde così dal viso ti s' invola.
Infin lassù la vide il patrïarca   70
   Giacob isporger la superna parte,
   Quando gli apparve d' angeli sì carca.
Ma per salirla mo nessun diparte
   Da terra i piedi.

*'We cannot ask the thing which is not there,
Blaming the shallowness of our request.'*

──────────── (XXXVI) ────────────

BY the Sunshine of Love Dante's petition is drawn from his heart. He would fain see the unveiled Countenance of St. Benedict. He is answered in words that must carry our faith beyond the region of Time and Space, even to the hidden summit of Jacob's Ladder. 'And behold the Lord stood above it.'—Gen. xxviii. 13. In that hidden Source of Love and Light he is told that his high desire shall be fulfilled, where all others and his own (Benedict's) shall be fulfilled, and where each desire is ripened and perfected and complete; where every fragment of a desire is, where it has ever been, in the unity of the whole. Here is the ground of our confidence, even the Heart of our Father; not in the apparent fulfilment at this moment or that of our ignorant request.

In time-conditions our answer may be just as much the response of Wisdom and Love when it is the 'No' that may seem to us like silent disregard, as when it is the fulfilment that we understand as the 'Yes.'

'The true doctrine of peace in Prayer is stated by St. John with perfect simplicity and clearness, namely, that no unanswered prayer is lost. Somewhere are laid up all those intercessions that seemed to be in vain—all answered, converted into better, sweeter, nobler things than it was in us to ask or think. "*Beloved, we know that we have*"—we know it—are aware of it as simple matter of fact—"that we are in possession of all the gifts we have begged of Him." Nothing more sad than to pray and agonize with all faculties day after day, and to rise, when all is over, and say: "He has not given it me. He knows best, I submit, but He has not heard my prayer." Nothing more strong, nothing more pure than the insight which John gives, "He *has* heard me, I know not how. I shall know. Till then I would not unpray one prayer. I do not fear to have been presumptuous. I could not bear to think of having prayed less or less intensely. I have the petition I have asked of Him. I know it."'—ARCHBISHOP BENSON.

The Contemplatives are swept up the Golden Stairway, Dante and Beatrice following in their train. They thence survey the Universe.

(XXXVII)

PARADISO, CANTO XXII. 97-105, 124-137.

COSÌ mi disse, ed indi si ricolse
   Al suo collegio; e 'l collegio si strinse:
   Poi, come turbo, in su tutto s' avvolse.
La dolce Donna dietro a lor mi pinse   100
   Con un sol cenno su per quella scala;
   Sì sua virtù la mia natura vinse.
Nè mai quaggiù, dove si monta e cala
   Naturalmente, fu sì ratto moto,
   Ch' agguagliar si potesse alla mia ala.   105

*   *   *   *   *

Tu se' sì presso all' ultima salute,
   Cominciò Beatrice, che tu dèi   125
   Aver le luci tue chiare ed acute.
E però, prima che tu più t' inlei,
   Rimira in giuso, e vedi quanto mondo
   Sotto li piedi già esser ti fèi;
Sì che 'l tuo cuor, quantunque può, giocondo   130
   S' appresenti alla turba trïonfante,
   Che lieta vien per questo etereo tondo.
Col viso ritornai per tutte quante
   Le sette spere, e vidi questo globo
   Tal, ch' io sorrisi del suo vil sembiante.   135
E quel consiglio per miglior approbo
   Che l' ha per meno.

> '*That my free soul may use her wing,*
> *Which now is pinioned with mortalitie,*
> *As an intangled, hamper'd thing.*'

──────── (XXXVII) ────────

WHEN St. Benedict ceased speaking, he with his circle of contemplative spirits who had descended the Golden Stairway to welcome Dante were gathered together and swept upward like a whirlwind.

Beatrice, as Celestial Wisdom, urged her disciple onward and upward in their track. It was in her strength and in her power of vision that his earthly heaviness was overcome, and that he found himself gathered up into the flight of those who went before. The laws of Spirit, at one now with his own essential being, carry on his upward tendency more easily and swiftly than the body on Earth is impelled by its own natural laws of motion.

Even before our spiritual faculties are developed, the companionship and the words of those above ourselves do, for a time at least, carry us into regions of thought, or hope, or love, or prayer beyond our own. Is not this a promise that we also belong to these heavenly hills, and may find our home there when our true nature is in right supremacy?

The ascent by this Golden Stairway of union with the ascended and ever-ascending Son of Man suggests neither effort nor difficulty; it is either impossible to a man, or it is a yielding to a force of Spirit beyond his own.

Line 124.—Before Dante becomes aware of any fresh revelation, even as he is being caught upwards, he is told by Beatrice that he is now so near the last Salvation, or his saving health, that he may look downwards with unclouded and piercing eyes, and behold the vast Universe at his feet. Such a vision will, she says, make his heart glad, and ready to beat in unison with the triumphant joy of the heavenly host above.

The Soul's vision of the Universe.

(XXXVII)

The marvellous picture of this transcendent survey may be contrasted with that shown to our Lord from the exceeding high mountain whence all the kingdoms of the world were perceived in a moment of time, their glory and authority laid at his feet and promised to Him by 'the World Ruler of this darkness.'—Eph. vi. 12, N.V.

The endeavour of that deceitful Magician was to magnify the importance of the world's allegiance in the eyes of Him who would indeed sacrifice Himself (but not Truth) to save the world loved by the Father. Here the Divine Wisdom would teach her Disciple to weigh and measure in the Balances of Truth, the Heavens, the Creation, and the World. In the light of God, he smiles at the 'ignoble semblance' of this world, ignoble not as to size alone, we are sure. He calls it 'the little threshing-floor that makes us so proud,' as if its chief purpose were to thresh the wheat of righteousness from the chaff of semblances; he would count its glories and honours as less than nothing to the wise. He is enlightened, also, concerning the vast proportions of the framework of Creation, things visible and invisible, and sees the little speck of the Earth in due relationship to the whole.

'That which we call vastness is, rightly considered, not more wonderful, not more impressive than that which we insolently call littleness; and the infinity of God is not mysterious, it is only unfathomable; not concealed, but incomprehensible; it is a clear Infinity, the darkness of the pure unsearchable Sea.'—J. RUSKIN.

The moral worth of man, incommensurate with Sense.

(XXXVII)

The inspired words of Isaiah may have been brought to his mind as they are to ours by this wonderful survey. 'He hath measured the waters in the hollow of His Hand . . . and comprehended the dust of the Earth in a measure, and weighed the mountains in scales and the hills in a balance. . . . Behold, the Nations are as a drop of a bucket, and are counted as the small dust of the balance; behold, He taketh up the isles as a very little thing. . . . Lift up your eyes on high and behold who hath created these, that bringeth out their host by number. He calleth them all by names, by the greatness of His might; for that He is strong in power not one faileth.'

The disciple learning, as Isaiah did, that Time and Space are nothing to the infinite, all-pervading Spirit, who is the Sustainer and Substance of the whole life, would at the same time be taught, as Isaiah was, that the moral worth of man is not touched by these finite measurements. In the midst of vastness he will not say, 'My way is hid from the Lord, and my judgment is passed over from my God,' for, as it is expressed at the beginning of the verses quoted above (Isa. xl.), the Infinite One 'feeds His flock as a Shepherd and carries the lambs in His bosom. It is He that giveth power to the faint, and to them that have no might He increaseth strength.'—Isa. xl. 12, 15, 26; also v. 11 and 29.

The bird awaiting the Sun-rise.

(XXXVIII)

PARADISO, CANTO XXIII. 1-15.

COME l' augello, intra l' amate fronde,
    Posato al nido de' suoi dolci nati
  La notte che le cose ci nasconde,
Che, per veder gli aspetti desiati,
    E per trovar lo cibo onde gli pasca,   5
  In che i gravi labor gli sono grati,
Previene 'l tempo in su l' aperta frasca,
    E con ardente affetto il Sole aspetta,
  Fiso guardando, pur che l' alba nasca;
Così la Donna mia si stava eretta   10
    Ed attenta, rivolta invêr la plaga
  Sotto la quale il Sol mostra men fretta:
Sì che veggendola io sospesa e vaga,
    Fecimi quale è quei che disïando
  Altro vorria, e sperando s' appaga.   15

    Dante has already twice taken his illustrations of God's living relationship with His creatures from bird life: once in Canto XVIII. 110,

'From Him doth flow
That power which makes each creature's nest its care'
(Plumptre's Translation),

or, in Longfellow's more literal words,

'From Him is remembered
That virtue which is form unto the nest.'

Again, in Canto XX. 74-78, the Lark's silent rapture in the last sweetness of her song is compared to

'The imprint
Of the Eternal pleasure, by whose will
Doth everything become the thing it is.'

'*How often would I have gathered thy children together, even as a hen gathereth her chickens under her wings.*'
—MATT. xxiii. 37.

(XXXVIII)

IT is remarkable that, immediately after the magnificent survey of the whole Universe, with which the last Canto closes, we should be led to concentrate our attention on the nest of the Mother-bird and her brood; perhaps lest we should be lost in the terrible interstellar spaces, and forget the intimate connection of the 'Inward Father' with each sentient creature of His creation.

In the Parable from Nature before us, satisfied with its perfection as a Poem, we might perhaps fail to read the spiritual significance of its details, and its relation to the preceding Canto.

The Mother-bird's care and love for her 'sweet brood' is dwelt upon; her fostering watch over them through the dark hours remembered; her yearning love to behold them again in the light, and her anxiety to feed them again, 'when her heaviest labours will be welcome to her,' are carefully noted. She is pointed out to us as keen to be on the wing, anticipating the dawn with eager outlook, and with ardent affection awaiting the sunrise. Such had been the fostering care of the disciple's spiritual life by Beatrice, as representative of the Divine Motherhood, and such was the rapt expectation he now read in her countenance, as she gazed towards the uprising Sun. He was taught, by beholding her thus, to desire, to yearn, and to hope with her. For by the ladder of heavenly Contemplation they have been translated into the Eighth Heaven, the Sphere of the fixed Stars, and they are here to await even fuller revelations of the knowledge of the Glory of God.

'The Power which built the starry dome on high
And poised the vaulted rafters of the sky,
Teaches the linnet with unconscious breast
To round the inverted Heaven of her nest.'
(Quoted in Longfellow's notes.)

The Vision of the Sun that kindles myriads of Lamps.

———————————— (XXXIX) ————————————

PARADISO, CANTO XXIII. 19-30.

E BEATRICE disse : Ecco le schiere
   Del trïonfo di Cristo, e tutto 'l frutto   20
   Ricolto del girar di queste spere.
Pareami che 'l suo viso ardesse tutto ;
   E gli occhi avea di letizia sì pieni,
   Che passar mi convien senza costrutto.
Quale ne' plenilunïi sereni   25
   Trivia ride tra le ninfe eterne,
   Che dipingono 'l ciel per tutti i seni ;
Vid' io sopra migliaia di lucerne
   Un Sol, che tutte quante l' accendea,
   Come fa 'l nostro le viste superne.   30

'The Lord cometh with ten thousands of His Saints.'—
JUDE 14.

(XXXIX)

THE vision of Christ as a lightning gleam upon the Cross, flashing forth in the whiteness of dawn in the midst of the ruddy Mars, was the only manifestation of Himself hitherto granted to the ascending Disciple. Regarding that experience his words were very few; he could find none, with all his genius, to utter that which his memory recalled. He had to appeal to those who take up their Cross and follow Christ to excuse his attempting to describe what he saw; for *they*, he says, have seen Him also, and *they* know the vision to be incommunicable. Those only who have the Spirit of Christ can behold Him, whether in His humiliation or in His glory.

The Revelation now made to the spiritual man is a further advance into the vision of Him as He is—the fulfilment of the Divine volition of Christ: 'Father, I will that they also, whom Thou hast given Me, be with Me where I am; that they may behold My glory.'—John xvii. 24. Beatrice's wistful yearning gaze, with which he has joined his own, has prepared him for this supreme effulgence. One more glimpse such as this, yet more wondrous still, is to be the Crown of all that has been vouchsafed to him. The three visions—the mystery of Christ on the Cross, Christ in glory with His victorious band of Saints and Angels, and Christ in the bosom of the Father—reveal to us the unmeasured reach of the blessed inheritor of the Kingdom of Heaven. After a very short pause of yearning hope and expectation the whole Heavens become more and more resplendent. Beatrice's glowing face and eyes of ecstasy are aflame with the reflected glory, as she exclaims:

'Behold the hosts
Of Christ's triumphal march, and all the fruit
Harvested by the rolling of these spheres.'

(*Continued from last page.*)

PARADISO, CANTO XXIII. 31-45.

E per la viva luce trasparea
   La lucente sustanzia tanto chiara,
   Che lo mio viso non la sostenea.
Oh Beatrice, dolce guida e cara!
   Ella mi disse: Quel che ti sobranza   35
   È virtù, da cui nulla si ripara.
Quivi è la sapïenza e la possanza
   Ch' aprì la strada tra 'l cielo e la terra,
   Onde fu già sì lunga disïanza.
Come fuoco di nube si disserra,   40
   Per dilatarsi sì che non vi cape,
   E fuor di sua natura in giù s' atterra;
Così la mente mia, tra quelle dape
   Fatta più grande, di sè stessa uscìo,
   E che si fèsse rimembrar non sape.   45

'Nothing is hid from the heat thereof.'

(XXXIX)

Above ten thousand burning lamps he saw 'A Sun that one and all of them enkindled'—the living Sun of whom our Sun is the faint image and emanation, the Kindler and Source of all Light. He beholds the Divine Substance through the living Light that vestures Him, and is overwhelmed by it; his eyes were not yet conditioned by the Light to bear the Light. Beatrice tells him that nothing can shield itself from the potency of this piercing Light. 'His countenance was as the Sun that shineth in his strength' are the words of the beloved Apostle who had lain on the breast of the Lord in His days of humiliation; yet, he says, after beholding Him in glory, 'When I saw Him, I fell at His feet as dead.'

Beatrice affirms that the thoroughfares between heaven and earth had been opened by the Wisdom and Omnipotence centred in the Light before him—'the Mystery which from all ages had been hidden' and yearned for (Eph. iii. 9), now made manifest to His Saints in the image of the invisible God, the first-born of all Creation (Col. i. 15). The Disciple knows that, as he gazed, his mind escaped its former boundaries; he was more than himself, but knows not what he became. He sinks under the overwhelming revelation, and in vain tries to bring it back to his mind, whilst he retains the emotion and wonder it has produced. Beatrice recalls his eyes to herself, for he must not gaze longer, and he is now able to bear her smile, after the glimpse of a glory that so far excelled all other. These things are unutterable; he says, further on, that he finds his way cut off from representing Paradise. He thinks, when the ponderous theme is realized, that he cannot be blamed if the mortal shoulder trembles under it.

> 'It is no passage for a little boat,
> This which goes cleaving the audacious prow,
> Nor for a pilot who would spare himself.'—(67-69.)

Beatrice directs the eyes of Dante beyond her face to the Garden of the Rose and the Lilies.

(XL)

PARADISO, CANTO XXIII. 70-87.

<pre>
PERCHÈ la faccia mia sì t'innamora,   70
    Che tu non ti rivolgi al bel giardino,
    Che sotto i raggi di Cristo s'infiora?
Quivi è la rosa, in che 'l Verbo divino
    Carne si fece; e quivi son li gigli,
    Al cui odor si prese 'l buon cammino.   75
Così Beatrice. Ed io, che a' suoi consigli
    Tutto era pronto, ancora mi rendei
    Alla battaglia de' debili cigli.
Come a raggio di Sol, che puro mei
    Per fratta nube, già prato di fiori   80
    Vider, coperti d'ombra, gli occhi miei;
Vid' io così più turbe di splendori
    Fulgorati di su da raggi ardenti,
    Sanza veder principio di fulgori.
O benigna virtù, che sì gl' imprenti,   85
    Su t'esaltasti per largirmi loco
    Agli occhi lì che non eran possenti.
</pre>

> '*O soaring Soul! faint not nor tire!
> Each Heaven attained reveals a higher!*'

(XL)

THE Eighth Heaven, called the heaven of the Fixed Stars, moved by the Cherubim, seems manifested as a region of Vision, rather than as an allotted stage of the differentiating glory of any one circle of Saints.

The Contemplatives had been swept up the Golden Stairway, and in their track the 'Soaring Soul,' urged upwards by the Celestial Wisdom. There seems to have been a descending stream of glory to meet this ascent.

The Beatific Vision was not even yet to be reached and endured by One who, notwithstanding the abundance of the revelations granted to him, was still under some of the limitations of the body.

The dazzling Glory had been withdrawn in loving kindness to give more scope to the eyes that were too weak to bear it. Beatrice counselled him to look around and behold the flowers of the Garden, blossoming under the rays of Christ. She points out the Blessed Virgin and the Saints; the first as 'the Rose in which the Word Divine became incarnate,' and 'the Lilies by whose perfume the good way was discovered' (73-75). A living thought indeed, and not merely poetic imagery, to those who, having been blind perhaps to the Truth, have yet been attracted to its Way by the aroma of loving and beautiful lives!

Dante must again make further effort to obtain the victory of the Spirit over his frail and over-tasked capacity of Vision. He tells us that, as he had formerly looked on a sunlit meadow of flowers, himself under the shadow of the cloud from which the rays had broken forth and illumined the meadow, in like manner he was enabled now to behold the blessed ones in the Garden of God, because of the gracious veiling of the dazzling splendour from his eyes.

Beatrice's intercession to the Elect for living water for Dante.

(XLI)

PARADISO, CANTO XXIV. 1-9.

O SODALIZIO eletto alla gran cena
　　Del benedetto Agnello, il qual vi ciba
　　Sì, che la vostra voglia è sempre piena;
Se per grazia di Dio questi preliba
　　Di quel che cade della vostra mensa, 5
　　Anzi che morte tempo gli prescriba,
Ponete mente alla sua voglia immensa,
　　E roratelo alquanto: voi bevete
　　Sempre del fonte onde vien quel ch' ei pensa.

'Steadfast in the Faith.'

———————— (XLI) ————————

THE intercommunion of those whom 'God hath quickened together with Christ and raised up with Him and made to sit with Him in the Heavenly places' (Eph. ii. 5-7) is fully realized and expressed in the opening lines of this Canto.

This quickened Spirit beholds the blessed Company at the great Supper of the Lamb, who is ever satisfying their desires. The '*immense desire*' of the soaring Soul to partake of some crumbs that fall from the plenitude of the Divinely spread Table is expressed for him by Beatrice, his Soul's Soul; she says:

'Ye drinking are
Forever at the Fount whence comes his thought.'

He says later, that he cannot picture the joyous movements and songs that responded to this invocation, for that our imagination is too coarse for such '*folds*' or involutions, and our language has too glaring tints. We know there are sounds in the physical world far too delicate for our organs of hearing, and colours that transcend our range of vision. How much more must escape our blunted spiritual capacities! Yet how apt we are, when we perceive nothing, to say there is nothing to perceive!

The three Apostles chosen by our Lord for beholding on Earth the deeper mysteries of His life, Peter, James, and John, were thought of in the early Church as Representatives of Faith, Hope, and Charity. 'These Three,' as it was said in the earthly Paradise, '*more profoundly see.*' With these the Disciple of Celestial Wisdom is to be brought into close Communion; and his convictions concerning the three Christian Virtues are unfolded to us in Canto XXIV, and the two following. It is hardly possible

(XLI)

(Continued from last page.)

PARADISO, CANTO XXIV. 130-147.

<pre>
Ed io rispondo: Credo in uno Dio   130
   Solo ed eterno, che tutto 'l ciel muove,
   Non moto, con amore e con disio.
Ed a tal creder non ho io pur prove
   Fisiche e metafisiche; ma dàlmi
   Anche la verità, che quinci piove   135
Per Moisè, per profeti e per salmi,
   Per l' evangelio, e per voi che scriveste,
   Poi che l' ardente Spirto vi fece almi.
E credo in tre Persone eterne; e queste
   Credo una essenzia sì una e sì trina,   140
   Che soffera congiunto *sono* ed *este*.
Della profonda congiunzion divina,
   Ch' io tocco mo, la mente mi sigilla
   Più volte l' evangelica dottrina.
Quest' è 'l principio, quest' è la favilla,   145
   Che si dilata in fiamma poi vivace,
   E, come stella in cielo, in me scintilla.
</pre>

'Persuasion and belief had ripened into faith, and faith become a passionate intuition.'

———— (XLI) ————

to make extracts from them without injuring their meaning; but a few characteristic lines are quoted from each.

St. Peter first addresses Dante, and draws out from him his confession of faith. His concluding words are given in the second Fragment before us (line 131). The thought is partly a physical explanation of the Universe. The immense velocity of the Primum mobile, which moves all the lower spheres, is itself caused by the desire to unite itself with the Empyrean, as the abode of God.

All physical motion is deemed to originate in spiritual desire and love towards the Unchanging Centre of all Life.

Dante will not prove his faith, he says, by physical or metaphysical arguments alone, but from the spiritual influences of Truth, as poured down through the channels of Moses, the Prophets, the Psalms, the Gospel, and St. Peter's own Epistles. In line 107 he says that, if Christianity were assumed to be only natural, the conversion of the world would be a greater miracle than any attested by its records. He declared his belief in the Unity of Essence and the Trinity of Persons of the Divine Being (line 141).

'When I endeavour to contemplate the One Eternal Glory, it resolves itself into Three; when I would gaze upon the Three, they blend into One.'—ST. GREGORY NAZIANZEN.

We are led in the last three lines of our portion for to-day to consider the relation between the spark of living Truth within and the sparks of external teaching and testimony; by this confluence, as it were, the vivid flame is engendered which becomes the abiding and lucent star in the soul's heaven. Compare 2 Peter i. 19.

Dante's Confession of Hope as the certain expectation of future Glory.

PARADISO, CANTO XXV. 52-57, 67-78.

LA Chiesa militante alcun figliuolo
   Non ha con più speranza, com' è scritto
   Nel Sol che raggia tutto nostro stuolo.
Però gli è conceduto che d' Egitto   55
   Vegna in Gerusalemme per vedere,
   Anzi che 'l militar gli sia prescritto.
   *   *   *   *   *
Speme, diss' io, è uno attender certo
   Della gloria futura, il qual produce
   Grazia divina e precedente merto.
Da molte stelle mi vien questa luce;   70
   Ma quei la distillò nel mio cor pria,
   Che fu sommo cantor del sommo Duce.
Sperino in te, nell' alta teodía
   Dice, color che sanno 'l nome tuo:
   E chi nol sa, s' egli ha la fede mia?   75
Tu mi stillasti con lo stillar suo
   Nella pistola poi; sì ch' io son pieno,
   Ed in altrui vostra pioggia ripluo.

'Joyful through Hope.'

(XLII)

THE Disciple, having shown himself as 'steadfast in the Faith,' is blest by St. Peter, and rejoiced over by him, in the Spirit of the Master who had welcomed the Apostle's own confession of God-revealed Truth when on Earth.

A few opening lines of this Canto express the memory of the beautiful Baptistery of St. John at Florence, where Dante was baptized into the Faith. A personal hope springs up as he glances backwards to that 'fair sheepfold, where, a lamb, he slumbered,' that his poem would overcome the hatred of his fellow-citizens, and that he might return to that very font and receive there the Poet's crown. From this touching visionary hope (unfulfilled, at least, as he pictured it) Beatrice recalls him by pointing out to him with ecstasy the Apostolic Representative of Hope. This is St. James the Greater, the son of Zebedee, who was supposed by Dante to be the writer of the Epistle of St. James.

Beatrice speaks to St. James of Dante as one who possesses as much Hope as any child of the Church Militant, and even affirms that it has been on this account that it 'was conceded to him to come out from Egypt into Jerusalem, before his earthly warfare is accomplished.' He is then encouraged to make known his definition of Hope, and his grounds for Hope. The living, glowing heart of Hope in St. James breathes answeringly back to him a new impulse of hope, for, as it has been said in an earlier line:

> 'What comes hither from the mortal world
> Must needs be ripened in our radiance.'

The ancient and the new Scriptures, Dante says, show him this sign (of Hope) 'in all whom God hath made His

(Continued from last page.)

PARADISO, CANTO XXV. 79-99.

Mentr' io diceva, dentro al vivo seno
  Di quello incendio tremolava un lampo   80
  Subito e spesso a guisa di baleno;
Indi spirò: L'amore, ond' io avvampo
  Ancor vêr la virtù, che mi seguette
  Fin alla palma ed all' uscir del campo,
Vuol ch' io respiri a te, che ti dilette   85
  Di lei; ed èmmi a grato che tu diche
  Quello che la speranza ti promette.
Ed io: Le nuove e le Scritture antiche
  Pongono 'l segno, ed esso lo m' addita.
  Dell' anime, che Dio s' ha fatte amiche,   90
Dice Isaia che ciascuna vestita
  Nella sua terra fia di doppia vesta;
  E la sua terra è questa dolce vita.
E 'l tuo fratello assai vie più digesta,
  Là dove tratta delle bianche stole,   95
  Questa rivelazion ci manifesta.
E prima, appresso 'l fin d' este parole,
  Sperent in te, di sopra noi s' udì:
  Al che risposer tutte le carole.

Hope in the ultimate Beatitude of Soul and Body.

(XLII)

friends.' We have all been baptized, and, may we say?, by our Church and our Parents *prayed into* the joyfulness of Hope—may we all find and patiently cultivate this our inheritance !

Dante applies to the 'friends of God,' sealed by Hope, some words of Isaiah lxi. 7, 'they shall possess double.'

> ' Isaiah saith that each new clothed shall dwell
> *With twofold raiment in his own true land,
> And that land is this life delectable.'—(91-93.)

One of our well-known hymns tells us that, in the bliss of Heaven, 'Hope is emptied in delight.' Can this be so, when the inexhaustible infinitude of God must ever extend above and beyond His offspring's reach ? Supersensuous Hope is 'based on the faith or insight into the knowledge of God and the Final Cause of His Creation. It is thus, as St. Thomas Aquinas explains it, "a sure expectation of future glory." 'It is to the will what faith is to the intellect. With the inequalities of insight and the vicissitudes of life, Hope supports the Soul during its nights and eclipses, giving steadfastness to the Will.'—T. W. HARRIS.

When the communing regarding Hope is ended, the disciple hears the very words he had quoted as the first that poured Hope into his heart 'echoed by all the dancing Sons of Light'; they are, as he said, 'by the chief singer unto the chief Captain' (sperent in Te), 'And they that know Thy Name will *hope* (Vulg.) in Thee, for Thou, Lord, hast never failed them that seek Thee.'—Psalm ix. 10.

---

* The glorification and beatitude of soul and body.

PARADISO, CANTO XXVI. 16-18, 25-45.

LO Ben, che fa contenta questa corte,
 Alfa ed omega è di quanta scrittura
 Mi legge amore o lievemente o forte.

*   *   *   *   *

Per filosofici argomenti,   25
 E per autorità che quinci scende,
 Cotale amor convien che in me s' imprenti;
Chè 'l bene, in quanto ben, come s' intende,
 Così accende amore, e tanto maggio,
 Quanto più di bontate in sè comprende.   30
Dunque all' essenzia, ov' è tanto avvantaggio,
 Che ciascun ben, che fuor di lei si truova,
 Altro non è che di suo lume un raggio,
Più ch' in altra conviene che si muova
 La mente, amando, di ciascun che scerne   35
 Lo vero, in che si fonda questa pruova.
Tal vero allo intelletto mio sterne
 Colui, che mi dimostra il primo amore
 Di tutte le sustanzie sempiterne.
Sternel la voce del verace autore,   40
 Che dice a Moisè, di sè parlando:
 Io ti farò vedere ogni valore.
Sternilmi tu ancora, incominciando
 L' alto preconio, che grida l' arcano
 Di qui laggiù, sovra ad ogni altro bando.   45

'*Rooted in Charity.*'

(XLIII)

'AND now abideth Faith, Hope, Love, these three; and the greatest of these is Love.'

A brighter Splendour now approached the Two who had hitherto discoursed with Dante, and Beatrice exclaimed (XXV. 112):

> 'This is the one who lay upon the breast
> Of Him, our Pelican; and this is he
> To the great office from the cross elected.'

The ardent gaze of Dante, bent on discerning the aspect of the Apostle of Love, consumed his power of vision. He turned in vain to Beatrice; he could not see her, 'though close at her side, and in the happy world.'

While thus blinded to all but the inner perception of Divine Love, his attention is concentrated on the words that issued from the burning Effulgence; he is told that his Lady shall restore his sight, and that in the meantime he is to express the aim of his soul and make known by what influence he had bent his bow to this aim. He answers (16-18) that the blessedness that satisfied that region ('Lo Ben'), the Supreme Good, even the knowledge of God, is the beginning and end of 'all the writing that Love reads to him, either in a whisper or aloud'—the Secret of Life—the secret, as he adds (lines 43-45), that the Gospel of the Apostle of Love, in its beginning, proclaims aloud— the Divine Word made known by the Lord of Love to be with God and in Man. He is asked again by what process his Soul was led to the true object of Love? His answer is, that Reason and Revelation alike give a basis for Love. The primal Love when comprehended must needs enkindle Love. No kind of good can exist apart from that Divine Essence.

> 'What else looks good is some shade flung from love;
> Love gilds it, gives it worth.'

(XLIII)

(Continued from last page.)

PARADISO, CANTO XXVI. 55-69.

Però ricominciai : Tutti quei morsi,   55
    Che posson far lo cuor volgere a Dio,
    Alla mia caritate son concorsi ;
Chè l' essere del mondo e l' esser mio,
    La morte che el sostenne perchè io viva,
    E quel che spera ogni fedel com' io,   60
Con la predetta conoscenza viva,
    Tratto m' hanno del mar dell' amor tôrto,
    E del diritto m' han posto alla riva.
Le fronde, onde s' infronda tutto l' orto
    Dell' Ortolano eterno, am' io cotanto,   65
    Quanto da lui a lor di bene è pôrto.
Sì com' io tacqui, un dolcissimo canto
    Risonò per lo cielo ; e la mia Donna
    Dicea con gli altri : Santo, santo, santo.

The manifold and all-prevailing cords of Love.

(XLIII)

Dante continues (55) that Love may capture the heart in many ways, and that many means have concurred to draw him from the restless 'Sea of perverse love' and to place him on the firm shore. He had been drawn to that shore by the life in the Creation of God, by his own life or being, by that death which Christ endured that he might live, by all that the faithful hope for with him, by a vivid consciousness of the truth revealed; all of these had turned his heart from perverse love to God's love.

As he speaks with blinded eyes we can imagine his glowing, and now inward, vision of the 'Garden fair' in which he stood, and to which Beatrice had lately directed his eyes; his heart was throbbing with love to the Chief Good, and therefore to all around him who were blossoming, as he had perceived them before his blindness, under the rays of Christ. He loves, he says, all the leaves that embower Christ's Garden, and he knows that the sap of each plant is derived from that Eternal Gardener; he is aware, also, that the love drawn from his own heart to each of these is just proportioned to the good each one of these plants contains of the Gardener's ingrafting.

When he ceased speaking the whole Heavens were filled with music and voices, Beatrice's amongst them, singing the words, 'Holy, Holy, Holy.'

*The Primum Mobile or ninth Heaven entered where
'they most know and most love.'*

PARADISO, CANTO XXVII. 100-114; XXVIII. 41-45, 70-72.

LE parti sue vivissime ed eccelse 100
Sì uniformi son, ch' io non so dire
Qual Beatrice per luogo mi scelse.
Ma ella, che vedeva il mio desire,
Incominciò, ridendo tanto lieta,
Che Dio parea nel volto suo gioire : 105
La natura del moto, che quïeta
Il mezzo, e tutto l' altro intorno move,
Quinci comincia come da sua meta.
E questo cielo non ha altro dove
Che la mente divina, in che s' accende 110
L' amor che 'l volge e la virtù ch' ei piove.
Luce ed amor d' un cerchio lui comprende,
Sì come questo gli altri ; e quel precinto
Colui che 'l cinge solamente intende.

* * * * *

Da quel punto XXVIII. 41
Depende il cielo e tutta la natura.
Mira quel cerchio che più gli è congiunto,
E sappi che 'l suo muovere è sì tosto
Per l' affocato amore ond' egli è punto. 45

* * * * *

Dunque costui, che tutto quanto rape 70
L' alto universo seco, corrisponde
Al cerchio che più ama e che più sape.

The Angelic Temple whose only walls are Light and Love.

(XLIV)

IF Love blinds the eyes, it is in order to bestow a deeper and further-reaching power of vision. The blinding of the Disciple passed away like a dream, every mote was chased from his eyes; his spiritual vision became clearer than before, through the radiance of the Celestial Wisdom, 'in whose countenance God seemed to rejoice.' This aspect of Beatrice impels Dante upwards into the next Heaven, the ninth, and the swiftest in motion.

We are here led away from semblances and similitudes, from locality, time, and space, into the Divine Mind itself, wherein is kindled the Love that moves and encircles this swiftly revolving Sphere.

In the physical Cosmos (of Ptolemaic Astronomy) this Primum Mobile moves with a marvellous velocity (as it is supposed) through its intense desire to unite itself with the calm, motionless Empyrean which is the dwelling-place of God.

'In the Spiritual Cosmos Love is also, in like manner, the cause of the rapid motion of the Innermost Circle of the Seraphim who excel in ove and are nearest to the Divine Presence' (Dean Plumptre).

'Be ye holy, for I am holy,' and 'Be ye therefore perfect, as your Father in Heaven is perfect' are commands of prophetic import, unfolding to us that we are born for perfection and can find no resting-place short of our Divine inheritance. This ninth Heaven represents, then, this Circle of perfection, where spirits are most purely conjoined with the Eternal Being of God. These are they 'who love most and know most,' who are the most ardently desirous of partaking, ever more and more, of His infinite Love and Truth—never satiated, but ever satisfied, in zealous activity and in profound vision.

Beatrice unfolds the mystery of the Hierarchies. Blessedness consists in the Vision that awakens Love.

PARADISO, CANTO XXVIII. 97-114.

E QUELLA, che vedeva i pensier dubi
   Nella mia mente, disse : I cerchi primi
   T' hanno mostrato i Serafi e i Cherubi.
Così veloci seguono i suoi vimi,   100
   Per simigliarsi al punto, quanto ponno;
   E posson quanto a veder son sublimi.
Quegli altri amor, che dintorno gli vonno,
   Si chiaman Troni del divino aspetto;
   Per che 'l primo ternaro terminonno.   105
E dêi saver che tutti hanno diletto,
   Quanto la sua veduta si profonda
   Nel Vero, in che si queta ogn' intelletto.
Quinci si può veder come si fonda
   L' esser beato nell' atto che vede,   110
   Non in quel ch' ama, che poscia seconda.
E del vedere misura è mercede,
   Che grazia partorisce e buona voglia;
   Così di grado in grado si procede.

'And like a Star in Heaven the Truth was seen.'

———————— (XLV) ————————

THE Polar Star for all hearts and minds is at length discovered. The false centre of gravity, Self, was left in the pit of dark isolation and death far below; the Soul has now found its own Country of Love and Truth, and knows the pulsation of circulating Life Eternal in God and in His harmonious and vital Universe.

> ' I heard them sing Hosanna choir by choir
> To the fixed Point which holds them at the *Ubi*'

(at the appointed place, or in true order).

Beatrice unfolds the mystery of the Hierarchies who encircle the Point of Light. Each Angelic Order moves the Heaven inversely correlated to it.

Those who desire to comprehend Dante's marvellous and complicated conception of the natural and moral scheme of the Universe are advised to study Chapter II. of Miss Rossetti's 'Shadow of Dante.'

These Angelic Hierarchies

> ' All have delight
> As much as their own vision penetrates
> The Truth, in which all intellect finds rest.'

Blessed contrast to the reiteration we hear as the restless waves of Time break upon our shores! What is Truth? What is Truth? The faculty of discerning the Truth is declared here by Dante to be anterior to that of loving the Truth.

Beatrice speaks of the Creation of the Angels in answer to an unspoken question of the Disciple's. The outburst of Creation as a glorious manifestation of Love, by some necessity of the Divine Nature, is wonderfully conveyed to

The Creation of the Angels.

(XLV)

(Continued from last page.)

PARADISO, CANTO XXIX. 13-21.

Non per avere a sè di bene acquisto,
    Ch' esser non può, ma perchè suo splendore
    Potesse, risplendendo, dir : Sussisto ;   15
In sua eternità, di tempo fuore,
    Fuor d' ogni altro comprender, come i piacque,
    S' aperse in nuovi amor l' eterno amore.
Nè prima, quasi torpente, si giacque ;
    Chè nè prima nè poscia procedette   20
    Lo discorrer di Dio sovra quest' acque.

The Eternal Love unfolded into new Loves.

(XLV)

us in these lines (13-18). To the three last (19 to 21) we may find a very helpful Commentary in some words of Tennyson :

> ' " Let there be light, and there was light "; 'tis so :
> For was, and is, and will be, are but is ;
> And all creation is one act at once,
> The birth of light ; but we that are not all,
> As parts, can see but parts, now this, now that,
> And live, perforce from thought to thought, and make
> One Act a phantom of succession : thus
> Our weakness somehow shapes the shadow, Time.'

The nature of the Angels is spoken of, and the fall of Lucifer through presumption ; he had been seen by Dante as 'one constrained by all the burden of the World.' The faithful Angels are described as 'modest' and so 'apt for more exalted vision.'

Memory is not necessary to them, it is said, for their vision of God's countenance has never been interrupted, and they read there all that was and is. In the Eternal Present of God, as well as His Eternal Presence, there is no room for the painful pathos of the Past.

Beatrice then deplores the distortion of truth below, where men somnambulate in their love of appearances, and shepherds are said (as in Lycidas) to feed their flocks with wind rather than with pasture.

We are constantly reminded, even in the very highest flights of the Spirit, that those on earth are intertwined with the heavenly hosts ; and the heavens are seen to blush at the wrongs done below, especially those done by the representatives of spiritual powers—'a devil's graft on God's foundation-stone.'

The Empyrean entered. Dante's vision quenched by overpowering Light, then rekindled with stronger power.

———————————(XLVI)———————————

PARADISO, CANTO XXX. 37-60.

CON atto e voce di spedito duce
   Ricominciò : Noi semo usciti fuore
     Del maggior corpo al ciel ch' è pura luce ;
Luce intellettual piena d' amore,   40
   Amor di vero ben pien di letizia,
     Letizia che trascende ogni dolzore.
Qui vederai l' una e l' altra milizia
   Di Paradiso ; e l' una in quegli aspetti
     Che tu vedrai all' ultima giustizia.   45
Come subito lampo che discetti
   Gli spiriti visivi, sì che priva
     Dell' atto l' occhio de' più forti obbietti ;
Così mi circonfulse luce viva,
   E lasciommi fasciato di tal velo   50
     Del suo fulgor, che nulla m' appariva.
Sempre l' Amor, che queta questo cielo,
   Accoglie in sè con sì fatta salute,
     Per far disposto a sua fiamma il candelo.
Non fur più tosto dentro a me venute   55
   Queste parole brevi, ch' io compresi
     Me sormontar di sopra a mia virtute ;
E di novella vista mi raccesi
   Tale, che nulla luce è tanto mera,
     Che gli occhi miei non si fosser difesi.   60

> *'Life's self is nourished by its proper pith,*
> *And we are nurtured like a Pelican brood.'*

(XLVI)

IN our last passage it seemed, indeed, as though the spiritual capacities of the New Man were enlarged to their uttermost to receive of the fulness of God; yet there is here a further entrance from the holy precincts into the pure Light Itself. The Truth is not now discerned as the Star above, but as an enswathing veil of living flashing light inbreathed, incorporating itself with the whole personality of this Child of Light. His former capacity of vision must again through this overwhelming experience be obliterated. Beatrice assures him that such is ever the welcome or '*perfect Salute*' given by Love into this Heaven of stillness —'To make the candle ready for its flame.'

Hitherto, perhaps, reflected light has been the only conscious portion of the New Man; though Christ, the Hope of Glory, burnt within, the Disciple could but feel that Christ was there as a Star imprisoned and entombed by his own limitations; but now the Child of Light is to be more than the Light-Bearer; he is to be himself a flame of light, every atom of body, soul, and spirit imbued with substance for the crowning, consuming flame.

> 'No sooner had within me these brief words
> An entrance found, than I perceived myself
> To be uplifted over my own power,
> And I with vision new rekindled me
> Such that no light whatever is so pure
> But that mine eyes would *meet it with repose.*'

To meet fresh Light with repose—knowing ourselves as to the manner born—is a glorious thought! The Light within and the Light without may be compared now to

> 'Two meteors of expanding flame,
> Those spheres instinct with it become the same,
> Burning, yet ever inconsumable;
> In one another's substance finding food.'
> '*Epipsychidion.*'

Dante's newly-kindled power of vision perceives the imagery which is preface to the Truth, as a River.

(XLVII)

PARADISO, CANTO XXX. 61-81.

E VIDI lume in forma di riviera
    Fulvido di fulgori, intra duo rive
    Dipinte di mirabil primavera.
Di tal fiumana uscian faville vive,
    E d' ogni parte si mescean ne' fiori,   65
    Quasi rubini ch' oro circoscrive.
Poi, come inebriate dagli odori,
    Riprofondavan sè nel miro gurge;
    E s' una entrava, un' altra n' uscia fuori.
L' alto disio, che mo t' infiamma ed urge   70
    D' aver notizia di ciò che tu vei,
    Tanto mi piace più quanto più turge.
Ma di quest' acqua convien che tu bei
    Prima che tanta sete in te si sazii:
    Così mi disse il Sol degli occhi miei.   75
Anche soggiunse: Il fiume, e li topazii
    Ch' entrano ed escono, e 'l rider dell' erbe
    Son di lor vero ombriferi prefazii;
Non che da sè sien queste cose acerbe,
    Ma è il difetto dalla parte tua,   80
    Che non hai viste ancor tanto superbe.

*'The new receptivity deserves
The new completion.'*

(XLVII)

WITH newly kindled power of vision, 'with the whole body full of light,' Dante is able to perceive undazzled the imagery which he describes.

A river of Light reveals itself to him, between two banks adorned with a wonderful Season of Spring; it seemed to him that living ruby sparks issued from the effulgent torrent and sank into the flowers on the banks, and again, as though inebriate with odours, they plunged into the living waters of Light. Beatrice tells him he has seen 'unripe' (acerbo) imagery only, which but 'dimly prefaces' the truths to be revealed later. She says this unripeness proceeds from his own incompleteness of vision. He must drink of that water of Light and Life, and bathe his eyes in it, before his great thirst to behold truly can be slaked. The river itself, clear and splendid as it is, he will find, when he has tasted of it and bathed his eyes in it, will broaden out into a wide circular Sea, and the lovely, sparkling, moving jewels will become living organizations. The heaven-taught eye of the true Seer will ever in its growing powers behold the enlargement of Truth, which can never be stereotyped, for it is Infinite. The Truth changes not (as Beatrice affirms), but 'we have to *grow up into Him* (Who is Truth) in all things.'

'In the higher world, it is not as in our dark dwelling-place, wherein sounds can be compared only with sounds, colours with colours, and a substance only with that which is directly related to it. There all things are more closely related with each other. There the light is sounding; melody produces light; colours have motion because they are living, and the objects are all at once sounding, transparent and moving, and can penetrate each other.'—ST. MARTIN.

Dante, after bathing his eyes in the River of Light, perceives it transformed into a circular Ocean.

―――――――――――――(XLVIII)―――――――

PARADISO, CANTO XXX. 82-99.

NON è fantin che sì subito rua
    Col volto verso il latte, se si svegli
    Molto tardato dall' usanza sua,
Come fec' io, per far migliori spegli   85
    Ancor degli occhi, chinandomi all' onda
    Che si deriva, perchè vi s' immegli.
E sì come di lei bevve la gronda
    Delle palpebre mie, così mi parve
    Di sua lunghezza divenuta tonda.   90
Poi come gente stata sotto larve,
    Che pare altro che prima, se si sveste
    La sembianza non sua in che disparve;
Così mi si cambiaro in maggior feste
    Li fiori e le faville, sì ch' io vidi   95
    Ambo le corti del ciel manifeste.
O isplendor di Dio, per cu' io vidi
    L' alto trionfo del regno verace,
    Dammi virtude a dir com' io lo vidi.

> '*Melting into this radiance, we blend,
> Mingle, and so become a part of it.*'

(XLVIII)

THE immature capacity of spiritual vision which Beatrice had told Dante was still his (in the last lines of our last portion) is now to be ripened by his stooping down and bathing his eyes in that effulgent river of Light. His whole will leaps to the reception of his long-sought element, even as a hungering babe to its mother's milk. This is the last of the many Baptisms of the mounting soul. It is self-administered, as none of his former baptisms have been; he now takes freely of the water of life. He has found this water as Ezekiel did, first reaching to the ankles, then to the knees, then to the loins, and lastly 'waters to swim in, that could not be passed over.' As his eyes are further opened, he finds the onward rolling river has become a 'Circular Ocean of Light,'—its circumference ' would be too large a girdle for the Sun.' Did he now behold Truth as the Divine Whole rather than as expressed in the succeeding moments of onward-rolling Time?

The sparks of ruby light and the flowers (as he had before thought them) he now perceives as manifestations of the two Hosts of Heaven: the Angels and the Saints. How they were raised in magnificence and joy! or rather, how much more truly his own opened eyes could perceive them!

Three times he uses the words 'I saw.' 'Io vidi,' 'io vidi,' 'io vidi,' as if never before had he seen! He places these words at the end of three alternate lines, as he always places the name of Christ. He saw not semblances, but realities, for he had indeed reached the 'triumph of the veracious realm.'

(XLVIII)

(Continued from last page.)

PARADISO, CANTO XXX. 100-108.

Lume è lassù, che visibile face 100
    Lo Creatore a quella creatura,
    Che solo in lui vedere ha la sua pace;
E si distende in circolar figura
    In tanto, che la sua circonferenza
    Sarebbe al Sol troppo larga cintura. 105
Fassi di raggio tutta sua parvenza
    Reflesso al sommo del mobile primo,
    Che prende quindi vivere e potenza.

(XLVIII)

Hitherto, Dante had but looked as it were upon masks. He finds he must appeal to the Splendour of God, which had given him power to behold, to give him power also to say in what manner he beheld these veracious things. It is this Light, he says, this wide-spreading circular Ocean of Effulgence like the glassy Sea, clear as crystal before the throne of God, which makes the Creator visible to each creature, 'who only in beholding Him has Peace.' All Vitality and Power issue thence, and impel the motion of the first moved Sphere, which transmits and reflects the transcendent beam.

Peace, Dante often affirms, is the primary condition for the Love and Knowledge of God, and for righteousness, liberty, and progress on Earth; from this conviction his intense desire arose for strong, orderly Government in Church and State. He says in the 'De Monarchiâ,' 'And since what is true of the part is true of the whole, and it happens in the particular man that by sitting quietly he is perfected in Prudence and Wisdom; it is clear that the human race in the quiet or tranquillity of Peace is most freely and easily disposed for its proper work, which is almost Divine, as it is written, "Thou hast made him a little lower than the Angels." Hence it is that not riches, not pleasures, not length of life, not health, not strength, not comeliness, was sung to the Shepherds from on high, but Peace.'

The beauty of the Saints mirrored in the 'Glassy Sea' of God.

(XLIX)

PARADISO, CANTO XXX. 109-132.

E COME clivo in acqua di suo imo
   Si specchia, quasi per vedersi adorno,   110
      Quando è nel verde e ne' fioretti opimo;
Sì, soprastando al lume intorno intorno,
   Vidi specchiarsi in più di mille soglie
      Quanto di noi lassù fatto ha ritorno.
E se l' infimo grado in sè raccoglie   115
   Sì grande lume, quant' è la larghezza
      Di questa rosa nell' estreme foglie?
La vista mia nell' ampio e nell' altezza
   Non si smarriva, ma tutto prendeva
      Il quanto e 'l quale di quell' allegrezza.   120
Presso e lontano lì nè pon, nè leva;
   Chè dove Dio sanza mezzo governa,
      La legge natural nulla rileva.
Nel giallo della rosa sempiterna,
   Che si dilata, rigrada, e redole   125
      Odor di lode al Sol che sempre verna,
Qual è colui che tace e dicer vuole,
   Mi trasse Beatrice, e disse: Mira
      Quanto è 'l convento delle bianche stole!
Vedi nostra città quanto ella gira;   130
   Vedi li nostri scanni sì ripieni,
      Che poca gente omai ci si disira.

'The Lord shall be unto thee an everlasting Light, and thy God thy glory.'—Isa. lx. 18, 19.

——————————— (XLIX) ———————————

ALL mirrored in the glassy, crystal Sea of the Light of God, the Seer now beholds in thousands of ranks the souls above 'who have returned thither from us below.' They have journeyed to no strange land, but have returned to their true Home!

The Spring-quickened banks of the Stream, reflected in the water, were the 'foreshadowing prefaces' of these Saints and Angels, mirrored in the Light of God. He changes his imagery again, and the thousands, tier above tier, of the white-robed saints appear to him like the petals of a snow-white Rose, of vastest amplitude, around its golden Centre of Light. The separate flowerets had passed away into one vital organization of beauty and unity. The Seer, with perfected powers, can behold the height and depth of the immeasurable fulness around him.

(118-121) 'My vision in the vastness of the height
 Lost not itself, but comprehended all
 The quantity and quality of that gladness.
 There near or far nor add nor take away.'

No natural law of space can hold in the spiritual kingdom. The only gulf of separation there is between those whose loves and aims are diverse.

The changing imagery we are studying, and such lines as those quoted above, make us feel as does the Seer himself, the futility of using the same language for the things of the senses and those of the spirit—unless, indeed, we understand the former to be only 'foreshadowing prefaces' of the latter. The scales and the measuring rods of each realm cannot be interchanged. Beatrice points out the vast circuit of the City that has no limits, and that is, notwithstanding, comprehended in one glance. She points out, also, that the allotted Seats are nearly filled, and says the number of the Elect must soon be completed.

*The Hosts of the Saints, the Bride of Christ,
seen as the Mystic White Rose.*

──────── (L) ────────

PARADISO, CANTO XXXI. 1-15.

IN forma dunque di candida rosa
   Mi si mostrava la milizia santa,
   Che nel suo sangue Cristo fece sposa.
Ma l' altra, che volando vede e canta
   La gloria di Colui che la innamora,   5
   E la bontà che la fece cotanta,
Sì come schiera d' api, che s' infiora
   Una fïata, ed altra si ritorna
   Là dove il suo lavoro s' insapora,
Nel gran fior discendeva, che s' adorna   10
   Di tante foglie ; e quindi risaliva
   Là dove lo suo amor sempre soggiorna.
Le facce tutte avean di fiamma viva,
   E l' ale d' oro ; e l' altro tanto bianco,
   Che nulla neve a quel termine arriva.   15

'*The Holy City, new Jerusalem, coming down from God out of Heaven, prepared as a Bride adorned for her husband.*'

——————————— (L) ———————————

THE Snow-white, Mystic Rose remains before the spiritual Poet's vision as the image of the Bride of Christ, made meet for Him by His outpoured Life-blood. He sees the hosts of Saints, in the unity of one vital organism of beauty, purity, and sweet perfume, expanding beneath the Divine rays of the uncreated Sun ; he sees the hosts of Angels with faces of vital flame and wings of gold, now sinking like bees amidst the living petals of the Rose, bringing with the fanning of their wings both Peace and Ardour, now re-ascending to the blessed Fountain of Life and Peace, where ' evermore their love abideth,' and whence they replenish their own powers. A glorious example for the Church below, of Service sustained and gladdened by Adoration !

The contrast of this Ideal of Light, Sweetness, and Unity with our dark, disintegrated, and tempest-tossed outward conditions, will not fail to awaken an Amen to the cry of the Seer in lines 27-30.

> ' O Trinal Light that in one Star sublime
> Dost with thy rays their souls so satisfy,
> Look down with pity on our storm-beat clime.'
> PLUMPTRE's Translation.

The Hosts of the Angels, like bees sinking into the Flower, carry Peace and Ardour into the White Rose.

———————————— (I.) ————————————

(*Continued from last page.*)

PARADISO, CANTO XXXI. 16-30.

Quando scendean nel fior, di banco in banco
   Porgevan della pace e dell' ardore,
   Ch' egli acquistavan ventilando il fianco.
Nè l' interporsi, tra 'l disopra e 'l fiore,
   Di tanta moltitudine volante,   20
   Impediva la vista e lo splendore;
Chè la luce divina è penetrante
   Per l' universo, secondo ch' è degno,
   Sì che nulla le puote essere ostante.
Questo sicuro e gaudioso regno,   25
   Frequente in gente antica ed in novella,
   Viso ed amore avea tutto ad un segno.
O trina luce, che in unica stella
   Scintillando a lor vista sì gli appaga,
   Guarda quaggiuso alla nostra procella.   30

'We are come ... to an innumerable Company of Angels, and to the general Assembly and Church of the Firstborn.'

──────────── (L) ────────────

It is not difficult, as we look within and around, to dwell on the dark side of 'poor shipwrecked Humanity.' We often picture its sufferings, sins, and feebleness concentrated, as it were, in one organism of failure and woe. May we not, on the other hand, by an effort of will and faith, lift our eyes to the other hemisphere of Humanity, and behold its nobler, transfigured soul, in separated consciousness of Love, Purity, and Vital Power, in the Sunshine of the Divine Ardour and Peace? Have we not had experience of some fragments of that other hemisphere? and if we venture to look into the darker heart of humanity, have we not our White Rose, also as a true vision of its Hope and Peace? 'Your Father Abraham rejoiced to see my day: and he saw it and was glad,' and many of the seed of the Faithful have seen the triumphant Day of Christ in the hearts of His militant Hosts, going forth with Him conquering and to conquer; not as a future 'Perhaps,' but as a present Reality. Many chapters of the roll of Faith's heroes might be added to that of Hebrews xi., for truly 'the time would fail us' also, in our own day, to tell of our 'Gideons and Baraks, and Samsons and Jephthas.'

PARADISO, CANTO XXXI. 64-78.

ED, Ella ov' è? di subito diss' io.
   Ond' egli: A terminar lo tuo disiro   65
   Mosse Beatrice me del luogo mio.
E se riguardi su nel terzo giro
   Dal sommo grado, tu la rivedrai
   Nel trono, che i suoi merti le sortiro.
Sanza risponder gli occhi su levai;   70
   E vidi lei che si facea corona,
   Riflettendo da sè gli eterni rai.
Da quella regïon, che più su tuona,
   Occhio mortale alcun tanto non dista,
   Qualunque in mare più giù s' abbandona,   75
Quanto lì da Beatrice la mia vista;
   Ma nulla mi facea, chè la sua effige
   Non discendeva a me per mezzo mista.

'*There was no more Near nor Far.*'

(LI)

THE Seer continues to gaze above, around, below, taking note of all he sees, even as a Pilgrim does in the holy place he visits, hoping to retell it on his return. Everywhere there meet his eye

> 'Faces . . . of charity persuasive,
> Embellished by His light and their own smile.' (49, 50.)

—words wonderfully significant of the union of the Divine with each human personality. What can be more characteristic of a friend than his own smile?

Beholding this illumination of Love in these faces, he is able 'to comprehend *with all Saints* the breadth and length and depth and height, and to know the love of Christ which passeth knowledge' (Eph. iii. 18, 19). He desires to ask Beatrice of things of which he is in doubt, and turns to seek her countenance. She has disappeared: he finds in her place by his side St. Bernard, 'an old Man habited like the glorious people,' who looks at him with the benign joy and the compassion of a tender father.

The extract for to-day continues the narration with Dante's startled, spontaneous exclamation, 'And She, where is she?' Pointed out by St. Bernard, the Seer beholds her in her own place by the side of the contemplative Rachel, who is a companion of the Blessed Virgin, and of Lucia, the ministrant of grace and compassion. No earthly eye could measure the space between himself and her, but he tells us the distance was nothing to him ('nulla mi facea'), because her image descended not to him 'through any misty medium.' In the innermost Sanctuary distance cannot be; in heart and soul the two are one in God. In her ascension to the place prepared for her we may read, by

Dante's Thanksgiving to Beatrice, and her last smile.

(*Continued from last page.*)

PARADISO, CANTO XXXI. 79-93.

O Donna, in cui la mia speranza vige,
   E che soffristi per la mia salute,   80
   In Inferno lasciar le tue vestige ;
Di tante cose, quante io ho vedute,
   Dal tuo podere e dalla tua bontate
   Riconosco la grazia e la virtute.
Tu m' hai di servo tratto a libertate   85
   Per tutte quelle vie, per tutt' i modi,
   Che di ciò fare avean la potestate.
La tua magnificenza in me custodi,
   Sì che l' anima mia, che fatt' hai sana,
   Piacente a te dal corpo si disnodi.   90
Così orai ; e quella sì lontana,
   Come parea, sorrise e riguardommi ;
   Poi si tornò all' eterna fontana.

'In the primal sympathy which having been must ever be.'

(LI)

the light of the Lord's Ascension, the Divine way towards a more abiding Presence than there can be under the misty conditions of the flesh.

The very Beatrice Portinari who had first awakened the soul of the Seer, and has been to him the representative of Divine Wisdom and Theology (sometimes, indeed, merged, as to her own personality, in these Powers), is now again realized, seen by him, as through her own special personal fitness, enthroned and glorified amongst her peers. He can now fully open to her the grateful homage of his heart, and tell over all the virtue and the grace he recognised in her ways and expedients for leading him from Slavery into the glorious freedom of the Child of God. His last words to her are these:

' Preserve towards me thy magnificence,
So that this soul of mine which thou hast healed,
Pleasing to thee, be loosened from the body
. . . . . . and she, so far away,
Smiled, as it seemed, and looked once more at me;
Then unto the Eternal fountain turned.'   88-93

> Leave me not, God, until—Nay, until when?
> Not till I be with Thee, one heart, one mind,
> Not till Thy Life is Light in me;
> And then—leaving is left behind!
>
> G. MacDonald.

*St. Bernard takes the place of Beatrice in directing
and instructing Dante's vision.*

PARADISO, CANTO XXXI. 94-99.

E 'L santo Sene: Acciocchè tu assommi
   Perfettamente, disse, il tuo cammino,   95
   A che priego ed amor santo mandommi,
Vola con gli occhi per questo giardino;
   Chè veder lui t' acuirà lo sguardo
   Più a montar per lo raggio divino.

   *   *   *   XXXII. 52-57, 142-151.

Dentro all' ampiezza di questo reame
   Casual punto non puote aver sito,
   Se non come tristizia, o sete, o fame:
Chè per eterna legge è stabilito   55
   Quantunque vedi, sì che giustamente
   Ci si risponde dall' anello al dito.

   *   *   *   *   *

E drizzeremo gli occhi al primo Amore,
   Sì che, guardando verso lui, penètri,
   Quant' è possibil, per lo suo fulgore.
Veramente nè forse tu t' arretri,   145
   Movendo l' ale tue, credendo oltrarti,
   Orando, grazia convien che s'impetri:
Grazia da quella che puote aiutarti;
   E tu mi seguirai con l'affezione,
   Sì che dal dicer mio lo cuor non parti;   150
E cominciò questa santa orazione.

Dante learns 'to mount along the ray Divine' and is instructed in the perfection of Divine Providence and the necessity of Grace and united Prayer.

(LII)

ST. BERNARD, the aged, mystic Saint, is to direct the Pilgrim's eyes, and to instruct his spirit, as he approaches the completing and consummate vision. Instead of Beatrice, Dante, the disciple of St. Thomas Aquinas, who was the Master of men's intellects, needed now the rapturous impulse from the Master of men's hearts, as St. Bernard has been called. Instead of Beatrice, the personally beloved, a universal representative of Woman was to be revealed to him through St. Bernard, the Virgin's faithful servant. He directs the Pilgrim, who has all but reached his Goal, to behold one Saint after another in God's Garden, and tells him this will discipline his sight 'further to mount along the ray divine'; he bids him observe the countenances, and listen to the baby voices (47) of the 'Festinata gente,' the hastened folk, as he calls the children who had died ere they knew right or wrong; and points out that each of these had his allotted place, and his own distinctive hair and crown; for in the Kingdom of God's Providence nothing is casual, but all is adjusted, as the ring fitted to the finger. He is then told to gaze into that face which most resembles Christ's, whose clearness will alone dispose him to behold Christ. Finally, he is instructed to direct his eyes to the Primal Love, and, as far as in him lay, penetrate himself with that effulgence. He must continue in prayer for needed influx of grace, uniting his heart with St. Bernard's words, lest (through isolation from communion) he should be only flapping his wings, without making upward progress.

*St. Bernard's Invocation of the Daughter and Mother
of Christ.*

PARADISO, CANTO XXXIII.

VERGINE MADRE, figlia del tuo Figlio,
   Umile ed alta più che creatura,
   Termine fisso d' eterno consiglio,
Tu se' colei che l' umana natura
   Nobilitasti sì, che 'l suo Fattore   5
   Non disdegnò di farsi sua fattura.
Nel ventre tuo si raccese l' amore,
   Per lo cui caldo nell' eterna pace
   Così è germinato questo fiore.
Qui se' a noi meridïana face   10
   Di caritate; e giuso, intra i mortali,
   Se' di speranza fontana vivace.
Donna, se' tanto grande e tanto vali,
   Che qual vuol grazia, ed a te non ricorre,
   Sua disïanza vuol volar senz' ali.   15
La tua benignità non pur soccorre
   A chi dimanda, ma molte fïate
   Liberamente al dimandar precorre.
In te misericordia, in te pietate,
   In te magnificenza, in te s' aduna   20
   Quantunque in creatura è di bontate.
Or questi, che dall' infima lacuna
   Dell' universo insin qui ha vedute
   Le vite spiritali ad una ad una,
Supplica a te, per grazia, di virtute   25
   Tanto, che possa con gli occhi levarsi
   Più alto verso l' ultima salute.

*The eyes of all the Blessed waiting on the Eternal Light
for Dante's illumination.*

PARADISO, CANTO XXXIII.

Ed io, che mai per mio veder non arsi
   Più ch' io fo per lo suo, tutti i miei prieghi
   Ti porgo (e prego che non sieno scarsi)   30
Perchè tu ogni nube gli disleghi
   Di sua mortalità co' prieghi tuoi,
   Sì che 'l sommo piacer gli si dispieghi.
Ancor ti prego, Regina che puoi
   Ciò che tu vuoli, che conservi sani,   35
   Dopo tanto veder, gli affetti suoi.
Vinca tua guardia i movimenti umani;
   Vedi Beatrice con quanti beati
   Per li miei prieghi ti chiudon le mani.
Gli occhi da Dio diletti e venerati,   40
   Fissi nell' orator, mi dimostraro
   Quanto i devoti prieghi le son grati.
Indi all' eterno lume si drizzaro,
   Nel qual non si può creder che s' invii
   Per creatura l' occhio tanto chiaro.   45
Ed io ch' al fine di tutti i desii
   M' appropinquava, sì com' io doveva,
   L' ardor del desiderio in me finii.
Bernardo m' accennava, e sorrideva,
   Perch' io guardassi in suso; ma io era   50
   Già per me stesso tal qual ei voleva:
Chè la mia vista, venendo sincera
   E più e più, entrava per lo raggio
   Dell' alta luce che da sè è vera.

Dante's Prayer for the rekindling of one spark of the Glory for the future people.

(LIII)

PARADISO, CANTO XXXIII.

Da quinci innanzi il mio veder fu maggio   55
   Che 'l parlar nostro, ch' a tal vista cede;
   E cede la memoria a tanto oltraggio.
Qual è colui che sonnïando vede,
   E dopo 'l sogno la passione impressa
   Rimane, e l' altro alla mente non riede,   60
Cotal son io, chè quasi tutta cessa
   Mia visïone, ed ancor mi distilla
   Nel cuor lo dolce che nacque da essa.
Così la neve al Sol si disigilla,
   Così al vento nelle foglie lievi   65
   Si perdea la sentenzia di Sibilla.
O somma luce, che tanto ti lievi
   Da' concetti mortali, alla mia mente
   Ripresta un poco di quel che parevi;
E fa' la lingua mia tanto possente,   70
   Ch' una favilla sol della tua gloria
   Possa lasciare alla futura gente:
Chè, per tornare alquanto a mia memoria,
   E per sonare un poco in questi versi,
   Più si conceperà di tua vittoria.   75
Io credo, per l' acume ch' io soffersi
   Del vivo raggio, ch' io sarei smarrito,
   Se gli occhi miei da lui fossero aversi.
E mi ricorda ch' io fu' più ardito
   Per questo a sostener tanto, ch'io giunsi   80
   L' aspetto mio col Valore infinito.

The concentration of all good in the pure ray of Light which rivets his gaze.

(LIII)

PARADISO, CANTO XXXIII.

O abbondante grazia, ond' io presunsi
   Ficcar lo viso per la luce eterna
   Tanto, che la veduta vi consunsi !
Nel suo profondo vidi che s' interna   85
   Legato con amore in un volume
   Ciò che per l' universo si squaderna :
Sustanzia ed accidente e lor costume,
   Tutti conflati insieme per tal modo,
   Che ciò ch' io dico è un semplice lume.   90
La forma universal di questo nodo
   Credo ch' io vidi, perchè più di largo,
   Dicendo questo, mi sento ch' io godo.
Un punto solo m' è maggior letargo,*
   Che venticinque secoli all' impresa,   95
   Che fe Nettuno ammirar l' ombra d' Argo.
Così la mente mia tutta sospesa
   Mirava fissa, immobile ed attenta,
   E sempre nel mirar faceasi accesa.
A quella luce cotal si diventa,   100
   Che volgersi da lei per altro aspetto
   È impossibil che mai si consenta ;
Perocchè 'l ben, ch' è del volere obbietto,
   Tutto s' accoglie in lei, e fuor di quella
   È difettivo ciò ch' è lì perfetto.   105

---

* It is supposed these lines imply that every moment of time is swallowing up the memory of the Beatific Vision, which belongs not to mortality, and which for ever rivets the gaze of Celestial Spirits.

His growing power of vision discovers Three Circles in the Light and our own Image depicted therein.

(LIII)

PARADISO, CANTO XXXIII.

Omai sarà più corta mia favella,
   Pure a quel ch' io ricordo, che d' un fante
   Che bagni ancor la lingua alla mammella.
Non perchè più ch' un semplice sembiante
   Fosse nel vivo lume ch' io mirava,   110
   Chè tale è sempre qual s' era davante ;
Ma, per la vista che s' avvalorava
   In me, guardando, una sola parvenza,
   Mutandom' io, a me si travagliava.
Nella profonda e chiara sussistenza   115
   Dell' alto lume parvermi tre giri
   Di tre colori e d' una contenenza ;
E l' un dall' altro, come Iri da Iri,
   Parea riflesso, e 'l terzo parea fuoco
   Che quinci e quindi igualmente si spiri.   120
Oh quanto è corto 'l dire e come fioco
   Al mio concetto ! e questo, a quel ch' io vidi,
   È tanto, che non basta a dicer poco.
O luce eterno, che sola in te sidi,
   Sola t' intendi, e, da te intelletta   125
   Ed intendente, te ami ed arridi !
Quella circulazion, che sì concetta
   Pareva in te, come lume reflesso,
   Dagli occhi miei alquanto circonspetta,
Dentro da sè, del suo colore istesso,   130
   Mi parve pinta della nostra effige,
   Per che il mio viso in lei tutto era messo.

PARADISO, CANTO XXXIII.

Qual è 'l geomètra, che tutto s' affige
  Per misurar lo cerchio, e non ritrova,
  Pensando, quel principio ond' egli indige ;   135
Tale era io a quella vista nuova :
  Veder voleva come si convenne
  L' imago al cerchio, e come vi s' indova ;
Ma non eran da ciò le proprie penne ;
  Se non che la mia mente fu percossa   140
  Da un fulgore, in che sua voglia venne.
All' alta fantasia qui mancò possa :
  Ma già volgeva il mio disiro e 'l velle,
  Sì come ruota che igualmente è mossa,
L' Amor che muove il Sole e l' altre stelle.   145

'Draw off thy shoes from off thy feet, for the place whereon thou standest is holy ground.'

——————— (LIII) ———————

THE closing Canto of the Paradiso must not be separated into fragments.

It is hoped that those who have followed some footsteps of the upward ascent in the preceding Selections will desire to study as a whole this magnificent conclusion in its own language.

In the Heaven of Heavens, the Empyrean itself, Dante learns that he needs yet more grace and power from the Fountain ere the 'Chief Pleasure' (the Sommo Piacer) can be revealed to his mortality.

For the full reception of this grace, he must not only himself aspire more ardently, but must be aided by the prayers of St. Bernard, the 'faithful Bernard' of the Blessed Virgin, as he calls himself, and at his request, by her intercessions also, and those of all the Blessed.

The Canto opens (1 to 39) with this Invocation of the Daughter and Mother of Christ, as he addresses her; perhaps, as Dean Plumptre notes, the most noble utterance that her Cultus has ever evoked.

If this utterance seems to us a more fitting invocation of the Primal Source of all essential and ideal life, than of even the purest embodiment of that life, we yet would not desire to criticise it here, but rather to stand with Dante, seeing where we can with his eyes, and learning as we may from his vision.

Dante must have intended to convey a special meaning in parting with Beatrice on the Threshold of the Goal to which she has been leading him. As the Celestial Wisdom, we might have expected Her to lead him to the Presence Chamber, in which, as Wisdom, She ever dwells; but in Dante's eyes Beatrice Portinari has resumed that personality

The low Estate of the Bond-maiden magnified by the Lord.

(now glorified) which he has known and loved from childhood, and has taken the place allotted to her amongst the august company of the Contemplative Saints. He has seen her farewell smile, and has rendered to her the grateful homage of his overflowing heart.

She was to him, as we know, the outward and visible sign of the Celestial Wisdom; he is now to behold the outward and visible sign of the Divine Ideal of Woman. This represented ideal of Womanhood is to be freed from all merely individual associations, and united with the name and character of Mary, known to all who know the name of Christ. She, who was pronounced by Heaven to be 'blessed amongst women,' by her close, pre-ordained, and manifested relationship to the Divine-Human flesh of the Son of Man, is through Him related to the redeemed and consecrated flesh of all the Sons of men. The sacredness of her Virginity and of her Motherhood, of her especial functions and ministry, is to become the inspiring and controlling ' Pattern in the Heavens ' of all thought and action with regard to all women.

In God the Woman is one hemisphere of the Divine Image, for 'God created Man in His own image . . . male and female created He them.' Feminine receptivity, lowly serviceableness and Motherhood, are revealed to be as truly in God as the masculine virtues and Fatherhood. The spiritual Man, represented by Dante, is on the verge of the all-completing, consummate vision of God and Man in unity. As the last preparation for the reception of this mystery in its fulness, he is to behold the Woman as an integral part of the Divine Humanity, personalized by the Blessed Virgin; he sees her distinguished from, yet in most

'My substance curiously wrought in the lowest parts of the Earth.'

intimate relationship with, her Divine Source; he sees her also distinguished from, yet in universal relationship with, the human race. The lowly Handmaiden of the Lord, evermore exercising her gracious ministries, which are, indeed, channels of grace, is the crowned Queen of angelic ministries in the very precincts of the Holy of Holies.

St. Bernard pleads the development of 'this man' (questi—22) from the lowest depth of the Universe through one after another of the spiritual lives, 'even as far as this,' as a claim for the gift of yet more power to uplift him higher towards the uttermost Salvation. May we not consider that these words point to the hope and destiny of the whole human race?

Not as an exceptional experience of one member of the human family would we interpret his vision, but as the promise anticipated in one of the first-fruits of the race for the whole of that race. 'For if the first-fruit be holy, the lump is also holy' (Rom. xi. 16).

Dante has made manifest to us, as, perhaps, no other has done, the immeasurable spaces to be traversed in the evolution of the human being. From the unconscious sleep in the dark and bitter Forest, dominated on awaking by wild animal life, he has descended (with others) by gradual steps of selfish desire to the dark, deep abyss of absolute, self-centred death; through the discipline of that painful self-consciousness (the initial point, however, of all progress), and through the experience of the necessary consequences of anguish and desolation in the evil choice, we have followed the emerging of his enthralled will in its upward struggles. His many cleansings of Water, of Fire, and of blinding Light, have been revealed. We have learnt through him of his inherited instructions from the Sages of Antiquity, and from the Prophets and Apostles and Saints; he has made known to us the awakened questions and answers of the living Spirit in his own heart; the diverse unfoldings of Providence and Nature; and the lavish ministrations and gifts of Heaven's Grace.

On the summit of the Mount of purification, that Sacramental region where the inward and spiritual and the outward and visible are at one, we saw him as anointed King and Priest over himself, and so fitted for that Eden environment, the very overflow and necessity of his sublimated life. There he is risen again with Christ. Since then we have been endeavouring to follow him with Christ in His Ascension through the 'Heavenly places,' to the central spiritual truths and causes that move the Heavens and the Earth, even to the Primal and Ultimate Truth and Cause Himself.

In this union with the Father, he is in his own measure with Christ to receive the right hand of Power for the succour of his Brethren.

These 'far distances' of ideal progression, symbolized by his first deep descent into the lower parts of the Earth, his long upward climb through the seven circles of the Purgatorial Mount, and his Ascension through the nine Spheres of the Heavens, force upon our minds some conception of the far-reaching purpose of God throughout the ages, in the fashioning of His Creation and of His Offspring out of the confusion and darkness of chaos into the order and light of union with Himself.

The concluding lines of the prayer of St. Bernard show him to us as expressing, not his own desires alone (though these, he says, exceed in ardour any he ever felt for his own

The New Man ascending with Christ to the right hand of Power.

salvation), but the desire of the whole Choir of the blessed, who join with clasped, uplifted hands their prayer with his. The eyes of the Virgin also are waiting on the Source of Light, in the self-same expecting hope. He for whom they prayed had exhausted every desire of his heart in this 'ultimate ardour': he needed not the sign that St. Bernard gave him to look upward, for this was the spontaneous attitude of his whole being. He is aware that his purified capacities of vision become more and more united with the pure Light which is Truth Itself.

> 'For as my vision to more pureness came
> Still more and more, it passed within the rays
> Of that high, bright, self-verifying flame.' (53, 54.)

We who read are like the people 'waiting for Zacharias while he tarried in the Temple. And when he came out he could not speak unto them: and they perceived that he had seen a vision in the Temple: and he continued making signs unto them and remained dumb' (Luke i. 22).

We know, as we perceive his signs, that we are not seeking to follow a Poet's dream that half eludes his grasp, but that we see One who has been grasped by an overmastering Power. The Vision has swept over him and has vanished; his memory cannot hold it. The 'distilled sweetness' of it alone remains in his heart; it is melting 'as the dazzling Snow in the sunshine, and is as the leaves of the Sibylline books scattered by the wind.'

67. Yet he cannot keep even that residue, that 'distilled sweetness' shut up in his own breast; he is mightily constrained to cry to the Supreme Light to re-lend a little to his mind, so that one single spark, even, of the glory may be

Essential Love at the core of the tangled knot of the Universe.

(LIII)

inherited 'by the future people,' and that a larger view of the Lord's Victory may be conceived. As he endeavours to recall it, he wonders how he could have endured the keenness of that living ray of Light. It seems to him it must have been through the concentration of his gaze on its infinite Potency (Valore) that he was able to bear it: had he stood aside, as it were, to scan the ray from his own separate position, with any measurement of it, or of himself, those scintillations would have utterly bewildered him; but he lent himself to their vibrations and ventured to join his sight with the Infinite Glory, and thus his sight was unscathed. Perhaps St. Peter's look at the waves, apart from the Divine Aspect, and the sinking that followed, may conversely illustrate the meaning here.

85. After his appeal to the Supreme Light, and his expression of thankfulness for the abundant grace which had emboldened him so to fix his eye on that Light, he again endeavours to reveal 'for the future people' and for their 'comprehension of Christ's Victory' that which he beheld in the Light and with the Light.

He saw 'bound together' in its depths, ' as in one volume, the Love that in its loose sheets or leaves is scattered through the Universe.' Love was perceived in the Self-existing Being, in all that is dependent on Him, and in all the properties and modes of operation outflowing from Him; and all were so marvellously interwoven and coordinated that one simple ray expressed to him this essential Love at the core of the tangled 'knot' of the universe (91).

He thinks it must, indeed, have been this great truth that he found, for in uttering it he feels his heart enlarged with

'*He that hath seen Me hath seen the Father.*'

more abundant joy. Joy, indeed, must be ever 'distilling' from this heart-knowledge which passeth knowledge!

106. And now, in answer to his prayer, something of the last and supreme reflection of that revealing glory—revealing, though 'dark with excess of Light'—is divinely relent to him. His words, he says, can be but the inarticulate sounds of the Babe at its Mother's breast.

Words of the intermeddling stranger should indeed be few here.

The mysterious Secret, which is the goal and the inspiration of the long Pilgrimage, is revealing itself to the spiritual eye—the Alpha and Omega of all Life in its fulness, of all Hope, of all Love—the revelation made not by flesh and blood, but by the Father Himself.

112. As he searched those deeps of Light with growing powers of Vision, the appearance of the Light seemed to the Seer to grow and change. Yet it changed not; it was his power of vision that was strengthening; he could distinguish in that Light Three Circles: Two as of a self-reflecting Iris; One as of Fire breathed forth from the Twain; and lo! within the Centre of that Unity, of the same colour as that Circulating Light, there appeared to be '*Our own image,*' the Sign of the Son of Man in the Heavens!

To know the mystery of the Union of God and Man in the Incarnation had been the hunger of the Seer through his long ascent. In the restored Eden he had seen the double nature of Christ reflected from the symbol of the Divine Man (the Gryphon) in the eyes of Beatrice; he had there also observed the apparent variations of the Unchanging One, now Man, now God. He was now more profoundly united with the wondrous Light, yet his wonder-

'Filled with all the fulness of God.'

ing flights of thought still fell short of that which he sought to grasp—the Manhood taken into God. This mystery was to be revealed in one lightning flash of intuition, and thus the Truth itself, in its totality of God, Man, and the Universe, smote in upon his soul.

The consummate moment passes and fades, and he strives not to retain it; for all his will, all his desires, are interpenetrated with the Supreme Will, an onward motion— a motion which is yet perfect rest; for it is one with the perfected harmony of the whole wheel of Life, inbreathed by the 'Love which moves the Sun and the other Stars.'

GLORIA IN EXCELSIS DEO!

Elliot Stock, Paternoster Row, London.

www.ingramcontent.com/pod-product-compliance
Lightning Source LLC
Chambersburg PA
CBHW020538300426
44111CB00008B/713